Sound for Digital Video

Sound for Digital Video

Tomlinson Holman

ELSEVIER

AMSTERDAM • BOSTON • HEIDELBERG • LONDON
NEW YORK • OXFORD • PARIS • SAN DIEGO
SAN FRANCISCO • SINGAPORE • SYDNEY • TOKYO

Focal Press is an imprint of Elsevier

Focal
Press

Acquisitions Editor: Elinor Actipis
Project Manager: Kyle Sarofeen
Assistant Editor: Cara Anderson
Marketing Manager: Christine Degon
Cover Design: Eric Decicco

Focal Press is an imprint of Elsevier
30 Corporate Drive, Suite 400, Burlington, MA 01803, USA
Linacre House, Jordan Hill, Oxford OX2 8DP, UK

Recognizing the importance of preserving what has been written, Elsevier
prints its books on acid-free paper whenever possible.

Library of Congress Cataloging-in-Publication Data
Application submitted.

British Library Cataloguing-in-Publication Data
A catalogue record for this book is available from the British Library.

ISBN-13: 978-0-240-80720-1
ISBN-10: 0-240-80720-0

For information on all Focal Press publications
visit our website at www.books.elsevier.com

06 07 08 09 10   10 9 8 7 6 5 4 3 2

Printed in the United States of America

To my students, who have taught me a thing or two.

Contents

Preface

This book is for those who wish to improve sound quality and make it more interesting for Digital Video productions. Some usual topics for sound books such as descriptions of basic sound, psychoacoustics, and descriptions of a wide range of media may be found in my book *Sound for Film and Television*. Instead, this book concentrates on the medium of Digital Video, with specifics for its use, and generally speaking in the context of single-system sound—that is, recording the sound along with the video on the same medium. As each major topic is introduced in turn, the fundamentals come first, then greater elaboration. So if you are coming to sound for the first time, you may find it easiest to skip through the book, starting on each topic and moving on to the next when you get enough information to do the job at that stage. In order to facilitate this approach, each chapter ends with a section called "The Director's Cut," which is the briefest possible statement of the ideas in the chapter. The notion behind my appropriation of that phrase was to alert sound people to "what the director should know." This is a firmly tongue-in-cheek extension of the tag line that has served well for a long time "what the director intended," a line meant to stimulate people downstream from film production to get exhibition right.

After chapters on basic concepts and an introduction to DV technology, there are three chapters on production sound. For those who must start a production just after picking up this book, Chapter 3 is probably the place to start. A core of the book, this is so important because if you have good production sound, then editing and mixing is relatively easy, whereas if you don't, at the very least you are going to spend more time and money getting a decent result.

Production sound is divided into three chapters of increasing complexity. The first chapter explains the various microphone techniques commonly employed, what can be done with an on-camera microphone, how to use the two channels, what to record on location besides speech. The chapter also covers microphone accessories. Then case studies are given of various techniques, along with their pros and cons. Next, raw production sound tracks available as extras on a commercially available DVD are analyzed, with information derived from an interview of the production sound record-ist. The boom operator's job is covered, and the chapter ends with some common problems, logging, and sound kit accessories.

Chapter 4 concentrates on microphones: their selection on the basis of how they do their job and how they respond to sound coming from various angles, powering, radio microphones, and so forth. Chapter 5 discusses dealing with the electrical voltage coming out of microphones, which may cover a very wide range that has to be accommodated by the following equipment to result in noise- and distortion-free recording. This includes especially information about how to set the level and where.

Chapter 6 discusses how to interconnect signals among pieces of equip-ment, whether analog or digital, hardwired or sent by light, as files or streaming transfers. You may never need this chapter, but if you do, it's probably because you have problems that may be solved by referring to it. Chapter 7 is a foray into sound design, a different way of thinking about sound tracks. Sound design is the art of getting the right sound in the right place at the right time, and this chapter explains that process.

Chapters 8, 9, and 10 cover sound editing, mixing, and mastering and monitoring—in one word, postproduction. Today the traditional areas of film sound production of editing and mixing are breaking down through the introduction of plug-ins for editing systems that allow editors what were traditionally mixers' techniques. The question today is: where do I optimally do these processes so that the project is run the most efficiently, with the best art applied in the least time? Some considerations for answering this question are given.

For a course in Sound for Digital Video, the work might start with Chap-ters 3 and 4 and then move back to 1 and 2, and then to 7 and so forth, with Chapter 6 being a reference. Still, for a person who wants a fuller explan-ation of the basic concepts and the medium of Digital Video, starting at the beginning and going straight through the book is perhaps the best ap-proach. This book is highly influenced by the large amount of activity in this field, but it would go instantly out of date if it covered even one digital-audio editing system in detail, for instance, because just as the book came out, version X.Y.Z of the software would be here! So this book tries to elucidate general principles that are useful with all editors and mixers so that it stands the test of time. That remains to be seen.

I want to acknowledge especially the help and encouragement of readers who made this a stronger work by providing feedback on drafts. Among these are Monica Kleinhubbert, Gary Rydstrom, and William Whittington. Eric Aadahl explained to me his sound design for the robots in *I, Robot.* Once again, Roger Dressler of Dolby Labs stepped up to the plate and this time vetted my scribblings on A.Pack. Amblin postproduction chieftain Martin Cohen put me in touch with production sound mixer Michael Barosky for an interview about his work on *To Wong Foo, Thanks for Everything! Julie Newmar.* Michael talked with me for hours, and we synchronized playback of copies of the DVD on the east and west coasts so that we could talk about what was going on, a fascinating experience—I wish I'd recorded it. Since the raw production tracks are available on the extras on this disc, they proved to be invaluable. This was chosen after listening to many discs as perhaps the best example of the range of problems encountered in production.

The book is, though, wholly mine in the sense that I am responsible for any errors, which you could bring to my attention for correction in future editions through writing the publisher. May this book help you practice good sound.

CHAPTER 1

Basic Concepts

Attend a shooting of *Will and Grace*, and watch one of the most accomplished directors in the world while the cameras are rolling, and you might ask the question: Where is he looking? James Burrows (*Mary Tyler Moore*, *Cheers*, and many more) is staring at the ceiling. He could be looking at the actors, but their routines have been blocked out days ahead, and they are highly accomplished. He could be looking at the monitors to see if the four cameras are covering the action as planned, but he has a fully professional crew and has been through camera rehearsals, so he knows they'll get it right. Why is he looking at the ceiling? Because he's *listening* to the delivery of the lines, the ultimate consideration of getting the show on film, constantly asking "is it funny?" The sound of the show is its bottom line. The question a sound person doesn't want to hear from such a director is "why is that distorted?" or "noisy?" or "reverberant?" This book explains how at each juncture— recording, editing, mixing, and mastering—mistakes can be avoided, sound quality improved, and sound design fit to the story.

It doesn't take a Hollywood studio environment to produce programs today. Digital Video is a revolution in making moving pictures, and it is well underway. For a few thousand dollars one can get started making programs that stimulate, amuse, inform, frighten, and do virtually all of the things that cinema and television have been doing for more than one hundred years. DV, as it is called, brings cheaper and better methods for storytelling to a wider pool of people than ever before. It is a time for great democratization of media, where large numbers of people have new access to storytelling tools, and so new visions of the world can be shared.

This revolution is digitally based, with camcorders producing digital tapes[1] that may be transferred with no generation loss into picture and

---

[1] Sometimes the camera and recorder are separate, and other media for camcorders are available, such as discs and RAM cards.

sound editing systems for manipulation, and then if desired into sound mixing systems for finishing. This is important because former analog methods often involved compromise and required extensive off-line/ online facilities that will be described later. When you copy a camera original tape over a FireWire[2] connection into an editing system, the source material for editing is a clone of the original, not just a copy.[3] When the program is subsequently put onto a finished medium such as an Edit Master tape or a DVD, once again over a FireWire or other digital connection, the output may also be a clone, shot-by-shot, of the original. The fact that such copies are literal clones means the work throughout the process is more visually and audibly true to the original than ever before, with the potential for no losses to occur along the path from the captured expression of an actor or documentary subject to the performance seen and heard by audiences. Of course, your objective may not be making perfect clones throughout the process, but rather modifying the original in aesthetic ways that add up to a whole greater than the sum of parts, but it is nice to know that the system is transparent when it needs to be.

However, a common misperception among producers is "now that it's digital, we don't need any postproduction, right?" The truth is that limitations on the quality of production sound recordings are caused by practical considerations such as noise on the set more commonly than the actual technical limitations of the digital recording. Furthermore, voices have to be recorded in different ways, potentially from shot to shot, and so that technical matters do not distract the listener, the recordings must be smoothly blended in postproduction. So even today there is plenty of work in postproduction, to improve on the original production sound recordings, add effects and music, and the like.

Although the media is at a new level of quality and simplicity of use today, the main item hindering better sound design and sound quality is, frankly, most often the training and experience of those doing the job, including not just sound-specific people but everyone involved in the task. Viewing art house films, produced on small budgets on video but with great passion, shows this to be true. Almost all of them have a look, formed by the synergy

---

[2] The Sony Corporation implementation of FireWire is called i.Link. Fire Wire/i.Link connections are called more formally IEEE 1394, the name of the standard that they follow.

[3] A clone is an exact bit-by-bit digital copy of an original digital recording to a new medium, meaning that all of the quality of the original is passed to the clone, whereas a copy is a more general term, with uncertain quality.

that occurs among location selection, production design, costume design, makeup, lighting, and cinematography, because everyone is aware, more or less, that these visual elements are important in the telling of stories through what is called a visual medium, whether fiction or nonfiction. However, less certain, perhaps because it is invisible, is sound quality, and the fit of the design of the sound to the story. The purpose of this book is to inform users of the potential for this medium and give information, both basic and subtle, about utilizing the medium better, all in the service of the story. Two famous filmmakers agree: sound is very important. From George Lucas to Michael Moore, a wide range of types of filmmaking is represented, yet each says how vital the sound experience of a movie is.

The range of productions covered by this book is from simple one-person shooting situations, but generally using cameras meeting certain minimum sound requirements, up through independent video productions shot for feature film release with larger crews. Included along the way will be tips that are useful for industrial and commercial information videos, meeting videos, event videos such as weddings, documentaries, and scripted videos designed for both film and television release. Note that the techniques given here, and inherent in the medium, are neutral with respect to their use, in a political and ethical sense. They could be put to good use by Leni Riefenstahl, had she had them to fawningly document Hitler's rise, just as well as they can be useful for the best documentaries and fiction films today. Technique is always only a means to an end.

Scope of Digital Video

Coming to digital video for the first time, most people probably lump the entire field together and think of it all as DV, a tape format. Yet in the categories of the variants of the basic DV format there are, for instance, cameras ranging from less than $400 (just plain DV or alternatively called MiniDV) to those costing many tens of thousands (HDCAM, DVCProHD). Some camcorders don't even record to tape but rather on fixed or removable discs, or memory bars. All share their basic method of recording pictures and sound to a medium—digital—and not too much else. Tapes from the two extremes of the range are not interchangeable, even though the lower-end tapes may play on a higher-end player. A low-end camera has a single image sensing device, its CCD, that delivers resolution or sharpness and range of color that is less than that of a good modern conventional video monitor, whereas a high-definition production camera has three high-resolution image sensors, covering a span of over 6:1 in sharpness.[4] The higher-definition cameras require tape formats that hold more information, thus the tape cassettes are typically larger and more expensive than those for consumer cameras—the range of cost today is from less than $4 per hour for low-end consumer cameras to about $75 per hour for high-end, high-definition cameras.

In the great middle ground between these extremes, prosumer cameras may rely on the one hand on consumer format tape or on the other hand on a tape format designed for professionals, with attendant cost increase for the tape, but with a more professional set of features. In fact, there are cameras that record to both consumer-based and to more professional format cassettes, depending on which type of cassette is loaded into them. The feature set changes depending on what type of cassette is used, and woe to the production assistant or end user who is sent out to buy tape and gets the wrong type, because the features of what can be done with the different format tapes are different. In some cases, knowing the camera model is not enough information; one must also know the tape type in use on a given production!

Minimum Standards for Audio

Although all camcorders record some kind of audio, just what audio they are recording is another matter altogether. Serious limitations are found for camcorders that record audio from on-board microphones only and have no available external inputs, and those that lack manual level controls. Lesser limitations sometimes occur even with cameras equipped for external inputs and with manual level controls in the form of the types of inputs available and their features.

The limitation to an on-board microphone as the only audio input to the recorder is just too great for practically any pro audio use, although a few things can be done this way that will be described later. However, to select a camera that only allows the on-board microphone to be recorded is just too great a limitation for most uses described in this book. This includes both

---

[4] There are a great many ways to measure this, and I had to pick just one for this comparison.

the simplest cameras and some of the more sophisticated, even high-definition consumer cameras. It is perhaps the first question for the sound-savvy person to ask of a camcorder: Does it have external audio inputs that can be substituted for the on-board microphone, if one is present?

The next most common limitation is lack of manual control over level. While some built-in automatic gain controls work reasonably well today, nonetheless their constantly seeking and changing gain according to the input level causes problems editorially. With automatic gain riding, one of the most common problems is that the level is turned up when things get soft, such as in long pauses in a speech. Then the automatic gain control (AGC), also called a compressor, turns the level back down when speech starts again. An operator, being smarter, will leave the level control alone when a long pause is being recorded. Later, in postproduction, an edit can be performed to cut from one pause to another with minimal problems if the operator leaves the manual level control alone. If the gain is constantly changing as a result of the use of AGC, the result is likely to be a jump in level at any particular edit, which must at least then be manipulated for smooth and continuous sound. And this problem could be repeated for every edit.

Another problem with compressors is called *pumping*, wherein the gain changes become audible within a word in speech, although some more modern AGCs seem to have eliminated this problem. Normally AGCs will limit your ability to make edit points just too greatly to be used for high-quality work. So it is interesting that finding manual level controls on a camera is a mark of a higher-quality camera; inexpensive ones are more automatic, both in picture and in sound, but higher-end ones allow greater manipulation of the image and sound by the user.

High-end professional cameras usually have balanced audio inputs, for both microphone and line levels. These are usually represented by the presence of XLR connectors (Figure 1-1) on the camcorder body or on a microphone input accessory. The reason to use balanced lines, with their two principal conductors covered by a common shield conductor, is that this type of wiring is less susceptible to the hum caused by magnetic fields associated with all kinds of power wiring. Alfred Hitchcock's first day of shooting the first British sound film was greatly delayed until it was sorted out that the microphone cables could not be run next to the lighting power cables, because otherwise the resulting hum was overwhelming. Balanced wiring tends to reduce such magnetic field–induced hum, so it is preferred in professional use over the more common unbalanced consumer wiring,

Figure 1-1 The presence of balanced input XLR connectors is the most readily apparent indication that the camera has separate microphone inputs. Note that other connector types may be used.

usually associated with the RCA phono pin plug such as that found on the back of CD players.

Consumer and prosumer cameras might have balanced microphone inputs, but they are unlikely to have balanced line-level inputs, which are more often provided by RCA phono pin plug connectors (Figure 1-2) for unbalanced inputs. Sometimes these connections are even bidirectional: used as input for recording, they become outputs for playback. The Canon XL series, for instance, uses the bidirectional approach.

The Four Dimensions of a Sound Track

There is a way to think about how sound works, how its representation works when recorded on a medium, and how it is perceived. Because this way of thinking about it spans the range from strictly objective measures into purely subjective ones, it is a valuable method of thinking about sound

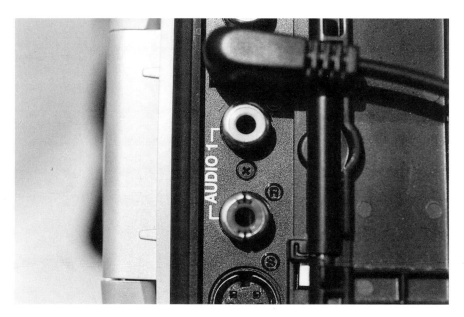

Figure 1-2 The ubiquitous consumer connector, alternatively called RCA, phono, pin, or Cinch plug, and sometimes combinations of these.

technology and design at one and the same time. I call it the four dimensions of sound: frequency range, dynamic range, space, and time.

1. *Frequency range.* Perceived as being from deep bass to high treble, frequency range has an objective basis—the frequency in cycles of a sound wave per second of time, in Hertz (Hz). It also is at the root for much subjective thought about sound: a low-frequency rumble during a clear summer afternoon means there is a threat around the corner, such as a thunderstorm that is perhaps an impending threat to our characters.
    The frequency range for sound perceived by humans is from about 20 Hz to 20 kHz (20,000 Hz), although these numbers are taken as averages of large numbers of listeners, and some young people can hear out to as high a frequency as 24 kHz (Figure 1-3). At the other end of this spectrum, sounds below 20 Hz are not usually heard but felt, if strong enough. Various devices deliver more or less of the frequency range: a telephone delivers a narrow frequency range, from about 300 Hz to 3 kHz, so lacks deep bass and high treble. This is why the letters "s" and "f" pronounced by a talker are easily confused over a telephone. The "s" sound lies principally at a higher

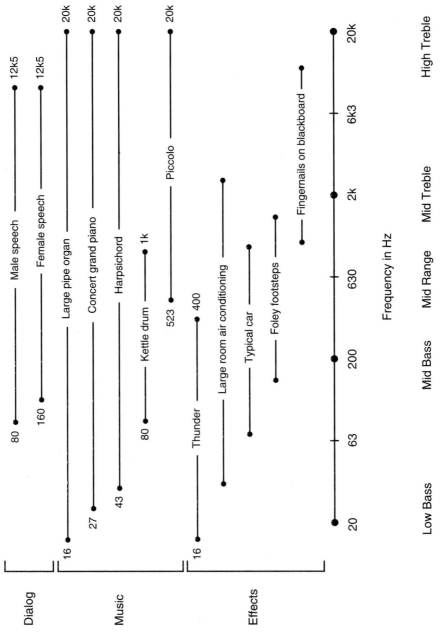

Figure 1-3 Frequency range, and some common sounds occurring within the range.

frequency than the "f" sound, and the telephone cuts off the higher frequencies, sometimes making the two indistinguishable.

2. *Dynamic range.* This is usually given as the range in amplitude from the softest audible sound, called 0 dB Sound Pressure Level (SPL), to the loudest sound tolerable, which is usually considered to be 120 dB SPL (Figure 1-4). Interestingly, older treatments call 120 dB SPL the threshold of pain, whereas because some stadium concerts and raves can operate at even higher levels, such levels are nowadays called the threshold of tickle in the ear; 140 dB SPL is now considered the threshold of pain, but it is also the point at which permanent damage may occur even for brief exposure.

A level of 85 dB SPL,[5] about twice as loud as normal speech in a movie theater, is tolerable for eight hours per day without long-term consequences to hearing,[6] but louder sounds are tolerable for shorter times. Noise exposure versus time that won't typically damage hearing is shown in Table 1-1.

Table 1-1 Permissible daily noise exposure.

dB SPL, L_{eaA}[7]	Daily Time Tolerable
88	4 hrs.
91	2 hrs.
94	1 hr.
97	30 min.
100	15 min.
103	7.5 min.
106	3.75 min.
109	1.875 min.

Decibels (dB) are a logarithmic scaling of the physical amplitude or size of the sound wave used to accommodate the very large dynamic

---

[5] Several items affect the sound pressure level readings used here: (1) frequency weighting, which gives more emphasis to frequencies to which the ear is more sensitive; (2) time weighting of one second, which is thought to match hearing damage more than a shorter time constant (faster metering); and (3) averaging of the one-second intervals over time, called equivalent level. Thus, in technical terms, what is described when speaking of hearing damage potential is called L_{eqA}.

[6] Except, perhaps, for the 1 percent of the population that is most susceptible to hearing damage from noise exposure. See ISO standard 1999.

[7] Ibid.

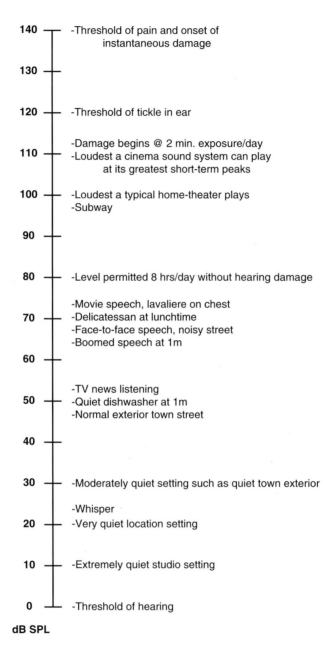

Figure 1-4 Average sound pressure level of typical sounds.

range of hearing. The softest sound one can hear, 0 dB SPL, is a million times smaller in amplitude than the loudest sound most of us can stand, 120 dB, but a scale dealing in numbers from one to a million is inconvenient. By compressing the absolute number scale logarithmically into decibels, one gets easier numbers to deal with. The character played by Walter Pigeon, Morbius, explains a log scale in *Forbidden Planet*, which is worth watching just for this scene. The meters on the wall behind him in the Krell inner sanctum show the power that is being used by the planet-sized machinery beneath him. He says, "Ten times ten times ten times ten, raised almost to infinity," explaining that each meter represents ten times the power of the previous meter. So it is with dB. Each meter on Morbius's wall represents 20 dB (10 times in amplitude), and a 120 dB range (or 6 meters on the wall) represents the whole of the human hearing range from just audible to the sensation of tickle inside the ear.

Dynamic range is used for artistic purposes by filmmakers all the time. James Cameron uses the extremes to great effect in *Terminator 2*: the playground just before the atomic explosion is made very quiet so that the extreme loudness of the explosion is exaggerated. Controlling the level range of the source to fit it within the capability of the medium is what we are doing when we set the level and even adjust it continuously, called riding the gain of the program to be recorded, and one of the worst failures that occurs is to record with excessive distortion (too high, over-recorded) or noise (too low, under-recorded) because these have been overlooked or done wrong.

3. *Space*. Conventionally called *mono* versus *stereo*, today that dichotomy is extended to include surround sound, such as 5.1 multichannel, which is prominent in cinemas and on DVDs. Two main effects arise when more than one audio channel is available on a release medium: sound localization and spaciousness. *Localization* means that you can point at the originating direction of a sound in space, and sound can be made to match the position of the corresponding visual source (or not, according to the aesthetic present for a particular style of sound), thus usually giving both sound and picture greater verisimilitude. *Spaciousness* means having a sense of the space in the recording. When reproduced over just two channels, spaciousness derived from stereo can provide a sense of listening into a space, perhaps from the next room with an archway between the space heard and the listener. Surround sound provides a means

of extending spaciousness to envelopment, the sense of being surrounded, of being in the same space as the source. Although high-end film production employs 5.1 discrete channels of audio to bring about these sensations of localization, spaciousness, and envelopment, nonetheless media with just two tracks can do a good deal of the same thing. This involves certain production techniques (which we will discuss later) and the use of an LtRt decoder such as found in cinemas (Dolby Stereo and others) and homes (Pro Logic decoding and others) on playback.[8]

On the production side of the equation, though, the use of left-right stereo original recording, while available on some model cameras, is not widespread. The two recorded channels are often used instead for two different perspectives on a scene, such as a boom mic and a radio mic on the principal actor. Such dual-mono is not the same thing as stereo, because for stereo the channels must be related in a particular way, generally as a pair intended for reproduction over left and right loudspeakers.

4. *Time*. How sounds are juxtaposed and evolve in time is the province of editors, who may simply maintain what was obtained at the time of shooting or may manipulate time across multiple tracks to great effect. We will discuss issues of time later in this book.

Digital Sound

Whether digital sound is good enough for a given purpose is typically answered at the time of conversion from analog to digital. Although the quality of the analog signal being converted is also all important and will be discussed later, three factors alone set the maximum quality level that can be achieved with digitized audio, and these factors grow out of the dimensions of sound directly. They are frequency range, dynamic range, and the number of audio channels. These three items are represented on cameras and recorders as the sampling rate of the digital audio f_S,[9] which is proportional to the frequency range; the word length, also known as bit depth or resolution, which is proportional to the dynamic range, 12 or 16 bits; and the number of channels, two or four.

---

[8] Chapter 10 covers the issues of surround 5.1 versus LtRt surround sound.
[9] Also notated (incorrectly) as F_s by some camera manufacturers.

The number of independent channels is the simplest of these three concepts to understand. The choices are two or four on most DV media, but the answer for that choice usually trades off against both the sample rate and the word length so that only some combinations of the three are available. Because a higher number of channels eats up the digital capacity of a medium, both sample rate and word length have to be restricted to reach the greater number of channels. As a result of the attendant quality limitations of the four-channel mode, most professional work in most formats is done with two channels, for reasons we'll see. However, two channels can be used in a flexible variety of ways that will be described in the next chapter, so this may not be as great a limitation as it first appears.

The four-channel mode is the most useful when several meeting participants must be recorded and no operator is available to mix the microphones together. By recording the microphone channels separately, it turns out not to be important that someone is fiddling with his microphone when he is not speaking, at least so long as there is a postproduction stage, because we can cut out or turn down that microphone during editing when this occurs. If the microphone channels are married (combined together) in a mixer, then recorded to one track, it is no longer possible to separate one microphone signal from another, which leads to limitations. So, a conference with one podium microphone and three additional ones could be handled by one setup using four channels, but this kind of example is about all at which the four-channel mode excels.

The sample rate determines the high-frequency limit of the audio that can be recorded. The rule is that the sample rate must be twice the highest frequency of the audio to be recorded, plus a little bit. The sample rates available on cameras are 48 kHz[10] and 32 kHz, but this choice is not independent of the number of channels: two channels are sampled at 48 kHz and four channels at 32 kHz. The corresponding frequency range is up to just under 24 kHz and just under 16 kHz. Because some humans hear past 16 kHz, even to as high as 24 kHz, there is an audible limitation for some listeners when sampling at the 32 kHz rate, but because people hear over a broad range of frequencies, losing just a part at the very top of the frequency range rarely causes much trouble. The sample rate is given prominence in camera menus and so forth, but the word length associated with the lower sample rate is the greater audible limitation in practice. That is,

---

[10] Sampling the amplitude of the signal 48,000 times per second.

the limitation to 12-bit audio is more important than the limitation caused by 32-kHz sampling. Table 1-2 gives the two prominent settings typically available.

Represented on media, dynamic range is from the point of noise on the quiet, small end of the scale to the point of unacceptable distortion at the loud end of the scale, in decibels. Most DV uses 12- or 16-bit digital representation of dynamic range. A bit is the fundamental unit of digital representation, a 0 or a 1, which is what is routinely stored and used by computers. With binary arithmetic, more familiar base-10 numbers can be represented for instance by using more digits, zeros or ones, to express the range from 0 to 9. Each bit of word length delivers approximately 6 dB of dynamic range, so you multiply six times the number of bits to get the dynamic range. With each bit delivering about 6 dB of range, 16-bit audio has roughly 96 dB range. This is only an estimate because a small amount of deliberately added noise called *dither* is needed to smooth the steps in the process that would otherwise cause low-level distortion. To cover the full capacity of human hearing, about 20 bits is needed, but in most practical recording situations, the background noise level is far higher than 0 dB, and the loudest sound does not approach 120 dB, so a 96-dB range (16 bits) is adequate most of the time.

Four-channel recording on MiniDV, DV, DVCAM, and Digital 8 is done at 12-bit word length. A 12-bit word length, however, delivers only about 72 dB of theoretical dynamic range. Thus, 12-bit audio falls far short of capturing the full range of audible sound. This means that if the loudest sound present in a program is recorded such that it does not exceed the highest level that can be represented without distortion—in other words,

Table 1-2 Audio record capabilities of DV (MiniDV), DVCAM, and Digital 8. (Not all cameras may support both modes, and some cameras will play back content recorded at 44.1 kHz, 16 bit.)

No. of Channels	Sample Rate	High-Frequency Limit	Word Length[11]	Theoretical Dynamic Range[12]
2	48 kHz	<24 kHz	16 bit	93 dB
4	32 kHz	<16 kHz	12 bit	69 dB

---

[11] Also known as resolution and bit depth.
[12] With dither, explained later.

the recording level is set right—and then played back at a standardized playback level, noise in the form of a hiss will probably be audible, certainly in a quiet environment. Perhaps for shooting situations where the acoustical background noise level of the environment is high, and the source being recorded is not too loud, this might be adequate, but it isn't much of the time.

Two-channel recordings on most of the digital formats are made at 16-bit word length, delivering a theoretical 96 dB dynamic range, but less on practical cameras,[13] far closer to the ear's capability than 12 bits, although still rather short of the full range of hearing. This problem is reduced by the fact that for most productions we rarely encounter sounds so loud as to stress the threshold of pain, and most environments we record in are not nearly as quiet as the softest sound we can hear, limiting the range we have to capture at the source. Thus, for most practical purposes, 16-bit recording is probably enough for production sound accompanying video. One format, HDCAM, records four channels of 48-kHz sampled 20-bit audio with a theoretical 120 dB dynamic range. Specialized recorders for sound only, typically used for high-end production sound or music recording, may record 20- or even 24-bit audio, with an actual dynamic range of 120 dB,[14] although such machines are not very common.

The bottom line of this discussion is that most pros would hardly ever use the four-channel, 32-kHz, 12-bit mode of MiniDV, DV, DVCAM, or Digital 8. If one or a few tapes were recorded in this format and then intermixed editorially in postproduction with others made in the two-channel, 48-kHz, 16-bit recording mode within one project, the problems range from being difficult to impossible to solve. So the first thing to look for on a camera is a menu that makes the choice between these modes, and set it for two channels, 48-kHz sampling rate, and 16-bit audio.

Higher-end formats may record more high-quality channels, mainly because of the space on the medium available in formats that consume more tape. The capabilities are detailed in the following section by format name.

---

[13] This is for their line-level inputs, not microphone inputs, and certainly not for on-camera microphones, which will be discussed later.

[14] The reason that 24-bit audio only delivers something on the order of 120 dB dynamic range, and not the 144 dB one would calculate, is practical: there are no converters with that much range.

Features of DV Format Tapes

Note that individual equipment may not address all of the possible variations that can be recorded within a format; for instance, some camera models may not have the capability to record all of the channels that the format has space for on the medium. However, as a general matter, the information listed in Table 1-3 applies:

Table 1-3 Audio capacity of various digital tape formats.

Formats that record two-channel, 48-kHz, 16-bit or four-channel, 32-kHz, 12-bit audio*	MiniDV DV (also known as MiniDV) DVCAM Digital 8
Format that records two-channel, 48-kHz, 16-bit audio	DVCPro
Format that records up to four-channel, 48-kHz, 16-bit audio	DVCPro50
Format that records up to four-channel, 48-kHz, 20-bit audio	HDCAM
Format that records up to eight-channel, 48-kHz, 16-bit audio	DVCProHD

*These formats can also play back two-channel, 44.1-kHz, 16-bit audio (the CD standard) when recording is made by way of a FireWire interface.

**The Director's Cut
(or what the technician hopes that the director knows)**

- Choose a camera with external microphone input capability and manual control over recorded level.
- Don't mix up tape types; choose one and stick to it. While DVCAM cameras can record in either DVCAM (more expensive with more features) or DV (Mini DV) modes (really cheap but lacking in features and not as robust), one would usually choose DVCAM for use on these cameras for a variety of reasons.
- Don't mix up camera settings; choose one and stick to it. Usually this will be 48 kHz, 16 bit, two channel.
- Watch your own exposure to loud noise, especially covering events such as concerts, car races, industrial sites, and the like.

CHAPTER 2

Introduction to DV Technology

This introduction to DV technology will describe some of the fundamental common features of all of the formats that make up digital video, as well as some of the distinguishing features among them. Chapter 1 covered the fundamental sound differences, and to delve deeper we will have to venture into the picture side of the equation because the distinguishing features among the formats are often related to the picture. Although there are some distinguishing sound differences among the formats, one would have to say that they are smaller than the range of picture qualities. Thus, a practical-sized sound book can cover a lot more formats than could a specifically detailed picture-related book, and learning about just a few distinguishing issues for sound formats allows one to cover the whole field. Today there are also camcorders available that record directly to DVD types of writable discs, to RAM cards, and to hard discs. These all share the same basic ideas as the tape-based media and have the same audio trade-offs involved, so they will not be covered separately.

Basic Digital

The basic process of capturing picture and sound to tape (or, more rarely, other storage media) for all digital formats involves conversion of the continuously varying signals[1] produced by the image and sound sensing devices (one or more CCDs[2] for picture and one or more microphones for

---

[1] What changes is the amplitude of the signal versus time. In the case of video, it is the varying brightness of the three-color components across an image that is converted to numbers. For sound, it is the moment-by-moment amplitude of the sound pressure versus time that a microphone converts into electrical voltage versus time.

[2] CCD is short for charge-coupled device, the type of image sensing device in most cameras today. In it, individual sites uniformly spaced along a set of regularly spaced parallel lines forming a grid are scanned rapidly for their voltage or current output, corresponding to the amount of light striking the sites. In a higher-end color camera,

sound) into numbers. The reliability of storing numbers rather than the smoothly and continuously varying signals that constitute analog directly is a primary justification for digital techniques. The advantage of the digital technique is that copies are literally clones of their masters if certain prerequisites are met: copies are then just as good as the original. This is never true with analog techniques, where each stage of copying exhibits some inevitable generation loss. Analog copies are like those from copy machines: if you copy an original, then copy that copy, and so forth, the picture will get fuzzier and have more contrast than the original through the generations, blurring the original variations in details and tone that made up the original work. Likewise, generational copying of analog video pictures and sound will result in reduced quality.

This difference between analog and digital makes digital techniques well suited to distribution channels, where getting it right for large numbers of copies is important. That is why the impact of digital on the sound industry in particular first happened with a distribution format, the CD. Later it was found that digital techniques were valuable in sound *production*, not just *replication*, once they were made to exhibit all of the qualities necessary. In digital video, the first users were high-end postproduction companies that needed to maintain quality among generations needed to make video masters. Later in the development came the explosion caused by the near-simultaneous introduction of DV and DVD. In digital video, just one advantage is that one particular color in a scene may be chosen, say that of grass skirts of Hawaiian dancers, and changed from green to chartreuse, without affecting anything else in the scene, something that conventional film chemical and exposure techniques could never achieve.

Finally, there's cost. While the minimum-cost consumer digital cameras are a little more expensive than the cheapest analog models today, the difference is fairly minor. More important perhaps is that a minimum cost is involved in obtaining a camera that has the features we want for recording good-quality audio, such as external inputs for microphones beyond the one on the camera, and manual level controls, but compared to shooting film or other professional video formats, the equipment is still

---

three CCDs may be used after the light has been split by a prism and filters into red, green, and blue component parts. Typically, conventional NTSC television cameras scan 480 active lines at 720 sites per line, whereas cameras for high-definition television scan up to 1080 lines at 1920 sites per line.

a great value. Although perhaps not yet rivaling the flexibility of film as a capture medium, video is advancing quickly, with high-definition, progressive scanning, cinema gamma, variable frame rate, and other developments all aimed at rivaling the best image making.

Operational Matters

Single Recording Speed Versus DV's SP and LP Recording Modes

The DV tape format (often called MiniDV) provides a means of lengthening playing time by trading it off against robustness. The Long Play (LP) mode records a smaller bit size on the tape than the Standard Play (SP) mode, making it more difficult or even impossible to interchange tapes and is not recommended (by the camera manufacturers themselves) for professional use. If use of the LP mode is absolutely necessary for recording time requirements, then playback on the same machine that made the tape is dictated. There are two ways to get longer recording times that don't involve this compromise:

1. The more professional DV formats using larger cassettes available on some camcorders and editing recorders allow much longer recording times than the LP mode of DV, so consider these formats if your usage needs long recording times, albeit at greater expense than DV but offering greater certainty of playback.
2. Certain DV camcorders provide a simultaneous output of audio and video to tape and to their FireWire port. Thus, an external FireWire-based recorder can be used in addition to the internal tape drive. This feature can be used to produce a continuous backup as the tape is being recorded. Or by switching back and forth between internal and external recorders, the recording time can be lengthened. The external recorder may record to tape or to a hard drive (which would then have its own time limitation). The rule is that DV records 25 megabits per second (Mb/s). Thus, every minute recorded requires 187.5 megabytes (MB). That is, 25 million bits per second, times 60 seconds per minute, divided by 8 bits per byte, results in the answer in megabytes. One gigabyte (GB) is 1,000 megabytes, so each minute is 0.1875 GB, and each gigabyte of storage equals 5.33 minutes of program.

Off-Line/Online

In one conventional method of working, video is first copied from source tapes at low resolution into an editing system, called an off-line system. The lowered resolution enables users to see what is happening but also permits users to keep a great deal of content available simultaneously because the trade-off is between picture quality and running time. The picture is then edited, and the result is an Edit Decision List, called an EDL. This EDL, in electronic form, is taken to an online facility, along with the original camera or other source tapes. The online system rapidly re-creates the cuts by selective recording from the source tapes to an Edit Master. This is done at the full resolution of the source media. Off-line time is much cheaper per hour than online suites, which offer not only higher quality but also special effects that have traditionally not been available in editing systems.

In contrast, today the FireWire connection from source machines—either the original camcorder or an editing deck—into an editing system carries the full resolution of the source tape, and thus the editor is dealing with a clone of the camera original. Full resolution permits users to see things better but still keeps a great deal of content online. The enabling technology is the picture recording, which employs compression between the CCD and the tape to get to a practical size for storage of 25 Mb/s, and the remarkable gains in storage capacity and its cost over the last several decades. Twenty years ago, I bought a hard drive that cost $2.43 per megabit, whereas today you can buy a drive for $0.0001 per megabit, an improvement in cost-performance of a factor of 24,000:1! This fact demonstrates why editing systems today can afford to handle full-resolution content, at least of the compressed format tape, when they formerly could not.

Time Code

All of the formats have the capability to record time code in the SMPTE format. The time code 05:15:22:23 means 5 hours, 15 minutes, 22 seconds, and 23 frames, marking a single frame with a number that may be used as an index address to that single frame. The numbers start at the beginning of a tape at 00:00:00:00 on most DV models; however, on some DV cameras, and on DVCAM and other formats, the starting number is presettable.

Time code is simple in the hours, minutes, and seconds digits, increment-ing upward serially just as a clock would, rolling over from 59 seconds to zero and incrementing the minutes counter, for instance. However, when it comes to the frames counter, things are a little more complicated because of the various video standards in use. Here, the counter increments from zero through 29, then back to zero, incrementing the seconds counter for NTSC television (U.S.) video standard tapes, and zero through 24, then to zero, for PAL television (Europe) video standard tapes. This process thus yields a nominal 30 frames per second (fps) for NTSC television and 25 fps for PAL television.

Interestingly, 24 P shooting (described in the Video section) does not store 24 fps of video on tape, but rather a nominal 30, so that the tapes can be played back on ordinary equipment. The process of getting from 24 frames to 30 involves a conversion akin to that used when 24-fps film is played on a telecine. In this case, certain half-frames called *fields* are repeated in a particular sequence called 3:2 in order to make the apparent speed-up.[3]

Now let us turn our attention to the word *nominal* in the foregoing discus-sion, when 30 fps was used as a term. The original black-and-white U.S. television system operated at precisely 30 fps, based on the underlying half-frame or field[4] rate of 60 fps. This, in turn, was based on the power line frequency of 60 Hz in the United States. When color was added, the frame rate was altered by being slowed down 0.1%—not a noticeable amount, but one that causes complications today. This was done to accommodate color in a signal that up until that time had only been black and white. The resulting frame rate, 29.97 fps, is the rate of all broadcast television and most video today. Note that we don't count in increments smaller than a frame, so the time code counting method was not altered: once 29 frames is reached, the next one is zero.

---

[3] This is a simplification of the process because for picture editing purposes there are several choices of how to repeat parts of frames in sequence on the videotape. See the manual for your camera because 24 P models vary.

[4] In interlaced video, each field consists of a set of lines, with odd-numbered ones scanned first in the first field and even-numbered ones scanned second. Interlaced video includes NTSC broadcast television, VHS tape, etc. The alternative is progressive scanning, which scans all of the lines in sequence and grew out of computer uses. Internally, the DVD is a progressively scanned medium, but on its conventional video output this is converted to interlace scanning for compatibility with conventional television sets.

However, because frames are now very slightly longer in playing time than ones played at precisely 30 fps, an error accumulates. The time code is running slow compared to a wall clock, thus playing out frames at this rate will result in the program running slightly long. One hour of time code will actually run one hour plus 108 frames of clock time. For many purposes, this error is unimportant. For such uses, the counting sequence that includes all numbers in the normal, incrementing sequence is used, and the tapes run very slightly long in comparing their time code to a wall clock. The name for this, rather unfortunately, is non-drop-frame (NDF) time code. I'll come back to why I say the name is unfortunate next.

Alternatively, if you are delivering to a broadcast operation, 108 frames per hour of error is very important. Thus, a means of keeping the time code in sync with a wall clock is needed, but it can't be if all of the frame numbers are used—a conundrum. The problem was solved by skipping 108 frame *numbers* per hour, jumping over them. No frames are in fact skipped, but rather the number sequence skips numbers, because if video frames were in fact skipped, you would often see the jump as a mistake. This is why I consider the name unfortunate, because this code sequence is called drop frame (DF) time code, when, in fact, no frames are dropped!

The counter frames 00 and 01 are skipped once every minute, which would yield 120 frames per hour, except in the minutes 00, 10, 20, 30, 40, and 50 for a total of 108 frames per hour. So the actual displayed time is not precise at many places in an hour but adds up to one displayed hour in one actual hour. So you can tell if a tape has been recorded DF or NDF by whether these numbers are skipped. A way of indicating DF code is to change one or more separators of the time code parts from a colon (:) to a semicolon (;).

The choice of NDF or DF code to be made at the time of recording depends on the editing system and the requirements of the delivery master. Most conventional television uses require DF time-coded master tapes, so real-time television operations can be timed by looking at the time code. Thus, this requirement backs up into editorial and even sometimes into the camera tape specification. At one time it was difficult for off-line editing systems to make the internal calculations necessary for counting frames with DF code, when some numbers were jumped over, and thus the most common way of working is probably still to record NDF code on the camera, work with it editorially, and then make the final delivery master with DF code.

Today more editing systems can handle DF code internally, so it is possible to shoot it on cameras and keep it throughout postproduction. As a sound person, this is something that should be brought up to producers: "What type of time code should we use, non-drop-frame or drop frame?"[5] The answer to this question is too infrequently known during shooting because most of the consequences occur in postproduction. One of the biggest problems occurs if the answer is not known during production and different parts of a production randomly choose DF or NDF code. In such a case, editing is at least greatly complicated, and sometimes made impossible on certain editing systems, by the mixed code.

The simplest code generators are used by DV generally. Most of them start at 00:00:00:00 each time a tape is inserted and each time a mounted tape is stopped and restarted if the power is turned completely off and back on. The standby power setting of some cameras like the Canon XL series keeps the time code generator at its last number, although otherwise off, so that when the camera is taken out of standby mode, the time code runs from where it was. On the other hand, if you rewind and play back a tape to see what you have, and then continue with recording after the recorded area, the time code generator loses track and starts over at zero, recording the same time code sequence a second time on the same tape—another potential difficulty for an editing system to sort out if trying to go back and find a particular clip of a source tape.

The resetting to 00:00:00:00 each time a new tape is used in most DV cameras is a nuisance for logging tapes, because the time code then can't be used to distinguish one out of a multiplicity of tapes for a given project. In one standard method of working, tapes are copied twice: once into an off-line editing system at low quality for editorial purposes only and a second time into an online editing system at high quality. An EDL, created by the off-line editing system, steers the online system to reproduce the edits made during the less expensive off-line time.

Because DV camcorders reset time code to zero for each tape, very good records must be kept of which tape is meant for each picture and/or sound edit, because the online editing system will ask for a specific tape by an identifier such as a six-digit code to be mounted into a playback machine and then will shuttle to the time code indicated. If it is not known what

---

[5] Unless the answer is prescribed by the format. Most DV cameras only support non-drop-frame; 24 P cameras only support non-drop-frame.

tape a particular time code event comes from, then the wrong tape and the wrong picture or sound may be inserted. If a given tape contains passages with identical time codes, separated along the length of the tape, ambiguity also occurs over what is meant.

Luckily, the need for fulfilling the bookkeeping requirements of the off-line/online method of editing is not as great as it once was because the full resolution of the DV tape formats is transferred into the editing system when using a FireWire interface. Thus, copies across this interface may be considered to be clones of the source tape, and the distinction between off-line and online quality does not exist.[6] Thus, there is no need to repeat the import of audio and video for an online session, and keeping track of sources is not quite so vital. Still, for backup purposes, it is always a good idea to know where the source video came from, in the case of an editing disaster, so labeling and logging tapes with a distinguishing code such as at least A, B, C—and, subsequently, to Z, AA, AB, AC—is good practice.

DVCAM, DVCPro, and others have the capacity for the user to set a starting time code, as do a few DV camera models. With settable time code, professionals will often set the hours counter, incrementing by one for each new tape so that the hours position indicates the tape number. This is complicated by the fact that some tapes may run more than an hour in length, and thus the time code generator will increment the hours counter when it passes one hour of tape time, and if a new tape is inserted and only incremented by one hour corresponding to the tape count, then there will be an overlap of code numbers, which again makes for potential editing ambiguities, in this case resolved by having unique tape identifiers other than starting time code.

For DV cameras, the time code generator typically runs when the tape rolls and pauses when the tape is paused. This is called Record Run (REC RUN,

---

[6] Although there may still be a finishing step in an online suite that can offer more extensive video processing than available in off-line systems. In this case, an export of a file containing the video is made from the off-line system to the online one. In the conventional case, all that is exported from the off-line system is an Edit Decision List (EDL), and the edits must be reproduced by the online system. Editing at full resolution in a DV-based system with a FireWire interface relieves the requirement of recopying from source tapes to the master during an online session and possibly eliminates the need for a session al-together.

R RUN) and it produces continuous code throughout a tape even with camera starts and stops, so long as the power isn't interrupted or the tape removed and put back in. Free Run (FREE RUN, F RUN) means that the time code generator typically is set to clock time and runs continuously, storing discontinuous code with each start of the camera, but providing evidence of the actual time of an event, sometimes needed for court requirements, for instance. Cameras recording to more professional formats than DV may be switched to REC RUN or FREE RUN, although REC RUN is used far more often. REC RUN is generally preferred because editing systems are then presented with continuous time code, and this is more easily dealt with than is discontinuous code.

Some cameras are able to read the code of an existing tape up to the point where no recording has been made and then pick up recording the time code from where it left off. Such a function is called REGEN, for regenerate. REGEN only makes sense when used with the REC RUN function and is typically enabled only when recording time code with this method. Some higher-end cameras do this automatically when the power is cycled. DV cameras generally do not have this feature, so restarts at 00:00:00:00 may occur within a tape if the power is interrupted. There is an important difference to be observed with cameras like the Canon XL series: if the camera is put in STANDBY, the time code generator remembers the current time code and picks up from where it left off, but if it is powered off, then the time code is forgotten. Because STANDBY consumes so little power, its use is to be encouraged.

A similar but distinct function is called JAM SYNC, the term for setting an internal time code generator from an external source. Jam sync is used when multiple cameras are used to shoot the same event, or double-system sound is in use, usually with a time code slate that has been jam-synced to the camera(s) time code. Higher-end cameras may also provide an input for a Genlock video input that permits sources shot on separate cameras to be matched precisely in time (the first line of video will start at the same time on each camera). Genlocking multiple cameras permits overlaying a graphic while switching between cameras in real time, for instance, whereas jam sync alone is not enough to accomplish this.

Within advanced video formats there are some limitations on time code. For instance, shooting in 24 P for coming as close as possible to the film look with video, and permitting simple transfer to film, permits recording only NDF time code on at least some cameras.

User Bits

Within the SMPTE specification for time code is a place for the user to note additional information, called user bits, or UB (sometimes wrongly and hilariously called the user's bit by manufacturers). This can be information regarding scene and take, time of day, particular filters in use, method of recording the frames, whether interlace or progressive and which type of progressive, and so forth. Because these are literally the user bits, they are not subject to strict standardization, and so mean different things on different cameras. DV generally does not allow the user to write user bits, whereas cameras recording to the other formats may, and what they do with them varies by the format and even by the specific camera models.

PAL Formats

Generally, PAL formats, those used in Europe and other 50-Hz power line countries, use 25 fps code and do not have the complications associated with 29.97 fps time code described previously. Frames are numbered with time code 00 to 24, and then increment the seconds counter and reset to 00. The time code runs according to a wall clock. One difficulty is that in order to transfer to film for theatrical exhibition, the 25 fps video must be slowed down by some 4 percent to achieve film standard 24 fps projection. Sound accompanying PAL video will also be slowed down accordingly in order to stay in sync; without correction this will result in all the pitches being 4 percent lower. This is noticeable even on actors' voices, so it should be corrected in transfer through the use of a hardware or software device called a *pitch shifter*.

Further Distinguishing Features Among the Formats

Locked Versus Unlocked Audio Sample Rate

Camcorders contain internal oscillators, much like those used in quartz crystal watches, to set various timings. They may use one master clock that is then divided as necessary down to various rates for audio and video, or they may employ two separate clocks for the audio and the video. The separation into two clocks makes the design somewhat simpler.

DV uses an unlocked audio sample rate, as do some of the other formats in various modes, one where the audio and video clocks are separate. Other formats such as DVCAM use locked audio, sometimes just with one sample rate but not another. In the case of locked audio, the audio and video clocks, those doing the audio sampling and making the video frames, run in a synchronized relationship to each other—they are hard locked. (For NTSC standard U.S. video at 525 video lines per frame and 59.94 Hz fps, every five video frames contain exactly 8008 audio samples.[7]) Thus, no matter what is done subsequently, even with audio and video played back separately, so long as certain conditions are met,[8] they will stay in audio-video synchronization, called *lip sync*.

Not having a strict requirement on audio sample rate makes cameras somewhat simpler and cheaper, so the DV format and others in certain modes employ unlocked audio in the interest of cost savings. This is unimportant if all one is doing is recording and playing back a tape because the audio will not go out of sync in any perceptible way; it takes around one frame out of sync for those looking closely to perceive sync errors, and because the audio associated with one frame of video is always played back from tape along with the video, there is no problem.[9] The tape paces the playback of the audio and the video, so there is nothing to get out of sync.

However, if the audio and video are separated, such as in an editing system, and separate clocks derived from the audio samples on the one hand and from the video on the other are used by the system to maintain audio-video synchronization, then problems can arise in longer takes. In an hour of tape playback, a typical amount that may occur in an editing system caused by having an unlocked audio sample rate is 20 frames out of sync. Because one frame out of sync is visible, and two frames is quite noticeable, 20 frames, or about two-thirds of a second, is quite bad. Most takes are not 60 minutes long, and a six-minute take would be two frames out of sync and would be on the edge of becoming unacceptable. However, transferring full-length tapes into an editing system all at once can result in later takes being badly out of sync. For this reason, Final Cut Pro has a

---

[7] Note that no smaller number of frames contains an integer number of audio samples.

[8] Namely, that the clocks doing the playback of the audio and video have the same time base, like setting watches to the same time before a mission ("synchronize your watches, gentlemen") in all those World War II movies.

[9] What is done to maintain sync is that the audio sample rate is sped up or slowed down by a small amount during playback of the tape to keep the audio in step with the video.

function that alters the playback rate of the audio samples to keep it in step with the video. This is called Sync Adjust Movies, or, formerly, Auto Sync Compensator.

Footprint

The size of the bits recorded on the tape representing the digital audio and video are usually of little concern to the user. However, they can make a difference in how robust the format is in the face of physical handling, dimensional variations caused by temperature changes, and interchange between machines. All other things being equal, a larger bit is easier to recover and play back than a smaller one. The DVCAM format records $15\,\mu m$ square bits on tape, whereas the DV format at SP speed records $10\,\mu m$ bits, so all other things being equal, one would have to say that DVCAM tapes are more robust than DV tapes, for instance. That is not to say that they won't perform identically for your purposes: they may well, but DVCAM is more forgiving than DV across a wider range of conditions. Thus, if you are always shooting interiors at room temperature and playing back on the camera, you are unlikely to see or hear any difference whatsoever resulting from format, but if you are shooting in the Arctic, DVCAM should demonstrate an advantage. It is a peculiarity of digital in general that this aspect of performance is somewhat obscure and is treated incorrectly in many places. At 25 Mb/s, both DV and DVCAM record identical quality pictures, although individual cameras may have a better or worse imager, for instance. The format selected is not responsible for quality differences, but individual cameras vary in their performance, and this issue of robustness may or may not affect you.

Previously described was the difference between SP and LP modes of shooting DV. LP is a consumer format with lower reliability that is rarely if ever used by professionals. Whereas SP records a $10\,\mu m$ bit, LP records a $6.7\,\mu m$ one, which illustrates the problem for interchangeability from machine to machine: it is simply harder to recover the smaller bits.

Interchangeability

DV tapes recorded in SP mode play in DVCAM machines, but LP tapes won't play. However, DVCAM tapes won't play in DV machines. There are such interchangeability issues all the way up and down the chain, but the general principle is that higher-end formats may play lower-end ones. A few camera models can record in both DV and DVCAM formats, depending on the tape inserted.

Note that it is possible for individual camera models to make available more or fewer features than are presented in Table 2-1.

Some Basic Video for Audio People

Frame Rates

Film and video share a common feature: both produce moving images as a sequence of frames taken at uniform intervals through time that are typically not seen separately, but instead blend together into continuous motion through our persistence of vision. A purely mechanical 19th-century invention, the Zoetrope, shows that blending still images together through time can produce the illusion of motion.

Theatrical films have used a frame rate of 24 fps ever since the coming of sound forced standardization in this area, around 1927. This is a universal standard, used around the globe. Actually, in most instances, each frame is shown twice on the cinema screen before being advanced to the next frame, so there are 48 flashes showing 24 unique pictures each second. The reason for this has to do with the perception of flicker. Shown at just 24 fps and at the brightness used in theaters, pictures seem to flicker (the term *flicks* used as slang to describe the movies probably originated from this effect).

U.S.-based NTSC video started out at 30 fps. The reason it could not be made 24 fps was the higher brightness of television than theatrical exhibition. Even showing each frame twice still produces visible flicker at 24 fps because human perception perceives more flicker at higher brightness, and television sets were routinely operated at some two to six times brighter than theater screens. So the black-and-white television standard adopted was 30 fps. Films shown on television used a convention of showing some of the frames twice in some of the video fields (or half-frames, described as follows), so that while the film traveled through the equipment at 24 fps, 30 video frames per second were produced. This is called a *3:2 sequence* (sometimes 2:3).

Table 2-1 Features of the various digital video formats.

Format Name, Bit Rate, Notes	Trade Name, Manufacturer	Bit Footprint	Max Tape Time*	Records Audio	Records Time Code for NTSC
DV aka MiniDV, 25 Mb/s	Many	10 μm (in SP mode) 6.7 μm (in LP mode)	DV 60/80 min.	Two-channel at 48 kHz, 16 bit, unlocked Four-channel at 32 kHz, 12 bit, unlocked	Typically NDF, starts at 00:00:00:00 each tape and if power is removed on most cameras.
ProDV 25 Mb/s	ProDV, JVC	10 μm	276 min.	Two-channel at 48 kHz, 16 bit, locked Four-channel at 32 kHz, 12 bit, unlocked	NDF or DF. May preset starting time. REGEN capability allows continuing the code on a partially recorded tape into unrecorded regions.

Continues

Table 2-1 *Continued*

Format Name, Bit Rate, Notes	Trade Name, Manufacturer	Bit Footprint	Max Tape Time*	Records Audio	Records Time Code for NTSC
DVCAM 25 Mb/s	Sony	15 μm	Minicassette 40 min.; std cassette 184 min.	Four-channel at 48 kHz, 16 bit, locked Four-channel at 32 kHz, 12 bit, locked	Ditto
DVC Pro (D-7) 25 Mb/s, plays DV	Panasonic	18 μm	Sm./med. 66 min.; lg. 126 min.	Two-channel at 48 kHz, 16 bit, locked; analog audio cue track	Ditto
DVC Pro 50 50 Mb/s, cameras switchable between Pro and Pro 50	Panasonic		92 min.	Four-channel at 48 kHz, 16 bit, locked; analog audio cue track	Ditto
DVC Pro HD 100 Mb/s	Panasonic		46 min.	Eight-channel at 48 kHz, 16 bit, locked; analog audio cue track	Ditto

Continues

Table 2-1 *Continued*

Format Name, Bit Rate, Notes	Trade Name, Manufacturer	Bit Footprint	Max Tape Time*	Records Audio	Records Time Code for NTSC
Digital S (D-9) 50 Mb/s, some models can also play S-VHS	JVC		124 min.		Ditto
Digital 8 25 Mb/s, consumer format, can also play 8 mm and Hi-8 analog	Many	16.34 μm	60 min.	Two-channel at 48 kHz, 16 bit, locked Four-channel at 32 kHz, 12 bit, unlocked	DF time code.
HDCAM	Sony		124 min.	Four-channel at 48 kHz, 20 bit, locked	NDF or DF. May preset starting time. REGEN capability allows continuing the code on a partially recorded tape into unrecorded regions.

*The maximum tape time may involve the use of a larger cassette, which may or may not be compatible with particular model cameras or editing decks.

Then came color. Color television standardization required that the color picture be fit into the same broadcast space on the air—called *bandwidth*—that black-and-white television had been using. The color component of the broadcast, transmitted as a subcarrier, could not interfere with the black-and-white broadcast, nor with the sound. In order to accommodate all of these requirements, among other things the frame rate was changed slightly, to 29.97 fps, for color broadcasts. An ordinary black-and-white set had no problem recovering a picture that was slightly off speed, and a color set could recover the color subcarrier and audio with minimal inter-ference, so this rate was standardized.

In Europe, the standard adopted for color television was 25 fps, and U.S. theatrical films are portrayed on European television by being played 4 percent faster, often with the attendant pitch increase in the sound. Only some titles are treated with pitch shifting to result in the correct final pitch. A recent introduction is an improved process for accomplishing this pitch shift, which formerly was thought to have had artifacts, limiting its use. The new device should be in widespread use and is available from Dolby Labs.

For film shot for theatrical release at exactly 24 fps, the conversion for postproduction editing to NTSC video involves the 2:3 field sequence of repetition to get to a nominal 30 fps, and a slow down on the telecine to 23.976 fps, together called 2:3 (or 3:2) pulldown. This means that sound recorded double system also has to be slowed down by the same amount to maintain synchronization. For analog, this is accomplished by using a reference for playback of the original tapes (recorded with a 60 Hz Pilot-tone) of 59.94 Hz. For digital, on higher-end portable production recorders of whatever medium (e.g., open-reel digital tape, DAT, hard disc, or optical disc), the recorder will be set to 48,048 Hz sampling. Then when copied into the postproduction editing environment and run at 48 kHz, it will maintain sync, having been slowed down the same amount as the picture. For such recording, 30.00 fps NDF time code is used, as it will be slowed down too to 29.97 fps, and match the video derived from the film. Note that this is even in the case where the camera is operating at 24.000 fps; the audio recorder is set to 30.000 fps time code.

The previous discussion demonstrates one of the difficulties of dealing with film originals in an environment that will include video postproduc-tion. Video original for video post is easier, but the standards are less universal, and adapting to them is potentially more complicated. For instance, if you shoot NTSC video and wish to release internationally, conversion to PAL can be complicated, expensive, and imperfect. An emerging method of making video more universal is to capture 24 fps and treat the video like a film original, as explained next.

Video Cameras

The most prominent camera feature is usually the number of CCD chips in the image sensor, one or three. Single-chip cameras are much less expensive but sacrifice resolution and color range (gamut) compared to three-chip models. A single CCD chip has alternating color filters over a line of receiving cells. This spacing is what reduces resolution compared to the three-chip approach, which uses a prism and filters to split the color into three component parts and illuminate three separate chips. Both types normally operate only at 29.97 fps in the U.S. NTSC system. Single-chip uses include surreptitious video when one is trying to look like an amateur and general carrying around in one's pocket. They rarely if ever have external audio inputs, relying on an on-camera microphone, which may be mono or stereo.

Three-chip cameras mostly operate at 29.97 for NTSC in interlaced format, as do single-chip ones, but there are some models described as follows that have added modes of operation. Interlace is the standard method of capturing video, where first lines 1, 3, 5 ... are scanned, and then 2, 4, 6. The complete sequence is recorded 29.97 times per second. The fields, one-half frames, are recorded 59.94 times per second.

Today some three-chip cameras have additional features:

- *16:9*. This refers to the aspect ratio of the pictures delivered. This wider screen aspect ratio (1.78 units of width per 1 unit of height) is more feature-film like than standard 1.33:1 video. It may be achieved several ways. One is simply cutting off the top and bottom of the picture with black bars, but this limits resolution of the remaining picture because of the loss of CCD area of 33.3 percent. A second way is to use a squeeze lens, an anamorphic attachment, that squeezes the image horizontally so that a 16:9 (1.78:1) picture fits in a 1.33:1 CCD, and then is unsqueezed in playback on a 16:9 monitor by shrinking the picture height but not changing the width. However, a conventional monitor shows the image squeezed, so this may be a problem. The third method is to use native 16:9 chips in the camera, which is typical of high-definition and a few standard-definition cameras such as the Canon XL-2.

- *High Definition*. Standard NTSC video uses 480 active lines. High-definition video may use 720 progressively scanned or 1080 interlace scanned lines (see definitions of progressive and interlace scanning as follows) for sharper images. Note that 1080 is not necessarily always better than 720; it is on fixed picture, but moving pictures are more complicated. High-definition cameras are generally of 16:9 aspect ratio, and much more expensive, although one prosumer model has appeared.

- *24 P*. In order to understand this emerging method of working, one first must understand the difference between interlace and progressive scanning of video pictures. The "P" in 24 P stands for progressive scanning.

Interlace scanning is the means traditionally used to make and distribute television pictures. For interlace pictures, first the odd-numbered lines (1, 3, 5, etc.) are scanned, and then, about 1/60th of a second later, the even-numbered lines are scanned (2, 4, 6, etc.), fitting in between the lines of the first vertical scan. The entire process takes about 1/30th of a second; each half-frame of an interlace image is called a *field*.

A problem with interlace scanning occurs when the picture moves noticeably between the first and second fields of a frame, making a vertical line that's moving into a zigzag, for instance. If you look closely, you can sometimes see this when the camera pans and then comes to a stop: once the pan is over, vertical edges are sharper than when the camera was moving. The laser disc version of *Jurassic Park,* which uses interlaced video, shows this effect when the bad guy is stealing the genetic material of the dinosaurs from the vault. The camera pans over the vertical lines of bars in the vault, and at its start and again when it stops, the vertical lines are sharp but when the camera is panning, the vertical lines are jagged when displayed on a conventional television with interlace scanning.

Progressive scanning is just what it sounds like: the scanning lines progress in order from the top to the bottom of the screen. Lines 1, 2, 3, 4 and so on are traced out in order. Computers use progressive scanning, whereas conventional television uses interlace scanning. However, both cameras on the one hand and monitors and projectors on the other are now on the market that do video in progressive scan, making the pictures more film-like.

Progressive scanning has another advantage over interlace: the lines written during the first half of an interlace scan are fading by the time the second half is written. We perceive this as lesser sharpness in interlace compared to progressive scanning. Thought of another way, interlace scanning produces one-half the scanning lines in 1/60th of a second, but progressive produces all of the lines in the same amount of time, so more information is presented per unit time by progressive scanning, and this is seen as better sharpness.

For these reasons, 24 P (24 fps, Progressive scanning) shooting of video is becoming important. There is a recognition that pictures from this format look more like they originated on film, because they lack the interlace artifacts of interlace scanning. The complication is that most NTSC video equipment expects a nominal 30 fps input, and while it will stretch to 29.97 fps, it won't go as low as 24 fps without complication. So what camcorders do is record 29.97 fps on tape, repeating some of the frames as is done with film on a telecine. So most cameras shooting 24 P are actually shooting 23.976 fps, and 24 P is simply a rounded-off number.

Such tapes play back in conventional decks and other camcorders because the recorded frames are 29.97 per second, but some of them contain repeats so that the rate of new frames is 23.976 fps. Another advantage of 24 P is that with specialized software, one can get back to the 24 original progressive frames each second and output a scan to 24 fps film directly, speed up by about 4 percent and output PAL for European distribution and to other parts of the world using the PAL system, or repeat fields in a particular way called 2:3 (also called 3:2) for NTSC output (as it is stored on tape) for the United States, Japan, and other parts of the world using the NTSC system. Thus, 24 P camera originals become source masters useful for film release and both main video standards, kind of a Great Grand Master.

As noted, when 24 P is mentioned, the actual frame rate is usually 23.976 fps and the number is rounded to 24 P for easy pronunciation. The reason for 23.976 fps video rather than exactly 24 fps is the direct relationship of 23.976 fps video through the 2:3 process to 29.97 fps video—the two run in the same overall clock time. Some professional high-definition cameras such as the Sony F900 make a distinction between shooting actual 24 fps and shooting 23.976 fps for better compatibility with NTSC video. When recording at one of these speeds and playing a tape back at the other, this difference is not noticeable,[10] but if the sound is separated from the picture and the assumption about speed is made incorrectly, the 0.1 percent difference could occur, usually in an editing system. The 0.1 percent difference isn't much, but it will cause audio recorded or reproduced at the rate opposite that of the camera to go out of sync visibly within a little over a minute. Whereas high-end cameras come equipped with a switch with separate 23.976 and 24 fps settings, lower-end cameras say 24 fps when they may well be operating at 23.976 fps. This is one of the many sources of potential problems for audio, because any sync problem that occurs is always an audio problem, right?

Under- and Over-Cranked Camera

Motion-picture cameras may be equipped with variable-speed motors, allowing them to shoot at a precise 24 fps most of the time, but also allowing for a wide speed range for special effects. Until recently, these effects were hard to come by with video, because all the timing signals and so forth in a camera are based on the frame rate—many things have to change together to vary the frame rate. However, high-end video cameras have now come on the scene, possibly with needed external processors that allow variable speed, at least in specific increments, offering slo-mo or sped-up action by over- or under-cranking the camera, respectively. Audio for over- or under-cranked situations is usually invented in postproduction, among other sources by possibly taking a separate recording of the same event recorded in real time and speeding it up or slowing it down by the same amount as the camera to maintain synchronization.

Interconnecting Video

Video consists of three color signals, but these may be portrayed on from one to five wires, with various degrees of quality and complexity as outlined in Table 2-2.

---

[10] Even by those with perfect pitch. The minimum noticeable pitch difference for the 0.01 percent of the population with perfect pitch on an absolute basis (not comparing side by side) is about 20 percent of a half-step, or 1.2 percent.

Table 2-2 Video interconnects.

Name	Connectors	Description	Upside/Downside	
Composite Video	Yellow phono connector; single BNC connector on pro gear	Complete color video signal on one wire	Simple, but combining color components together causes artifacts; useful for field monitoring, but never used if possible for production purposes.	
S-Video	Four-pin mini DIN connectors	Separate luminance (the black-and-white part of the picture) and chrominance (the color part) on two conductors	Better than composite and still simple to connect, but limited bandwidth and thus resolution of color channels compared to component connections.	

Continues

Table 2-2 *Continued*

Name	Connectors	Description	Upside/Downside	
			good for monitoring, but not production standard where subsequent matting is necessary, for instance.	
Analog Component Video	Three to five phono or BNC connectors: three colors plus potentially vertical and horizontal sync signals	Three separate color signals plus possible sync signals	Best for bandwidth of each component color; useful for postproduction; used on high-end DVD players.	
Analog Component Video Progressive Scan	Same as analog component only progressively scanned	Same as analog component video	Rarer, but useful for eliminating interlace artifacts; available on DVD players, for instance.	

Continues

Table 2-2 *Continued*

Name	Connectors	Description	Upside/Downside
DVI–Digital Video Interface	Separate digital color component video on customized connector, potentially progressively scanned		
FireWire	Digital signal on custom connector		

Conclusion

The principal differences among the various tape formats are (1) the foot-print of bits on tape leading to differences in robustness, (2) having a locked versus an unlocked sample rate, and (3) the ability to handle only simple or more complex time code requirements. Interestingly, none of these is the basic audio quality, which is fixed by the choice of the combination of sample rate, word length, and number of channels. Normally for profes-sional production, this is set to two-channel, 48-kHz sampling rate, 16-bit audio, and thus audio quality is more determined by the degree to which a given camera comes close to the ideal than by the format. A distinguishing feature of more expensive formats is the availability of more audio channels at 48 kHz sampling and at 16- or even 20-bit word length.

While the more professionally oriented formats do have things to offer that are greater than the basic consumer DV format, the tape cost is certainly higher, and so for those on a budget, DV, accepting some limitations, may be the best choice of format, whereas for others, the differences will be worthwhile.

The Director's Cut

- Be careful to choose and stick to a single choice of standard format because intermixing types is next to impossible. NTSC is U.S. standard video; PAL is European standard video. NTSC records at 29.97 fps, and thus it is difficult although possible to get a film output at 24 fps. PAL records at 25 fps, and may simply be slowed down 4 percent to make a 24 fps film output. While PAL recording for film out is useful, it is being supplanted today with the introduction of 24 P recording.
- Aspect ratio: 4:3 standard television or 16:9 widescreen are the choices.
- Understand interlace versus progressive scanning. Most video is inter-laced; most computer work is done progressive. Emerging 24 P video is recorded progressively scanned, which leads to better film outputs if ne-cessary. 24 P in effect mimics the universal nature of 24 fps film that may be released as film or transferred to PAL video at 25 fps by a 4.166 percent speed-up, and NTSC video by a slowdown to 23.976 fps and the introduc-tion of a 2:3 repeating field sequence resulting in a video frame rate of 29.97 fps.

Director's Cut (*Continued*)

- Don't use LP recording on DV except in absolute emergencies.
- Understand time code terms such as non-drop-frame (NDF), drop frame (DF), Record Run, Free Run, and Regen, described in the text. Choose one method of working and stick to it throughout a production. For multi-camera shoots, use GenLock if possible.
- Know that audio may go out of sync in some editing systems for DV tapes because of its use of unlocked audio. A table of which formats record which way is given.
- Understand interchangeability: For instance, DV tapes recorded at SP speed play on DVCAM machines, but not vice versa.
- Interconnecting video ranges from one-wire composite video, with compromises, through S-Video, to component video, each step with less of a compromise.

CHAPTER 3

Production Sound I: General Considerations

For many programs, the quality of the sound picked up on location is the principal determining factor in the overall sound quality. Good technique can make a program, while bad technique can, at the very least, cause a lot of extra time, effort, and money in postproduction. Any reality-based program is unlikely to be able to replace dialogue in postproduction, so microphone technique and recording is all important for these programs. In some cases, vital performances or reality situations that cannot be repeated may be lost. Of all the information in this book, these chapters are probably the most important, because once sound has been picked up badly, it is difficult and expensive, if not impossible, to rescue.

The First Big Step: A Dedicated Sound Person

In many instances, DV videographers have to be one-man bands, doing their own producing, directing, camera operation, and sound recording. However, when just a second person is added to the crew, that person almost naturally becomes the sound person. It is common in documentary production, for instance, for a two-person crew to be separated into the responsibilities for directing and sound, on the one hand, and videographer on the other. The videographer lights the scene, or chooses to manipulate available light, sets up the tripod and camera, white balances it, and so forth. Meanwhile, the director is getting to know the subject and setting up the sound. Fiction filmmaking with minimum crew may follow this breakdown of jobs as well. It is fair to say that the needs of the picture often dominate on location, just because a picture is being shot and pictures tend to dominate thinking over sound, which is, after all, 50 percent of the experience. With a second person responsible for sound, it is less likely to be overlooked or compromised.

However, it is still important, even in a two-person crew, for the camera-person to be able to aurally monitor the ongoing events. If necessary, this means equipping the camera operator with headphones,[1] because framing the picture, determining when to zoom in, and so on, particularly in documentary films, depends on what is being said. As the scene grows more intense, it is usually desirable to push in to a close-up, for instance, but the camera operator can't know that intensity is occurring unless he or she can hear and respond to the action. On the part of the sound person, observing the focal length of the zoom lens by looking at a zoom stick[2] will tell with practice where the boom mic may go. Alternatively, the boom mic can have a small video screen attached and wired to the camera output, so that the boom operator can see the shot and know how close the boom can be (and it is usually best to get it as close as possible to being in the frame).

There is an associated factor in video compared to film: the viewfinder of a video camera provides no area above the picture to see the potential intrusion of the boom. In a film camera, the eyepiece optics display more area than the picture aperture, and the eyepiece ground glass is marked with the frame line for the format in use. Thus, the cameraperson has an early warning of when the boom may intrude into the picture. There is no such capability with video, because the cameraperson is looking at a video monitor through the eyepiece, and every scanned line is portrayed, but no more. Thus, video camerapeople get good at looking through both eyes: one at the viewfinder for the composition, framing, focus, and even in some cases audio level, and through the other eye at the overall scene, to know where items are about to intrude into the picture, especially the boom mic.

That having been said, if the crew can only be one person, certain measures should be taken to get good sound, which will be discussed.

Location Scouting

Feature films always scout locations before shooting, partly because of the complexity of handling their large crews and equipment. However,

---

[1] Using a Y-adapter for the connectors in use to extend monitoring to both the camera and sound persons.

[2] A stubby stick that screws into the zoom ring on the lens, indicating by its angle the current focal length. If your lens lacks such a provision, white marker tape can be used, set in a triangle to point at the current focal length.

location selection is too often based just on what a location looks like: they are often chosen by selecting from stills made by a location manager or even from a database with no one from the production visiting the site. Although a camera can pan off an offending modern structure in an otherwise quaint neighborhood, sound does not have the hard frame line that picture enjoys. Microphone selection, placement, and aiming can only produce tendencies, not such a hard decision as a frame line. Thus, if a jet flies overhead and you are out in a quiet desert shooting, the picture may be fine, but the sound is likely to be ruined.

The two main items to watch out for in scouting locations for sound are noise and reverberation. Once we had a student film shoot in a perfect location for picture—the shot contained a lot of graffiti—but the location was essentially impossible for sound—it was underneath a freeway. Likewise, shooting a large museum interior, one wants to start out showing the scope of the place with a wide shot, but the corresponding reverberation of the large, hard space causes sound problems. So common sense dictates that if an irreplaceable event is going to occur in a large reverberant space, like a wedding to be covered from the back of the church, then special sound considerations apply. One solution for this is radio mics, but their peculiarities also lead to some problems, which are discussed later.

Coverage

In filmmaking, the term *coverage* refers to the number of different ways that a scene is photographed, from wide master shots, through two-shots, to over-the-shoulder and full-face close-ups. When I first saw the flying wing sequence of *Raiders of the Lost Ark* during postproduction on the dubbing stage, I was sitting next to Michael Kahn, Steven Spielberg's long-time editor. I was astonished at the variety of cuts and the naturalness of the edits in the scene, and I said to him, "Michael, that's brilliant cutting." His reply was, "It's nothing—coverage, coverage, coverage." A little like "location, location, location" in real estate, this mantra is good guidance for filmmaking in general.

In the case of fiction filmmaking where the action of the scene can be repeated a number of times, this usually takes on a fairly formal structure, with a scene being divided into setups, each being a particular camera position, framing, lighting, and so on. In documentary filmmaking, no such formal structure exists, but nonetheless the job of the cinematographer is to cover the scene, with a variety of shots for making editable footage. For instance, having some visual to cut away to provides a means to compress an otherwise real-time interview, without suffering from a jump cut, a discontinuity in a basic on-camera interview. Sound carries the story in such a scene because the sound is being cut so the story is told linearly, while the picture is cut to support the sound, and not the other way around. Such supplementary visual material is sometimes called B roll, in the jargon of news coverage.

Here we want to take the term coverage and apply it to sound: how to sort out what is the desired sound moment-by-moment within a scene, and how to concentrate on that sound, while reducing less important or even annoying sound, is the job of the location recordist. It is always possible to add reverberation and background ambient sound later in postproduction, but it is extremely difficult to reduce excess reverberation in particular, and noise in general, that accompanies original recordings. All too often, excesses spoil production sound recordings in one or both of these factors. The job of microphone technique is to reduce both of these to manageable amounts that make sense in the context of the scene. This requirement is what leads to our wishing to move the microphone off the camera body whenever possible, and get it up in the air over the principal action, and/or place microphones on the talkers or hide them on the set close to the talkers.

Not only is it the responsibility of the sound person to minimize noise and reverb, but on fiction films, almost everyone in the crew gets involved one way or another:

- Set dressers hang blankets, say on C-stands, out of camera view, to soak up excessive reverb

- Grips make dolly motion quiet

- Costume people provide cloth booties for actors to use in scenes where their feet don't show, and provide places for radio mics in costumes

- Gennie operators site generators for minimum noise

- Assistant directors maintain a quiet and disciplined set.

Inexperienced crews will not necessarily know the importance of capturing good production sound, and one of the primary skills of the sound people is to make their needs known to others who may not understand the effect they have on sound, without being obtrusive. The previous examples just begin to explore the range that might be required as suggestions, but there are surely many more. While many productions combine skills into fewer people, thinking that the job of production shooting is capturing good picture *and* sound goes a long way toward making better sound.

The obvious thing to capture in a scene with dialogue is the speech of the actors or documentary subjects. Usually we want the sound quality to be on mic, that is, having not much recorded reverberation or noise, and miked in front of the actor, most often from overhead (as being the position that most sounds like the actor's natural voice, for reasons that will be explained later). On the other hand, there are certain relatively rare times when we want to hear an actor sound off-mic. This might occur when we concentrate on the face of an actor in a scene listening to another speaking, for instance, and may be an indication that we are on the way into the thoughts of the actor who is being seen, not the one being heard. So alternative microphone perspectives can be used as a storytelling element. However, principal on-screen dialogue deserves to be covered sounding as such, and this most often means that an on-camera microphone won't do, but there are exceptions described later.

In original recording accompanying a picture, there are many possibilities for what is important and what is not. Filmmakers who have gained some experience come to realize that what one typically is capturing, whether for a fiction or nonfiction film, are the bits and pieces that can be edited together into a seamless whole. This means perhaps paradoxically that the best training for production personnel—camera and sound people—is picture and sound editing. The smallest productions do this because it is the same person doing all the jobs, and feedback from editing and mixing will inform production sound, at least on your second show!

Normally, good production technique calls for edits within a scene to not be jarring. Continuous sound across picture edits indicates to the audience that the scene is continuous too: while we may have changed point of view, we are anchored in the same space before and after the edit. This is complicated by the fact that we may not be cutting between similar shots, but from a wide one to a close-up, for example. While the sound recording can exhibit some difference between these two perspectives, if we were, for example, just to use the on-camera mic for a wide shot and a close-up, the difference in sound perspective when the picture and sound cuts between the two would be jarring, even though the picture cut makes sense. A much smaller difference in perspective, such as both being covered by a boom mic, but with the wide shot a little looser perspective and the close-up somewhat tighter, makes a good sound track.

Another part of getting sound recordings is to obtain sound not just of the principal action but also room tone that can be used to bridge gaps in the action, cover up momentary noises, and generally smooth edits. In shooting years ago, a pause would be taken by the cast and crew to record room tone specifically. This is rare today because digital audio workstations can be used to find fragments between the speech elements and other set noises where the background is said to be clean that can be looped and thus extended to the length necessary.

In sound for picture, image usually takes precedence over sound, so the requirements of picture, such as not having a microphone visible in a shot, usually takes precedence over sound capture. The job becomes recording the best sound on location that can be smoothly blended together in postproduction to form a cohesive whole, with minimal outside interference, under a set of given conditions of camera angle and other factors. This means that microphones are rarely allowed within the field of view of the camera, among other things.

Scene Coverage

Conventional dramatic television shows are a good thing to watch to understand scene coverage in the conventional sense of the term. Start with the sound down, and note how scenes often progress, from a wide shot possibly tracking the actors into a locale, to closer shots over the course of a scene. The idea is to establish the geometry of the space in which the action occurs for the audience first, and then to use a certain set of grammatical rules about film shooting and editing to produce a continuous-appearing whole scene that progresses to a climax.

The three main microphone techniques in use to produce coverage are boom, lavaliere on the actor/subject, and planted mic on the set/location. The relative strengths and weaknesses of the various techniques are given in Table 3-1. Normally, the boom mic is preferred, if it can be used. This is commonly done for feature films and even for documentaries such as *Spellbound* (2003), for which more than 90 percent of the production sound was from a boom microphone.[3] For situations where the boom simply can't be used, lavaliere microphones often have to be resorted to. This might occur if there were such a wide shot, for instance, that for any usable placement of the boom microphone, the recorded sound would simply be too noisy and/or reverberant.

Planted microphones have their place too. In situations where an actor or subject is moving through a set or location, there may be positions where a boom can't follow, such as through a doorway where it would have to duck into the picture. In such a case, a skillful production sound recordist may be able to smoothly cross-fade from the boom mic on one side of the door, to a planted mic over the door in order to get through it, and then back to the boom. Another example of the use of a planted microphone is where the action occurs far upstage from the camera, and the boom can't reach the area needed.

For content that is boomed, matching the microphone perspective to the action is something that occurs rather naturally, because the microphone is farther away in the wide shots and can be closer in the close-ups. This is one area where lavaliere radio mics are at a disadvantage because they cannot match the perspective of a shot. If an actor wearing a lavaliere turns his body and faces away from the camera, the sound is largely unchanged, when it really should change. Matching microphone perspective to camera perspective is usually a good thing. This is why microphone placement is preferred above the frame line, and not to one side or the other of the side frame lines. If the mic was on the left side of the frame, and the actor turned during the scene and spoke to the right, they would be going too much off-mic, revealing that the microphone and camera perspectives don't match. The position above the frame is preferred to below the frame because voices sound better on or above a horizontal plane through the head than they do below that plane, where they tend to sound chesty, with

---

[3] The producer Sean Welch was boom operator, while the director Jeffrey Blitz operated the camera in production. Postproduction editing and mixing was by Peter Brown and Joe Dzuban.

Table 3-1 Common microphone techniques for production sound.

Method	Pros	Cons	Special Considerations
Boom	Best sound in most situations—most representative voice timbre and ability to match camera perspective.	Obtrusive: can make documentary subjects and even actors nervous; potential exists for boom shadow; more susceptible to reverb and noise than the lav.	Needs operator separate from camera operator and coordination between camera and sound personnel.
Lavaliere (wired), on chest	Closest to mouth, thus less influenced by room noise and reverberation typically than a boom (unless compared to a mic held up to the mouth or a headset mic); mic can perhaps cover more than one subject/ actor if they are close together.	Mic can't see mouth and mounting on chest both change timbre for the worse; lacks match to camera perspective if subject moves; subject to clothing noise, subject touching chest; invasive to place the microphone on the actor/subject.*	Wire tether restricts movement but is a more reliable link than radio mic.
Lavaliere (radio mic), on chest	Same as above.	Same as above.	More freedom of movement at expense of less reliable connection; more information is to be found in Chapter 4 under the heading "Use radio mics."

Continues

Table 3-1 *Continued*

Method	Pros	Cons	Special Considerations
Lavaliere in hair or hat	Commonly used Broadway method; potentially less costume interference than on chest; perspective stays the same when actor turns head.	Difficult to place and wire; timbre requires equalization; more subject to perspiration than chest-mounted mic.	
Planted (hidden mic on set)	Works well for certain situations.	Inflexible.	

*Even an actor as experienced as Tony Curtis said in an interview that he didn't like being touched by people doing hair, makeup, costume, and sound.

a mid-bass emphasis. Sometimes, however, it can be necessary to compromise and shoot from below the bottom frame line and make up for it in the mix. Such an instance might occur if the camera is set low with a wide-angle perspective, showing lots of headroom (literally) above the actor.

Shot-to-shot matching of sound perspective is usually a good thing to do. This means that if we are shooting coverage of two people speaking in alternating over-the-shoulder medium close-ups, we will record the actor whose face is being seen on-mic, and the actor not being seen will be recorded off-mic. The editor doing sound can then choose to construct the sound from all of the on-mic lines, covering the sound for the shot over the back of an actor's head with their on-camera lines (the lips should not be seen or otherwise sync problems will arise). A problem for this technique is dialogue overlaps, which are hard or impossible for actors to control equally on each take. In the case of overlaps, the recordist or boom operator then has to choose to weight the on-mic versus off-mic actor at up to 50/50 in the microphone perspective, ultimately by recording from the side of the frame favoring the face view of the actor. This is an example of where a rule given above (don't record from the side because if the actor turns it won't match camera perspective) should be violated for the better good (matching both on- and off-camera actors so that dialogue overlaps can be used).

When the shooting must be unobtrusive, such as for a documentary where the subjects may be spooked by the presence of a camera or boom close to them, then a new set of rules apply. For example, reality TV today relies greatly on radio microphones, with one on each subject. This captures their dialogue no matter where they are, but does have certain problems:

- *Clothing noise often arises.* This problem can be minimized using tape to surround the lavaliere microphone, then tape it to the chest, and use a second double-stick tape to adhere the mounted assembly to the clothing, all the while not obstructing the sound ports on the mic (see Figure 3-4).

- *People often fiddle with their clothes near the microphone or the microphone itself.* This could include chest beating, which too often occurs right on the microphone. The worst case ever seen was of a new baby in the arms of her mother, who proceeded to reach up and play with that shiny object during the morning television news show *Good Morning America.*

- *People embrace.* When they do, the voice sound becomes at least muffled and often noisy through contact, a dead giveaway that a radio mic is in use.

- *The subjects usually remember they're wired.* Hidden, on-set microphones overcome this problem.

What Can Be Done with an On-Camera Microphone?

This is a great limitation, as has been outlined before. Shooting a wide shot from the back of a church, and expecting the on-camera mic to record the wedding vows is just crazy. However, some things can be done, even with an on-camera microphone:

- If all that happens within a shot is establishing a locale, for instance, and no principal dialogue occurs, then an on-camera mic may be okay. Such *establishing shots* give a pause or bridge in the ongoing action, helping to anchor placement in time and space. Such shots are helped by the sync between picture and sound that makes them seem more real. For instance, my students once shot a documentary about an artist who worked with large Magic Marker–style pens. Choice of a quiet location and use of a directional mic allowed them to pick up the sound of the marker on paper. The sound effect, especially its in-sync nature, added a real sense of being there for that scene. Hearing it as the only sound emphasized the lonely nature of the task of creating art; one thought that if you can hear that, it must be quiet!

- Feature filmmakers call this type of sound Production Effects, and they cut one or more tracks specifically for them. This is as opposed to ambience or backgrounds, which is general sound of a like space laid over a shot or, more likely, a series of shots constituting a scene. Ambience is an aural space for the movie to live in, but Production Effects are potentially even more powerful because of their sync nature. In order to make ambience seem more real, hard effects can be cut over the top of it on other editorial tracks, portraying particular events in the picture with sound. Foley effects, too—those made synchronously in a studio while watching the picture—have the same effect: sync sound sells. So feature films go to a lot of trouble to build a sonic environment that matches what you see in the picture: ambience, hard effects, and Foley all may play a role. Still the cheapest route to obtaining the advantages created by all of these layers is often Production Effects if they can be captured cleanly at the time of shooting.

- If a documentary subject can be isolated from others and shot in close-up, with the camera only two to three feet from the subject, then a high-quality, directional, on-camera microphone may do. This means limiting the shooting style in order to accommodate the method of sound recording, but it is effective. I made a short documentary for the 66th reunion of the Mt. Morris (Illinois) High School class of 1936. The lunch was around a big table with lots of gabbing. While I shot that for coverage, I also arranged to take each of the 12 alumni into a quieter corner and asked them questions in close-up. The close-up shots provided not only a part of the picture coverage, but also the sound that was used as principal voice-over, covering the wider shots of the group at lunch. It worked because I limited the kind of shooting I would do in the interviews to being quite close up, not only in framing, but in actually being close to the subjects, so that I could capture decent sound.

- On a fiction film with good actors, it is possible to shoot the picture with accompanying bad sound just for sync purposes (called a scratch track) and then go back and shoot the lines again for sound only, with the camera and its microphone in a preferred position for sound recording. Called *wild track*, this method requires tedious work in postproduction to resync all of the performances in the wild track to the scratch track, but it is possible to do. A key to it is getting the actors to perform in much the same way for the microphone as they did for the picture.

- It is generally a bad idea to shoot MOS (for "mit out sound," a term coined by early Hollywood sound recordists, who tended to be German), because even the on-camera mic sound may prove useful in postproduction, if for nothing else then for a guide track as to exactly what was said. For scripted productions there are deviations from scripts that make looping or replacing dialogue difficult when there is no precise record of what was said. For documentary films, having some sync sound available instead of putting in a general ambience makes editing easier.

- The camera is a sound recorder too, and often the only one on the location. It can be used as a sound recorder only, with the picture just along for the ride, which may be used to document where the sound was taken. With the low cost of tape, and decent sound recording quality, this option is potentially much better than using a separate cassette audio recorder, for instance.

Another problem of on-camera microphones is that the mechanism of the spinning drum that writes and reads the dense audio/video data on tape causes mechanical vibration that is inevitably transmitted through the camera body to the microphone and induces noise there. You might not hear this in a quiet room from two feet away, but if you put your ear in contact with the camera body, you will hear it. This noise is what the microphone hears, and various microphones are more or less isolated from their camera bodies to influence how much is picked up. In one case, the Canon XL-1 series, several accessory devices are sold[4] in the aftermarket to isolate the microphone better from the camera body than the stock equipment and reduce the noise. This usually is heard only in very quiet shooting situations though.

Louder camera noises can also occur intermittently with zoom lens motors and other camera functions. Because these relatively soft noises are located very close to on-camera microphones, they can be a real nuisance. The largest help for them is spacing the microphone away from the noise source.

How to Use the Two Channels

The first chapter described why use of the two-channel mode in normal shooting is preferred over the four-channel mode. This gives us two channels to record on, yet there are several ways to use the two channels:

- *Record the same signal from one microphone—or possibly more mixed together usually external to the camera—to both channels, providing redundancy.* This leads to only a little potential confusion in postproduction, and it is simple, but it doesn't provide the most flexibility. This is one setting for

---

[4] By Lightwave Audio Systems (www.lightwavesystems.com) and by K-Tek (www.mklemme.com).

the Sony DSR-PD170 and similar models with its accompanying single-element microphone; we might call it redundant track recording.

One advantage of recording the same signal to two channels on some model cameras is the ability to stagger the levels between the channels—call it redundancy with a twist (of the knob!). The input levels can be adjusted for perhaps a 15 dB difference in peak levels, and if the channel recorded to higher levels becomes distorted, the editor can cut to the lower gain channel (with appropriate level compensation) in the editing system and save the recording from bad distortion. This may require an external Y-adapter.

• *Record a left-right stereo pair from a stereo microphone.* This is the method used by the Canon XL-1 series. A single microphone body contains two pickup elements, in this case, one facing forward and one facing sideways of particular types. Through electronic manipulation, these are turned into a left-right pair. Stereo recording can potentially sound more real than mono recording, because sounds are reproduced in space in a way that matches the picture. Comparing stereo original recording with mono often finds an advantage in openness as well as angular matching between picture and sound. However, editors must be aware that they must keep the two channels together and treat them as a left-right pair, and there can be subjective complications at edits, where the sound jumps around spatially, when we have come to expect dialog, for instance, to generally be delivered from center screen.

One way to use the two channels from the Canon's particular stereo microphone type, called MS stereo for mid-side, is to do further manipulation of them in postproduction to obtain signals corresponding to the original microphone elements forward and sideways facing. Then we have the principal sound in the direction that the camera is looking and a second channel that represents the ambience of the space—that which the camera is not looking at. The first channel emphasizes the sound of an actor that the camera is framing, say, while the second channel literally rejects the actor in favor of hearing the room reverberation and ambience. This can be useful later in postproduction mixing, to be able to manipulate how close or far away the actor sounds by changing the relative balance of the now center-front and surround instead of left-right channels. An aural zoom is possible, by cross-fading between the side and front elements, to make sound seem at first far away, and then moving closer, for example.

However, having discussed stereo production sound recording, it must be said that typical Hollywood feature films long ago gave up on a stereo approach in favor of the dual mono approach discussed next, largely because of editing and mixing concerns. This may be rather unfortunate because well-cared-for stereo sound tracks do have things to offer, but they also add some complication, so editors and mixers must know what to expect.

- *Record dual mono.* Two separate microphones are recorded on channel 1 and channel 2. This system allows greater potential editorial freedom than recording the simpler dual mono. However, the picture and sound editor(s) need to be clued in as to what the coverage plan is so they don't reject something based on what they hear on just one channel, usually the first, which is normally what editors concentrate on. In a variation, two separate *types* of microphones may be mixed together to form one channel, such as putting a boom on channel 1 and two lavs mixed together on channel 2.

Various cases can be considered. If there is only one principal source to cover, it can be covered by two techniques simultaneously. This double coverage of the same activity provides greater redundancy than even dual mono, because if one of the techniques should fail, for example through the subject beating his chest while wearing a radio mic, then the other mic can be relied on for a clean signal. Second, the editor is given the choice as to which combination produces the best sound: one, the other, or both used together. The boom approach typically provides the best timbre and perspective. The lavaliere approach typically provides the tightest sound, with the least reverberation and room noise, which is both good and bad: good because it is probably the most intelligible sound, and bad because of the limitations caused by the lavaliere placement on timbre, naturalness, and with the potential of handling noise, and being muffled from placement underneath costumes. The best sound might result from using a little of each microphone in the final mix, although because there is likely to be a difference in the time of arrival of the direct sound at the two microphones, a frequency response notch or notches can arise, which may sound like the recording has been made in a barrel. All of these choices are postponed until post-production, when there is more time to contemplate and listen to them with this approach than if the microphones were combined to mono in production.

An example of dual mono usage is coverage of a wedding. Conventional thinking might use two radio mics, say one on the bride and one on the officiator, recorded on the two channels, the groom being picked up by the bride's mic—after all, it's her day. The problems with this coverage are that there is no perspective of the wedding space—the sound is rather dull, although the words can be heard. Additionally, the wedding gown's layers make noise. Better practice is to record two radio mics, one on the officiator and one on the groom, whose tuxedo jacket is a lot less noisy than a wedding dress and on which we can pick up the bride adequately, to channel 1; and record a boom mic, or even the on-camera mic, on channel 2. The principle is to group mics having the same type of perspective on separate channels, for best use in postproduction. Another principle illustrated here is to put the best sound on channel 1 because many video editors will typically only listen to the first channel. These two perspectives allow for postproduction mixing to determine how loose or tight sounding the final product is; without the boom or on-camera mic on channel 2, there would be no way to loosen up the overly tight perspective of the lavs alone, especially considering there are other elements of sound, such as the music, to record.

If there are two main sources of sound, then one source may be recorded on each channel. An example is a documentary subject and a questioner. Although a documentary director/questioner will often say "don't bother to record me, we're going to cut out the questions," you'd be surprised at how many times this turns out not to be true, and even if the questions are all cut out, it is still useful to have a clean record of them for transcriptions to know exactly what the questions were. Another example is scene coverage used for a fiction film that has multiple speaking parts. A single boom mic might not be able to cover all of the action simultaneously because of various distances and angles from the camera. Two boom mics could well be the best answer in such a situation, rather than trying to stick to the one boom/one lav scenario that is quite common. The freedom this offers editorially is that both mic channels do not need to be cut simultaneously, and this permits better continuity by having greater potential to conceal sound edits.

Coverage with two spaced microphones such as at a podium so that the talker is covered leads to problems. If they are spaced, it is likely that for at least some of the time the distance to each microphone will be different. Adding together signals with different times results in comb filtering, selective enhancement and diminution of various frequencies, which can even result in a swishing sound as the time changes. A better approach is to use two mics close together, for redundancy and to reduce combing.

Other Items Recorded During Production Sound

Until now we have concentrated on capturing voice in production sound. The reason for this is that the story most often depends on it, and dialogue recording is usually what separates the good from the bad in location sound. Another reason comes by way of an analogy. Color television engineers say that you only have to get the colors of skin, grass, and sky right; nothing else matters nearly as much. That's because skin, grass, and sky have familiar colors, whereas you aren't as familiar with your shirt color. These three elements are used to form absolute color judgments because we have day-to-day experience with them. Dialogue is rather like skin, grass, and sky, so familiar that changes to it are easily perceptible. Such changes include variations in level, timbre, location, and amount of reverberation. Thus, typically the job is to minimize these changes. However, occasionally changes in, say, reverberation are useful to establish and change the apparent distance to a character.

Production sound effects can show wider variations from recordings that are correct in the sense of being the best recorded, and still be very useful. That is, they may have compromised timbre because the microphone isn't in the correct place, or be a little too dry (lacking reverb) or too wet (with excessive reverb) without suffering from these distortions as much as voice would. Thus, it is useful to roll sound on virtually everything because you don't know what will be useful to build tracks in postproduction. Sound effects recorded on location are sometimes of unrepeatable events, like blowing up a building. While in a Hollywood feature, such an explosion might well be enhanced with sound effects from libraries; sometimes the event being recorded is so rare as to be unique. For expected loud sounds, the information given in Chapter 9 will be useful.

Microphone Accessories

Booms/Fishpoles

Hollywood studios traditionally used large, heavy, floor-mounted booms, principally Fisher Booms. These aren't typically used in production nowadays because so much of it is done on location and moving such large equipment is too difficult. Their use has mostly given way to fishpoles, which are typically operated from the floor by a boom operator. There are a great many fishpoles on the market, with cheaper ones made of aluminum tubing and more expensive ones made of carbon fiber for lightness. Some considerations in the selection of a boom are needed length and corresponding weight to hold up (coarsely speaking weight × length = torque, the more important matter than simple weight), internal or external microphone cable, potential articulation (poles with a joint that can be rotated), possible counterweights, and ruggedness (Figure 3-1).

Good fishpole operation means getting the microphone to where it needs to be, aimed correctly, and silently. Professional boom operators are often overlooked for their contribution to sound, but production sound mixers

Figure 3-1a Pictures of good and bad boom technique. (a) Good position and technique.

Figure 3-1b Poor position: under the frame line sounds generally sound worse by being chesty, although the recording can be rescued with appropriate re-recording equalization.

Figure 3-1c Poor position: off the axis of the talker is generally poor recording and probably cannot be rescued.

Figure 3-1d Be careful not to hit the talent in the head with the boom mic; it is easy to do this if you are distracted.

of Hollywood movies know and appreciate their extreme mechanical versatility, their ability to memorize the script quickly and follow the action, their ability to get the microphone where it belongs to match the camera perspective and to have the right amount of reverberation, their ability to remain completely professional in the line of fire because they are the closest to the actors and must not distract them, and so forth.

One common problem with booms is operating them so that the cable, either internal or external, does not move relative to the boom and make noise while in action. Internal curly cords like those on telephone headsets may work well. If an external cable is used, it is generally wrapped around the boom for a few turns and held taut with the operator's hand nearest the bottom of the boom.

Shock Mounts

Shock mounting of microphones to be used on booms or other places is essential when mechanical vibration can be transmitted to them through their mounting (Figure 3-2). Even tapping a little finger on a fishpole

Figure 3-2a A shock mount showing the flexible rubber parts responsible for suspending the mic freely.

Figure 3-2b The lead dress allows the cables to be freely suspended in air—they do not touch each other nor the windscreen when it is in place. This particular mount uses two different cable diameters: one connected to the mic for best flexibility and one out of the assembly for ruggedness.

results in loud output from the microphone if the shock mounting is poor because of the size that this vibration represents at the microphone compared to sound. A typical problem with shock mounting is to short-circuit the effect of the shock mount by having too stiff a microphone cable pulled too tightly. The microphone should ride in the shock mount in a completely springy way. Also, the compliance or springiness of the spring, which is usually made of rubber or plastic parts, needs to be correct for the weight of the microphone in use. If the rubber is too stiff, the effect of the shock mount will be minimal; if it's too loose, then the mic may bounce too much and actually hit other suspension parts when moved.

It is important to maintain shock mounts (and windscreens) so that all mechanical connections are tight. Even slightly loose small parts can cause audible rattles because the components are so close to the mic or even in physical contact with it.

Windscreens

Windscreens are essential in virtually all video applications because just moving the mic even indoors creates wind that can cause obvious low-frequency disturbances (Figure 3-3a). Wind disturbance is usually heard first as low-frequency noise, which progresses up through being so bad that the signal from the mic may intermittently bobble or be cut off as the wind blows the diaphragm into extreme positions. There are several degrees of windscreening, and some require matches between microphone types and windscreens for best effectiveness. Even drafts caused by air handlers indoors can cause small amounts of low-frequency noise to be added to microphones, so there are just not many uses one can have for an unwindscreened mic. The degree of windscreening needed depends on the wind velocity expected. All windscreens alter the sound somewhat, with more aggressive ones offering more protection but altering it more. Thus, you should use the minimum amount of windscreening that works.

Because of their principle of operation, omnidirectional mics may use a foam windscreen that encapsulates the microphone fully. A larger-diameter screen will be more effective. However, this type of foam windscreen is typically unsuitable for directional mics. Note that camcorders with directional mics are often supplied with a simple foam windscreen; these

Figure 3-3a Windscreen types. Shown are differing basket-type windscreens with an internal free air volume for best performance—such types are a virtual necessity for directional mics. A Windjammer used to cover one of the basket-type windscreens for ultimate wind protection is shown as well.

are certainly far from being good, and the aftermarket supplies many different solutions[5] (Figure 3-3b).

For all directional mics, the best idea is to encapsulate a volume of air inside the windscreen, where the velocity of the air may be minimized. Such ball or zeppelin-style windscreens are often made of silk to form an enclosed place to protect the mic. Larger-diameter ones may produce better results, with consequent increases to size, weight, and price.

In more extreme cases outdoors, the silk windscreen can be covered with a Windjammer, a furry covering that progressively reduces the air velocity as it encounters denser fur toward the inside of the device, slowing down the air velocity with which the internal windscreen must deal.

---

[5] Such as those from www.lightwavesystems.com and www.rycote.com.

Figure 3-3b Aftermarket windscreen and added shock mount for the Canon XL series cameras offer greater reduction of camera and wind noise than the stock solution.

Pop Suppression

For close miking, particularly using a directional mic like a cardioid in a music studio miking a vocal, a stretched silk diaphragm commonly called a Popper Stopper placed between the vocalist and mic can reduce or eliminate popping the mic on plosives.

For instances of coverage of people talking at podiums, a good idea is to use an omnidirectional microphone close to the talker, with a small foam windscreen. These will be unobtrusive compared to a full rig with a directional mic and a Popper Stopper. The reduced susceptibility of the omni to popping, and having no bass boost when used close as all directional mics do, make up for the fact that this mic type is not directional. While you can't convince many so-called public address experts of this, who insist on using directional mics up close for feedback suppression, nonetheless it is true. One can simply work an omni mic closer without problems than a directional one.

Case Studies

Mounting Lavs

In mounting a lavaliere microphone on a subject, several issues need to be considered (Figure 3-4). First is the basic position: too low and it's too far away from the mouth, but too high and the microphone is in the acoustic shadow of the jaw. The optimum place is typically in the range of 6 to 9 inches below the jaw line. It is desirable to place the lavaliere somewhere around the centerline of the chest if the talker is facing the camera because then turns to one side or the other will be going off-mic. If it is a two-person interview situation, the lavaliere can be cheated offcenter toward the other person so that when speaking straight ahead or toward the interviewee, the interviewer stays on-mic.

It is desirable to have the microphone see clear air and not be buried under dense clothing, and some extremely small types are available that can be pushed through a buttonhole and remain unseen. With a little larger type, it is desirable to place them under the minimum amount of clothing. A test is blowing air through the cloth; the easier it is, the more sound transmission occurs.

There are several ways to tape the lavaliere to the talker to minimize the effect of clothing rustle. One such way is shown in Figure 3-4.

Radio Mic Usage

Several sections in this chapter have emphasized the pros and cons of lavaliere microphones, discussed how to mount them, and discussed considerations regarding the radio-frequency part of the system. All that background having been said, typically the biggest problems most often heard in film dialogue are caused by problems with radio mics. So Table 3–2 is a guide to solving such audible problems.

Disposable Mics

Occasionally you see a shot in a movie that seems as if the camera must have been destroyed as some large object attacked it (and the audience!).

Figure 3-4a Wrapping a bandage around a lavaliere provides secure mounting.

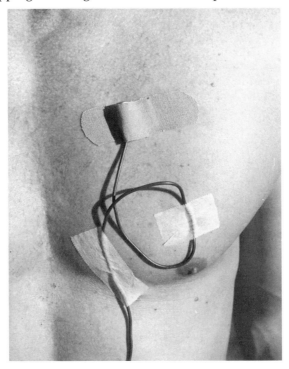

Figure 3-4b The mic is taped to the chest in the position shown (higher to the chin more shadows the sound; lower the direct sound falls off). The loop in the wire is to provide flexibility so that the assembly is not strained as the actor moves.

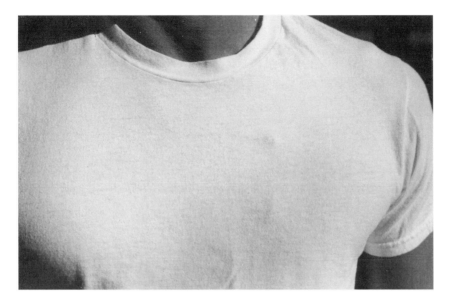

Figure 3-4c Even under a T-shirt, the microphone is not very visible.

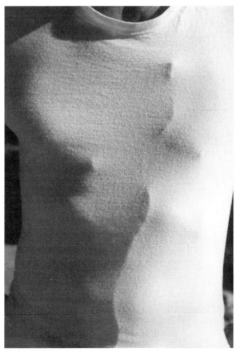

Figure 3-4d In cross light with poor cable dress, the assembly can become obvious.

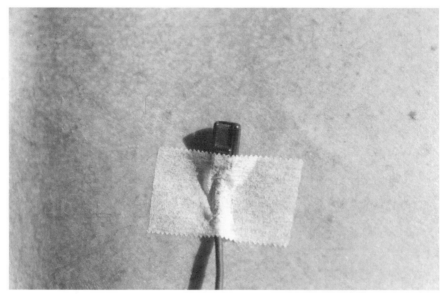

Figure 3-4e Newer side address microphones are flat and therefore somewhat easier to conceal.

Table 3-2 Radio mic problems.

Audible Problem	Possible Explanation/Solution
Problems originating in the audio domain	
Sound is muffled, indistinct	• Lav placed underneath too much clothing: try thinning out the clothing over the microphone. A test is that if you can blow air through it easily, the clothing is acoustically transparent; the harder you have to blow the air, the harder it is for high frequencies to get through. If visibility of the mic is the problem, try using one of the smallest types, such as the Countryman B6, which is small enough that it can be stuck out a buttonhole and not be seen in an ordinary shot, and it comes in a variety of colors.

Continues

Table 3-2 *Continued*

Audible Problem	Possible Explanation/Solution
	• The lav may be in a poor position, such as at the top of a turtleneck pullover, where the sound is shadowed by the chin; this lav needs equalization in addition to the high-frequency boost equalization supplied by most lavs. • If the sound track has already been recorded, then equalization can be applied, which can range from improving the sound somewhat all the way up to making the sound good.
Sound is chesty	Virtually all radio mic recordings benefit from equalization (described in Chapter 9).
Sound is distorted when actor shouts	Gain and limiter settings have to be right for the loudest section of the performance. If the radio mic channel is overloaded by shouts, at least limiting will take place, putting a cap on the maximum level but potentially producing distortion of its own.
Sound has clothing rubbing noise	Use 3M Surgical Clear double-stick hairpiece tape* on skin and around the mic, as per Figure 3-4. Stick it to skin and clothing. Stick multiple layers of clothing together.

Problems originating in the radio domain
(further treatment of this topic is found in Chapter 5)

Sound has intermittent electronic swishy noise or dropouts	Multipath is the cause. Locate and/or orient receiver antenna for better reception. Try vertical versus horizontal orientation. Use Yagi receiving antenna cut for the frequency of the transmitter.** (The boom operator can operate the antenna in scenes where only radio mics are in use.)
You hear signals other than the microphone, such as tones, speech, clicks, or other noises	Radio-frequency interference is the cause. With a frequency-agile system, try a new frequency. With a fixed-frequency system, sometimes moving the receiver to be closer to the transmitter can overwhelm the interference. Remember, you need not necessarily put the receiver where the camera is; if the camera is fixed, a long mic cable can be run from the receiver, which can be close to the transmitter.

*Or moleskin available from drugstores.
**Books are available on how to do this at www.arrl.org.

These shots may be made with a sacrifice camera, a cheap camera that may be destroyed in getting a unique shot. For instance, you may need to plant a microphone in an animal's lair to get the super close-up sound that is going to convince us of the reality of a shot, and yet you may potentially have to sacrifice the microphone. With the microphones discussed so far, this would be an expensive proposition. For this purpose, small electret capsules are available for just several dollars that can be fashioned into a complete microphone with a battery, a resistor, and a capacitor, as shown on their data sheets. These can even be used successfully underwater when wrapped in a condom and well sealed.

Production Sound Example

It is very useful for those studying how production works to be able to hear what it sounds like at various stages. Finished films only tell so much because we don't know what scenes have been ADRed[6] if it's done well, for instance. DVDs provide us with a means to hear what things sound like after picture editing has been performed, but before sound postproduction has taken over, in the extras on some discs in scenes that have been deleted. It is commonplace to shoot more scenes than are finally needed and to remove some after screening for the filmmakers or studio. However, because these scenes are removed from the film before the meticulous sound postproduction is done, they provide us with a means to hear the sound at essentially the dailies stage of the process. A particularly good example are the bonus features from *To Wong Foo, Thanks for Everything! Julie Newmar*, a 1995 Universal theatrical release now on DVD (production sound mixer Michael Barosky and boom operator Linda Murphy). The scenes contain only production sound as it came off the set or location and edited by the picture editors.[7] There is a mix of types of scenes, particularly both interiors and exteriors. In some cases, you can compare the production sound with the finished track by listening to the main feature in contrast with the bonus feature presentation (Table 3-3).

---

[6] That is, had their dialogue replaced in a process called Automated Dialog Replacement, a system wherein an actor watches a picture of the scene and listens to synchronous dialogue in headphones, and repeats the performance, in sync to the picture, in a quiet and dead studio environment, for use as a substituted dialogue track, eliminating the noise and reverberation of the original environment.

[7] They also appear to have been copied through several generations, possibly U-Matic, leading to greater hiss than the original, but they are otherwise very useful for our purposes.

Table 3-3 An analysis of production sound on *To Wong Foo, Thanks for Everything!*
Julie Newmar

Bonus Features Scene Title	Notes
Extended Restaurant Scene	Interior. Boom mic Schoeps Mk41. Two booms in use on some wide shots, requiring two operators on final scene that is in the film, due to Robin Williams' ad libs, among other things (Chapter 4). Hiss due to multigeneration analog postproduction dubbing, not representative of the original.
Style versus Substance	Exterior, day, Queens, New York. Radio lavaliere mics made necessary by the very noisy location. In New York, if police hold traffic, then drivers honk their horns! The first line "This will make it to California, no problem" muffled due to radio mic placement (fixable with equalization in postproduction). This scene probably required at least some ADR due mostly to the noisy location. There are ticks and clicks, but their source is unknown.
The First Step to Queenliness	Exterior, day, quiet mountain setting. Lavaliere radio mics on the three planted in their ample fake bosoms. Wide opening of shot and wind noise prevents use of boom. With equalization and ambience, this would be fine.
Chi Chi's Charms	Interior. Room sound of small room. Hiss probably from post dubbing. Note level of footsteps on stairs is high relative to voice.
A Day with the Girls	Muffled radio mic sound due to placement, fixable with equalization. Excessive footsteps on gravel around the line "Miss Noxie..." This was a preproduction discussion, with the problem pointed out by the location manager and key grip in scouting (sound didn't scout this remote location, but others were looking out for it).

Continues

Table 3-3 *Continued*

Bonus Features Scene Title	Notes
	The road was raked, and rubber mats put down out of sight, but if the scene evolved to where they would show, they couldn't be used. Some of the footsteps heard are those of the camera operator running the Steadicam, not just the actors.
Salade Nicoise	Interior, kitchen, day. Stockard Channing on her knees scrubbing the floor. Boomed. She sounds reverberant, whereas Patrick Swayze is closer on a second boom. Might need ADR. As scene evolves and Stockard crosses to the sink, it gets better.
Beatrice's "Red and Wild"	Exterior evolving to interior, day. Lavs sound a little dead. Need equalization and ambience, and possibly some added reverberation in the barn. These are good raw tracks for postproduction.
A Women's Place	Exterior, dusk. Two guys in a wide shot, radio miked. A one-er (scene shot in one master shot). If close-ups were shot, their sound on a boom could be used over the master, by syncing up editorially. "Career" is distorted, but could possibly be fixed with pencil tool in Pro Tools. This may be a multigeneration dub problem and not be present in the original.
Taking a Chance	Interior, day. Good scene shot all on boom. One floor creak from camera move, possibly editable. Production sound crew helped by the quiet location, the shot choice, the placement of the generator, and so forth.
Extended Goodbye Scene	Footsteps cover the line "you take care honey." First shot complicated by camera moves. Radio mics when used need equalization. Crowd wide shot as car exits shows why you should always shoot sync, as it is useful. Some wind sound and distortion on radio mics of three of them leaving.

Listening to these scenes, and the corresponding ones in the final film for those that are present, shows just what production sound can and cannot do when enhanced with postproduction techniques. Most of the scenes work, with equalization for lavalieres, added ambience and in some cases music, and occasionally added reverberation. On the other hand, there are scenes that are just about impossible to cover with production sound alone because the background noise level is just too high. Take the car lot exterior. It's real, but it needs a lot of sound postproduction work. In older Hollywood productions, this would have been shot on a controlled back lot. In today's world, no one has the time and budget for such meticulous staging, so it is shot on location, with sound consequences heard in the bonus features segment.

The Boom Operator's Job

The boom operator has an important job. Although not as technical as the production sound mixer/recordist, it nonetheless contributes greatly to the track. Among the considerations for the job are the following:

- Hold up the fishpole for extended periods of time and move it silently.

- Learn the dialogue for fiction films as well as anyone on the set so that they can emphasize the right thing moment by moment. For documentary films, they must stay on the ball to cover the person speaking and anticipate the next one to speak.

- Match the microphone perspective to the camera shot. This means knowing the focal length of the lens in use, or if a zoom, where it is set, knowing where the frame line is and avoiding it, and making the distance to the actor appropriate for the acoustics of the space for the shot.

- Be front-line person for the sound crew because they are closest to the actors. They will often be involved in positioning radio mics.

- Not distract the actors/subjects by making eye contact.

- Boom operators must learn the translation from headphone listening to loudspeaker listening. Headphones exaggerate background noise, making almost any intrusive noise audible, which may not be too much trouble to reduce in postproduction. There is a long learning curve with this skill. Unfortunately, you cannot trust most editorial setups to tell you whether there is good or bad sound. The answer doesn't emerge until later in the process, with wide frequency range calibrated level monitoring, and most boom operators are long gone from the show by this time, so a valuable feedback loop is lost.

As noted earlier, video has one problem for camerapersons that film doesn't have that affects boom operators. The viewfinder shows more than the photographed area on a film camera but exactly the captured area (if that, as there could be overscan in the monitor) for video. This means there is no warning of when a boom will be in a shot in video. One possibility is for the fishpole to have mounted to it a small LCD monitor, showing the frame. This involves one cable from the camera's composite output to the monitor and clamps to hold it to the fishpole. In this way the boom operator can be certain of the frame line.

Common Problems

Some gotchas are as follows:

- High-end cameras often combine channels in their monitoring circuits. Thus, you may send it two channels and expect two back for monitoring with an external mixer, but get the two channels mixed. Interestingly, this is not a problem with some semi-pro models.

- Level setting can be complicated by the use of different types of meters in use on mixers versus cameras. Professional cameras will indicate −20 dBFS as the reference level for tone on a digital peak meter, whereas prosumer cameras may show −12 as reference level (this is described in detail in Chapter 6, Connecting Up and References).

- DV cameras with nonlocked audio may produce no sync problem played from tape, or even from the first stage editing system, but, depending on how subsequent processes handle the audio-video sync, could come apart later. Systems that interleave picture and sound bits will normally be okay, whereas ones that separate the files and then try to put them back together later may suffer from sync problems. One way to ensure sync is to test the full path you are going to use, from camera capture through picture editorial, to sound

DV Production Sound Log[8]

Prod #		Prod Name		Shoot Date	
Camera Op.		Sound Op.		Roll #	
❏ Two-channel, 48-kHz sample rate, 16-bit word length ❏ Other					
SMPTE Time Code: ❏30 fps ❏ 29.97 fps ❏ 25 fps ❏ 24 fps ❏ 23.976 fps ❏ NDF ❏ DF Starting code: : : : .					
Scene	Take	TC Start	TC End	Track 1	Track 2
Head tone and bars				Tone @ –20 dBFS	
Circled takes good. A.F.S. = after false start. TS = tail slate. For dailies indicate ❏ Do not sum tracks. ❏ Sum tracks.					
IF FOUND, please call					

---

[8] Copyright modified for this page: it may be copied by original producers for their use when accompanied by this notice: Original © 2005 Tomlinson Holman. Used with permission.

editorial and layback to the picture master, and even to the final output, such as a DVD. If you make a tape with a clapperboard slate every minute for the length of your program, then put it through all of the processes you are going to use, and you can be assured that the final result stays in sync.

Logging

In conventional film production, keeping logs is quite important because picture and sound are separate and must be sunk up in post, and it is a waste to print takes that are no good. In DV production, because it is a single system, this is less of a strict requirement, but with many hours of footage, it is a good idea to know where scenes are located on tape. Thus a camera assistant, producer, or script person can keep track of what the general time code for specific scenes is.

Sound Kit Accessories

- Location sound logs

- Tape for lavaliere mounting: 3M Surgical double-stick, hairpiece tape (from costumers), or moleskin

- Tape, Gaffer's, cable tie down

- Bungee cord for holding cables

- Carabiners (mountain climbing clamps) for holding cables

- Spare mechanical parts for boom and mic suspensions

- Greenie, a small Xcelite screwdriver (model P3321) used for XLR connectors, small adjustments, etc.

- Tweaker, an adjustment screwdriver tool especially used for 10-turn potentiometers

- Needle-nose pliers, small

- Diagonal cutter, small

- Soldering iron, small, and solder

- First-aid kit.

The Director's Cut

- If at all possible, designate a sound person during production whose principal responsibility is sound.
- Scout locations for sound as well as look. You can pan off an offending sign, but you can't pan off an offending noise nearly as well.
- In fiction pieces, make everyone aware of the need to get good production sound.
- Obtain coverage. That is, shoot production sound of the event well, but fill in by recording room tone; in fiction filmmaking record wild lines if possible for the parts not able to be covered well.
- Boom microphones are typically greatly preferred. Radio mics are possible but have several drawbacks.
- A few things can be done with an on-camera mic: ambience, for example.
- Use the two channels for redundancy, staggered levels so you get the widest clean dynamic range, or two differing mic perspectives.
- Use shock mounts, windscreens, and fishpoles effectively to produce silent microphone moves.
- The boom operator is much more than "a big kid out of high school with strong arms," as one producer exclaimed to me. Professional production sound mixers know that skilled boom operators make their job infinitely simpler by learning the scene, tracking the action, and so on.

CHAPTER 4

Production Sound II: Microphones

There are many different types of microphones in the world today, from sophisticated and expensive ones used for high-end film production and music to millions of simple ones used in telephones and answering machines. While the range is large, only a few types are prominent in film and video production, and this chapter will concentrate on these types.

There are two main factors that characterize microphones, beyond their simple visible characteristics of size, mounting, and so forth. The first factor is the method by which the microphone changes acoustical energy, sound, into electrical energy, represented by changing voltage versus time at the electrical output connector of the microphone. The generic name for a microphone is *transducer*, meaning a device that changes from one domain to another. A loudspeaker is also a transducer, at the other end of the audio chain, converting electrical energy back into sound.

The second factor that is important to users is the directional characteristic of the microphone, whether it accepts sound equally from all angles practically speaking, or whether it has a directional preference, picking up sound from one range of directions while discriminating against sound from other directions. This directional property, called a microphone's *polar pattern*, is in many cases the most important property in choosing a microphone.

Many other factors can be important in microphone selection, but these two factors are usually the first to be thought about. Other factors include the susceptibility of particular microphone models to wind and handling generated noise, how well particular models of microphones cover the frequency range from deep bass to high treble without discrimination, how well the polar pattern is maintained across frequency, power requirements, environmental susceptibility to temperature and humidity, ability to handle loud and soft sounds, ruggedness, and others.

The main method of transduction used in microphones for film and television production today is called *electrostatic,* and these are commonly referred to as capacitor or condenser microphones. In this method of transduction, a stretched diaphragm of flexible material like a drumhead is moved in and out by impinging sound energy, usually by an incredibly small distance. Typically the moving diaphragm hovers over a fixed internal back plate. The changing distance between the diaphragm and the back plate is analyzed by measuring the changing electrical capacitance between them, using one of several means.[1] There are several things for users to know well:

- All electrostatic (condenser, capacitor) microphones require a power source somewhere because of the basic principle of operation.

- All electrostatic microphones should be kept dry because moisture can short circuit the insulation on which the ability to measure the capacitance between the diaphragm and back plate depends and can cause crackling in the output or gross failure.

Power

Power is supplied to electrostatic microphones in several ways, dependent on the model of microphone in use. Microphones physically built into the body of cameras have their power supplied as part of the general power supply of the camera, but those mounted externally fall into two categories: those supplied with the camera and those separately marketed as accessories to cameras. For those sold with the camera, normally the camera will supply the power, but for microphones treated as accessories, the camera may supply the power, or one of the methods described as follows may be used.

The most direct way of supplying power to an external microphone is a battery in the microphone body, or often with lavaliere microphones in the shell of the connector supplied by the microphone manufacturer that resides at the other end of a cable from the microphone. The type of battery used

---

[1] *Capacitance* is a measure of the ability of a device to hold an electrical charge. In this case, an insulator, such as air, separates two conductors: the diaphragm, which may be metal or plastic coated with metal, and a metal back plate.

varies widely, and it is a necessity to have spares available, especially when working away from sources of supplies of particular and sometimes-rare battery types. Also, it is easy to overlook such batteries at the end of the day and leave them running in microphones overnight. While microphones can operate a long time on some of the battery types, they may be found to be fully discharged just when they are needed. A related way of powering electrostatic microphones is by using a small separate box that can house the battery and into which the microphone plugs; the output of the box is another connector that can be plugged into a cable destined for a microphone input of a camera or mixer.

The consequence of diminishing battery voltage at the end of battery life is potential distortion, and perhaps less overall output level from the microphone. Distortion usually affects loud sounds first, and as the battery voltage goes down, the effect will be heard with lower and lower levels of sound, until the battery dies completely. It is a good idea to time batteries in use and replace them before distortion becomes potentially audible. A curiosity that is important to know is that battery life may range from 20 hours for one particular model of stereo microphone using an AA battery (Sony ECM-MS5) to 5,000 hours for a lavaliere (Sony ECM-55B) *using the same battery*. Thus it is important to know the rated battery life of a particular microphone you use.

A second method of powering is by a direct power connection, separate from the wires carrying the audio signal. The microphone supplied with the Canon XL series, for instance, has a connector with two adjacent plugs: one for the signals from the microphone (the one segmented into three parts called tip, ring, and sleeve for left signal, right signal, and ground, respectively) and one for power (the one segmented into two parts: tip for power and sleeve for ground). The camera supplies power to the microphone by way of this second connection, and because this is a somewhat unusual method of powering, the microphone as delivered is only suitable for use with these model cameras. Powering an external microphone from the camera is simpler for the user because he or she does not have to remember a separate battery.

A third method of powering is used with a wider range of professional microphones. Called *phantom powering*, often designated in the microphone model number with a "P" suffix. In this case, power is supplied on the audio signal wires in a particular way. The signal runs from the microphone to the camera or external mixer, and the power runs the other direction, from the camera or mixer to the microphone. Again, this is fairly simple for the user in practice because it means there is no additional battery to remember. However, the input to which the microphone is connected must supply power, and it is often switchable on and off because applying phantom power to other microphone types might result in damage. Also, the voltage of phantom supplies is not standardized; although 48-V phantom is the most common, 12-V phantom supplies are also found. So to use a microphone with phantom power, the user must switch on the power and set the voltage of the camera or mixer to match the microphone requirements. Forty-eight-volt phantom power is the method used by the Sony PD-150 and 170 camera microphone accessories, for instance.

A similar but not interchangeable method is called "T" or "A-B" powering; it is considerably more rare than phantom powering, but its widest use has been in production sound for film, so you may encounter it. Usually designated by a T suffix in the microphone type, it is an older method used particularly on some models of Schoeps and Sennheiser microphones, but is rarely if ever encountered with DV equipment. Still, external mixers like the Shure FP-33 are internally switchable between T and P powering, and the user must match the switch setting in the mixer to the microphone type in use for it to work. Just to confuse things further, T-powered mics were traditionally supplied in two polarities. Normally they had pin 2 of the XLR connector for positive (+) voltage and pin 3 for negative (−) voltage. Those with a red dot and some others perhaps unmarked were meant for connection to Nagra tape recorders, the film production standard for many years, that had pin 2 (−) and pin 3 (+). If you encounter a microphone with a red dot, you may use a polarity reversing (also called polarity inverting) cable, or build one, to interchange the leads for pin 2 and 3 to connect such microphones to conventional T-powered inputs. The Shure FP-33 mixer supplies phantom power at 12 V and 48 V and T power at 12 V in the standard polarity, so a microphone formerly used for film sound, connected to a Shure mixer, may not work, and polarity is usually the reason.

Dynamic Microphones

Another method of transduction is the electrodynamic principle, with microphones built in this way called simply dynamic ones. These work like a conventional loudspeaker, only in reverse. Sound moves a diaphragm attached to a voice coil, which resides in the field of a magnet, causing an electrical voltage to arise directly, using the same principle as do electric generators. These types require no power, and models can be built that are quite rugged. Their output voltage for a given level of sound is usually lower than for electrostatic mics, and their uniformity of responding to all frequencies from bass to treble is often not as good as for electrostatic types. However, there are several places where they excel and are virtually needed: news operations where they can better stand the effects of weather and abuse, and as a backup for electrostatic microphones. When all goes wrong with insulation because of high humidity, battery supplies, and so forth, with electrostatic microphones, a rugged dynamic microphone will almost always still work. Thus, documentary filmmakers carry a dynamic microphone with them to be sure that they can get sound under practically all conditions encountered.

Generally, connecting most dynamic mics to phantom power will not damage them, but T power may because in this case the voltage is applied across the voice coil. Connecting another type of microphone transducer using the same principle as the dynamic mic for transduction but using a different construction, a ribbon microphone, to either phantom or T power is likely to damage it, thus the need for microphone power switches on units like the Sony PD-150 and 170 microphone input. Separate mixers intended for more general purposes may have switching for both phantom and T power, potentially of different voltages. Of course, if these are left off, electrostatic microphones of the correct type, P or T, will not work; if they are switched on and fed to a microphone that doesn't match their type, the result could be microphone damage.

Polar Patterns

The term *polar pattern* describes how a microphone responds to sound from various directions. The simplest polar pattern is omnidirectional. The smallest microphones, such as lavalieres or microphones built into telephones, and larger microphones that can be identified by having only one entrance for sound are typically omnidirectional. They accept sound equally from all directions, except perhaps at the highest frequencies, where the size of the microphone makes it discriminate somewhat for sources in front rather than behind the mike. Thus, they generally need not be aimed precisely, but on the other hand, they discriminate the least against undesired sound.

Where microphones have to be small, an omnidirectional polar pattern is usually the only option. This is true of almost all lavaliere microphones, which gain their utility by being located close to the source rather than by discriminating sound from various directions. We'll examine how these are related below.

All other types of microphone polar patterns show a directional preference. While none of them can be said to magically reach out and record something at a distance, they do attenuate sound off their main pickup axis in various degrees, depending on their polar pattern, while maintaining their sensitivity to sound along the principal axis of pickup. In real rooms and locations, off-axis attenuation has the effect of reducing environmental noise and reverberation. This typically leads to a preference for directional microphones over omnidirectional types for microphones that are on cameras, booms, or planted because omni mics are at a disadvantage when it comes to discriminating against noise compared to more directional types.

Any directional microphone can be aimed such that a desired sound source is put on-mic; that is, the microphone is pointed toward the source, and undesired sound is placed in the null or cold side of the polar pattern. Although almost everybody understands intuitively that a microphone is better aimed at a source than not, almost everyone also overlooks the second fact: that aiming the side of the mic that discriminates against undesired sound is perhaps equally valuable. Shooting a scene outside a nightclub for a documentary about music on noisy Sunset Boulevard in Los Angeles on Saturday night means getting the most directional mic the closest to the subjects possible, aiming it at them, and keeping the back side of the mic to the street, thus reducing the noise of the street cruisers as much as practical.

Another type of noise insofar as production sound recordings are usually concerned is reverberation. *Reverberation* is sound that has bounced around a space several times such that individual reflections have merged into a foggy cloud; reverberation arrives at the microphone distinctly later than the direct sound and from virtually all directions. Reverberation can be helpful in small amounts to set the feeling of distance, because recordings with no reverberation at all, called dry, sound like they come from outside the space of the movie, like narration. However, in larger amounts, reverberation can be damaging to speech intelligibility because sound emitted produces reverberation that tends to cover up later emitted sounds.

Contrasted with reverberation are direct sound and early reflections. *Direct sound* is the sound that originates at the source and propagates in a straight line to the microphone, assuming nothing is in the way. *Early reflections* are the several reflections of direct sound off walls, the floor and ceiling, and so on that work like balls on a pool table, bumping off the edges in a defined way, and eventually making it to the microphone. Each of these reflections has distinct direction(s) associated with it, and thus directional microphones can be used to emphasize them, or deemphasize them, depending on where the microphone is placed and which direction it is pointed.

A demonstration of appropriate reverberation on a voice in an interior compared to voice-over narration occurs in the first scene of *Apocalypse Now*. The first voice is that of Capt. Willard, in voice-over, as we hear his interior thoughts. This voice recording is on-mic and dry. Then when the officers arrive to pick him up, they are heard in the hall of the Saigon hotel. Their voices, doubtlessly from production sound, are more reverberant; they are real.

Although used appropriately in *Apocalypse Now*, excessive noise and reverberation on voice is one of the biggest problems exhibited by many movies, shot on DV or film. This arises because of the routine use today of location sets, particularly in sparsely furnished modern housing. Kitchen scenes are often particularly bad because all of the surfaces are hard, and thus the room is quite reverberant. This is also demonstrated by the large, hard interiors of Savannah, Georgia, mansions in *Midnight in the Garden of Good and Evil*. Many lesser films have the effect even worse, to the point where the words become difficult to understand. Basically, it is impossible to remove reverberation in postproduction, and relatively easy to add it, so production concentrates on getting the voice without excessive reverberation because it always can be added but not subtracted.

There are basically two ways around picking up excessive noise and reverberation: get the mic close while aiming it properly, and make it directional. The case of the lavaliere is covered later; for boom and planted mic operation, we typically want the most directional mic we can use without side effects dominating. The types of polar patterns are as follows (Figure 4-1):

- *Omnidirectional.* This type accepts sound equally from all directions. As such, it must typically be closer to sources in order to pick up an adequate amount of direct sound compared to reverberation. It is the

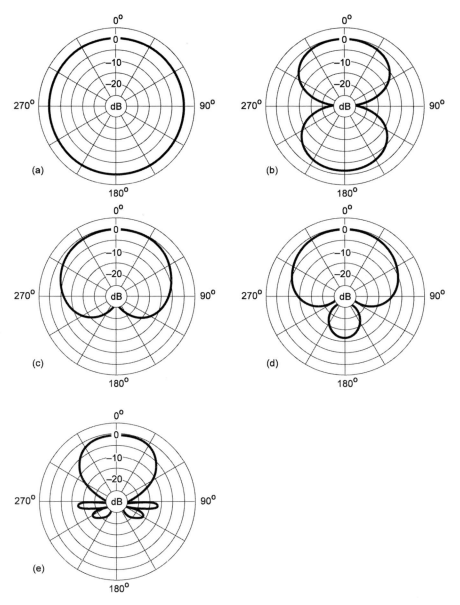

Figure 4-1 Microphone polar patterns. (a) Omnidirectional. (b) Bidirectional. (c) Cardioid. (d) Hypercardioid. (e) Interference tube. Although these are shown in two dimensions, the actual polar pattern is the two-dimensional pattern rotated through three dimensions along the main pickup axis of the microphone.

simplest construction and thus is found in the smallest microphones, such as lavalieres, that also are placed close to the source of sound.

- *Bidirectional*. This type prefers sound from the front and back but nulls out sound from the side. Its main use in film and video sound is in making the side-facing component of single-point stereo microphones. Random sound energy like reverberation originating from all angles is attenuated to a factor of one-third of the level of on-axis sound.

- *Cardioid*. This type has a broad frontal acceptance and a null at 180 degrees from its principal direction. Although this polar pattern is probably the most often found among directional mics in the world, film and video boom mics are usually more directional, such as the following types. Like a bidirectional mic, random sound is picked up at about one-third the level of on-axis sound. There is also a subcardioid available in some types, with its polar pattern between that of an omnidirectional mic and a cardioid.[2]

- *Hypercardioid/supercardioid*. These types have a little narrower frontal acceptance than a cardioid, being somewhat more attenuated at 90 degrees than a cardioid, and they have a null in the shape of the surface of a cone, at an angle from the front of 110 degrees or 126 degrees. There is a small rear lobe of sensitivity. These are the most directional types of simple microphones, with random sound being picked up at a level about one-quarter that of on-axis sound. Because the null is off the rear axis, these types can be put on a boom and aimed at the actor, while the null is aimed at the camera, and not be in the field of view of the camera.

- *Shotgun*. These types vary in their polar pattern depending on their length, from a fairly narrow club shape (about ± 30 degrees about the axis) for short shotgun models (meaning about a foot in length) to very narrow (about ± 10 degrees) for those around 3 feet in length.

---

[2] Specific models of subcardioids like the Schoeps MK-21 g have an interesting property: they pick up direct sound arriving from one direction and reverberant sound arriving from all directions, with nearly the same frequency response. In other words, their bass to treble balance is the same for both sound fields. Omnis roll off highs off-axis, while other directional mics vary; they are usually less uniform than the subcardioid.

Because their angle of acceptance is so narrow, it is critical that they be aimed correctly. Sounds from off the axis are colored because of the principle of operation. The short shotguns only develop their directional property at higher frequencies, so they do not discriminate any better than a hypercardioid/supercardioid at bass to midrange frequencies. In practice, they *must* be aimed if the subject is allowed to move at all, so they require a boom operator in most instances. With these potential drawbacks in mind, they are probably the most used film and video production microphones, followed by hyper- or supercardioid types.

Long shotguns are really only suitable for outdoor use unless they are used in a large, dead studio like a Hollywood shooting stage because through their principle of operation, their off-axis sound—which constitutes a large fraction of the energy received at the microphone in a normal room—is so colored that the problem becomes obvious. On the other hand, they can be useful in outdoor tracking dolly shots, for instance. For such a shot, lavalieres have a peculiarly intimate quality that does not match the picture well, whereas a long shotgun mic on a boom may get perfectly usable sound.

Differences Between Microphones Having Various Types of Polar Patterns

All other things being equal, an omnidirectional mic will be less susceptible to wind and possibly to handling noise than nondirectional types. In fact, most omnidirectional mics are less wind susceptible than most directional mics. For building a microphone system with maximum wind noise rejection, see pg. 137.

A corresponding fact is that omnidirectional mics have less sensitivity to pop effects. Try this experiment: hold your bare arm up vertically with your hand about six inches in front of your face. Pronounce a "P." You should feel a puff of wind in your hand. Now pronounce a "T." You may now feel a puff of wind on your wrist or below. "P's" and "T's" are called *plosives* in speech. They create these puffs of wind when pronounced, and how microphones handle them distinguishes how useful they are on close-miked speech. Omnidirectional microphones have an advantage in close miking because they are less susceptible to pops.

Directional microphones have a potential problem in that they exhibit boosted bass when the source is close to the microphone, called the *proximity effect*. This can exaggerate a woofy quality in voice when used close, for instance.

Here is advice in short form:

Use omnis:

- Where the source-to-microphone distance is small, so that the fact that it is nondirectional does not cause a severe disadvantage

- Where the source is a talker and the microphone can be very close, right in front of the talker, for two reasons: this type demonstrates less susceptibility to popping and no bass boost from close use

- Where wind is a significant problem

- Where you must because of the requirement for small size, such as lavaliere use and for planting hidden microphones, where the size must be kept small

- Using multiple spaced omnis is one type of stereophonic recording that may be particularly useful with certain large-scale effects (e.g., a train going past the microphones).

Use cardioids:

- Where you can differentiate the sound field into desired sound coming from one direction and undesired from 180 degrees away from the desired, such as placing a microphone near a talker on a street and pointing the mic at the talker and its back side at the street.

- However, note that cardioids, which in the wide world are the most common directional microphone, are not as widely used in filmmaking as in music recording or public address systems, because hypercardioid and supercardioid mics are more directional, and thus discriminate against noise and reverberation better than cardioids

Use hypercardioid or supercardioids:

- Where you want to discriminate the most against reverberation in a mic having a relatively small body

- Where the source of noise can be placed in a null in the range of 110 degrees to 126 degrees from the front, and the desired source on axis, such as on a boom capturing an actor on-mic and placing the camera in the null (typically more important with film cameras than video ones)

- These considerations lead to the selection of these types for boom microphone use.

Use short shotguns:

- For greater discrimination against reverberation and noise at high frequencies than hypercardioids or supercardioids, although in the bass and midrange they are equal to those types

- When, if the actor or event is moving, a boom operator can accurately aim the mic, because off-axis sound is poor

- This is probably the most often used boom microphone.

Use long shotguns:

- For the greatest discrimination against off-axis sound over a wider frequency range than the short shotgun

- Out of doors, for wide shots, dolly shots, and so forth

- Indoor use is not generally recommended, because the interaction of the complex polar pattern of this mic type with room acoustics leads to coloration.

The following continues recommendations, but not about specific polar-pattern types; rather they are listed by microphone technique.

Use boom mics:

- Whenever practical, because they produce better timbre and perspective than lavalieres.

Use dead-hung mics:

- This is a type of inflexible boom mic that might be used in a fixed setting, such as the set of a sitcom; it is useful where it makes sense for coverage, such as upstage away from the reach of a conventional boom, but in a well-defined place.

Use on-camera mics:

- For ambience or establishing shots with sync sound

- For close-ups if there is no boom operator

- As a last resort for a scratch track.

Use planted mics:

- In conventional car interiors, on the headliner, positioned so that the sound makes sense relative to the picture

- When set pieces clog up the working space for a boom and the position of the actor is well defined, such as for Norm seated at the end of the bar in *Cheers*.

Use radio mics:

- When there is no practical way to use a boom mic and the problems with them have been considered

- When a wired lavaliere won't work because of the needs of actors/ subjects to move about:

Problems with radio mics include:

- The sound perspective never matches the camera perspective. If an actor turns and faces away from the camera, the sound doesn't change, when it should. This isn't always important, because a news-reader for instance is not shot at a variety of angles, but for most fiction and documentary work it is important.

- Noise from clothing rustle and the direct connection of clothes to the microphone body is troublesome.

- The microphone is in a poor position for picking up voice—it can't see the lips. Many lavaliere microphones exaggerate high frequencies, effectively turning up the treble to try to overcome this effect, but the effects of putting a microphone on a chest instead of in front of a talker are to color the sound in a more complex way than can be compensated for with a simple treble rise. The sound is literally chesty and lacking in certain midrange to high frequencies, while emphasizing others. Methods of dealing with lavaliere sound are described in the Chapter 9 on mixing, but all in all, lavalieres have to be said to be a compromise, from small to severe.

- For fiction filmmaking where the microphone cannot show, burying the mic beneath layers of costume tends to muffle the sound.

- For documentary filmmaking, putting lavalieres on subjects invades their personal space. For small crews, the director does this. Running the mic cable outside of clothing where it shows is bad form, even for news coverage, and so it is normally placed under clothing. Actors are very used to being handled by makeup, hair, and costume people, so they usually don't find the addition of dealing with a radio mic to be much trouble, but for documentary subjects it may be a strange experience.

However, sometimes the only solution for a given shot is to use one or more radio mics. In a large space with a wide shot from a low angle, there is literally no place to put a microphone that won't be seen in the shot. In an exterior street scene in a busy city, there may be no way to conceal the actions of the crew, such as a boom operator, from bystanders without use of concealed radio mics, and thus other techniques draw more attention to the filmmaking than might be desirable.

The Radio Part of Radio Mics

The term *radio mics* used in film and video sound usually means lavaliere microphones attached to belt-pack transmitters, often used with similar sized receivers placed directly on the camera (Figure 4-2). However, there are other instances, such as handheld microphones with the transmitter internal or external on a plug-in called a butt plug and receivers that are rack mounted for fixed installations. You can pay between $130 and $7000 for a radio mic, so what distinguishes them? You might think that it could be the transmission power, because more power will reach farther, but that is unlikely to be the main difference because of strong Federal Communications Commission (FCC) regulatory limits on transmitter power.

The distinguishing features across the wide range of radio mics have to do principally with the reliability and sound quality of the transmission system. You can beat any of these systems with microphone cable

a

Figure 4-2 A typical radio microphone transmitter (a) and receiver (b).

Continues

b

Figure 4-2 Cont'd

hardwired, but you would be giving up the freedom of movement that is so cherished among actors and subjects. Here are some qualities that make radio microphones have such a wide price range:

- *You typically pay a premium for being on radio transmission frequencies that are less likely to be occupied by others,* such as television transmission, paging systems, industrial radios, government channels, and so on. Higher-frequency radio mic systems that work at UHF frequencies may be more costly than VHF because the technology is a little more difficult, and you might be willing to pay the difference because the frequency spectrum is less busy at higher frequencies and thus less likely to have unanticipated sources of trouble. A competent seller in a particular market will know the frequency coordination issues of that market and sell or rent you a radio mic that isn't on the same frequency as a powerful UHF digital television transmitter, for instance. This is why local knowledge is important in the use of radio mics, to know what is found in a particular market.

- *Transmitter and receiver may employ a fixed frequency, or they may have agile frequency tuning.* A fixed-frequency system is the simplest and may well work, but in case interference develops on that channel, a frequency agile system can be set to a new frequency. Some are even smart enough to scan across the frequency range and find an available channel without interference. Others offer a spectrum analyzer function, showing a graph of all the radio frequency transmissions occurring across a band of frequencies so that you can choose one where no one else is broadcasting.

- *More expensive systems typically will work under more difficult situations.* This is because the filters in them that separate the desired signals from undesired ones will be more elaborate in more expensive mics and do a better job. If you were to use one radio mic in a rural environment away from sources of radio frequencies, then an inexpensive one may do, whereas if you needed 10 radio mics in a city near a transmitter, then you've got a much bigger problem, perhaps an insurmountable one for a given budget.

- *The transmission method commonly employed for radio mics is FM, and it suffers from the potential for multipath reception.* That is, the receiver may get one principal signal from the transmitter, but also a reflected signal off a building, say. That reflected signal could come in at just the right delay relative to the direct transmission so that the sum of the two signals adds up to nothing—we say they are out of phase with respect to each other. This is the effect you hear when listening to FM in a big city while driving around in a car. The momentary noisy dropouts are caused by multipath reflected off the buildings. You can even find that if you drive up to a red light that there may be no signal at all or a distorted one, and then you move a foot or two and the signal is restored. This is the result of multipath.

The way to minimize multipath problems is called *diversity reception.* Here, two[3] antennas and receivers physically spaced apart are scanned and the output selectively chosen as the one having the best signal, moment by moment. The idea is that although the signal may drop out at one point in space because of multipath, it is much less likely to drop out at two points in space. Full diversity reception is as described, with two full receiver systems used, in one or several chassis. Antenna diversity systems attempt to add signals from two antennas together to achieve a similar goal, but such efforts are rather limited in quality.

Another way to minimize multipath is to use directional receiving antennas tuned to the frequency range of the transmitter and aimed at

---

[3] Or very occasionally more.

the source transmitter,[4] thus reducing the multipath signals strength. Such directional receiving antennas work rather like directional microphones, picking up signals along one axis and attenuating signals from off the axis. In some such cases, if a boom mic is not in use, then the boom operator will aim the antenna to follow the action. This method is sometimes used on feature film production, but it is uncommon.

- *Because of the nature of noise on FM, transmitters and receivers use companding noise reduction, with the transmitter variably boosting the highs before sending and the receiver cutting them back in an equal and opposite way.* The attempt is to hide the noise of the channel behind the program content. The companders used are of various levels of quality because this is a tricky process, varying in time, and can add artifacts to the voice, so a more expensive mic is likely to be a better one, although that might not always be true.

- *Audio performance varies from model to model.* Because the dynamic range of the radio-frequency channel is limited, it is commonplace to employ an audio limiter, capping the maximum loudness of sound. These limiters can range from benign to obvious in use, depending on their design and how hard they are pushed.

- *Recently, more expensive systems have switched to digital transmission from FM transmission,* with claimed benefits in reliability of the channel, which is what radio mics are all about. In order to do this, the audio must be strongly coded to fit in the channel, and this coding may or may not be audibly transparent, so it is a good idea to audition these systems before you need them.

- *The most elaborate digital systems employ encryption to prevent someone from tapping the transmission.* With high-profile movies, this may be a consideration, but it probably doesn't affect most producers.

- *So far all known radio mic systems use FM or digital transmission assigned to one particular frequency* (for the carrier; the audio-modulated radio frequency signals extend out around the carrier). In the future,

---

[4] Books on this subject are available from the National Association for Amateur Radio at www.arrl.org.

spread spectrum systems may be expected to come on the market. Spread spectrum means putting out radio frequency energy over a very wide band of frequencies with a particular method of coding such that the transmitter and receiver are synchronized to one another—there is no one carrier frequency, and this is what keeps the system more immune to multipath and less likely to be detected by an interloper. In a bizarre turn of history, the co-inventor of this technique was the film star Hedy Lamarr. Kept as a government secret for many years, Lamarr's method of communications was to use something very like player piano rolls synchronized in both transmitter and receiver to determine their carrier frequency moment by moment and to thus frequency-hop the carrier so the transmission could be hidden. The largest use of a related technology dating back to Lamarr's World War II invention in the world today is the global positioning system (GPS).

It is important to start level optimizing by setting the level at the transmitter rather than at the receiver. This is because the transmitter audio gain control best matches the range of the actor's voice to the available dynamic range of the channel. Overmodulation will run into limiting and possibly obvious distortion, while undermodulation will make for noisy recordings. Often two LEDs are provided, perhaps marked SIG for signal, indicating some noticeable activity in the channel, and OVLD for overload, so much signal that distortion is risked. The idea is to set the manual transmitter level control so that the SIG LED flashes often but the OVLD flashes little. A whole performance must be included, because overload of radio mic channels upon actors shouting is all too common. In fact, in many films, excessive limiting of the transmitters is often the most audibly identifiable part of there having been a lavaliere in use, because of the artifacts surrounding the gain changes.

There are a great many radio mics on the market, and perhaps a simple system will do for your purpose, but it should probably be tested in the conditions of use to prove that. One way to tell what systems seem to work is by consulting film/video sound-specific rental houses for big urban areas, such as www.coffeysound.com and www.locationsound.com in Los Angeles, or similar companies in your area.

The Director's Cut

- Microphones have two main characteristics: how they convert sound to electrical energy, and their directional properties. Electrostatic (condenser, capacitor) microphones require a power supply, so the need for special batteries is a consideration for some of them. They are typically more delicate than the other main type but generally have the best sound quality. Dynamic (electrodynamic) microphones do not require power and are generally more rugged.
- The only directional types usually used for boom mics are super- or hypercardioid, or shotgun, because these are the most directional types, and the idea is to reduce noise and reverberation and pick up the voice, best separating it from the background.
- In high wind, omnidirectional microphones perform better. Most lavalieres, being omni and covered with costume cloth, can have an advantage in windy locations.
- Use of radio mics requires professional advice pertaining to the location where they may be used.

CHAPTER 5

Production Sound III: Dealing with the Output of Microphones

Microphones are called as a general class *transducers*, changing acoustical energy, sound, into electrical energy, voltage. They typically put out much lower voltage levels than most audio gear, so they must be amplified by a microphone preamplifier to get to usable levels. A typical amount of voltage delivered by a professional microphone is 13 mV (0.013 V), a rather small voltage, for 94 dB SPL,[1] a rather loud level. Thus, microphones must be connected to microphone inputs, and the converse is true too: line-level devices like CD players must be connected to line-level inputs. If a line-level device is connected to a microphone input, the result will typically be overload or bad distortion. If a microphone is connected to a line-level input and the gain is raised high to hear it at all, the result will typically be noisy or hissy. This is complicated by the microphone attenuate (MIC ATT) switch on some cameras that allows high-level microphone outputs (when encountering loud sound) to be accommodated by low-level (sensitive) microphone inputs.

This chapter will give you the details needed to scale the voltage output of the microphone as needed to the input capability of the microphone preamplifier, whether in a camera or an external mixer. Before taking these steps, it is important to understand that over-recording digital is a very bad thing to do, as the onset of audible distortion is very quick when the maximum level is exceeded. The maximum recordable level without distortion is 0 dBFS. Figure 5-1 shows a good recorded level for dialog. The bar on this Canon XL-1 indicates the current peak level, and the separated section indicates the recent peak level. Here, the signal is somewhat

---

[1] Sound Pressure Level, dB relative to the threshold of hearing, which is a pressure of $20\,\mu N/m^2$.

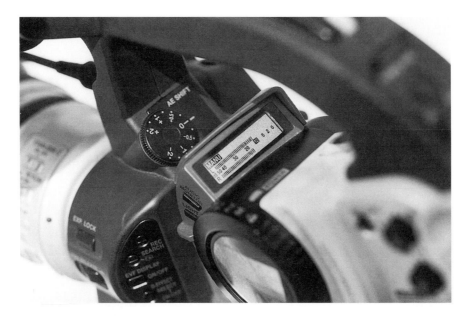

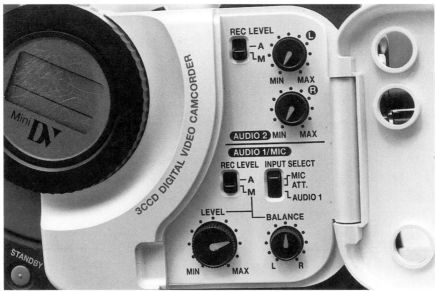

Figure 5-1 The audio meters atop the Canon XL series show left and right channels' peak levels, both currently (the bar) and in the recent past (the separated line sections). This peak level is good for dialogue recording.

dominant in the left channel, indicating that the sound source was off center to the left somewhat, and the peak levels for the dialogue passage do not exceed −12 dBFS, leaving 12 dB headroom for unexpectedly loud sounds.

While in cinema the name *Cries and Whispers* normally refers to the Bergman movie of that name, in sound we can use the phrase to describe being able to record very loud sounds without distortion and very soft ones without excessive noise, at least of the electronic variety. Accomplishing this is a matter of matching the dynamic range of real life to that of the recorder.

Real life has the potential for wide dynamic range. While the span of the quietest sound you can hear to the loudest sound you can normally tolerate is about 120 dB, even perfect 16-bit recordings (of which DV is capable) can produce only 93 dB range,[2] and actual practical cameras set to 16-bit recording have much less range. Measuring a Panasonic AG-DVX100Ap through its microphone input to its analog audio output showed it to have 58 dB dynamic range, and from its microphone input to its FireWire output to have 69 dB range.[3] The analog Nagra 4.2 recorder used on many feature films, measured a similar way, has a dynamic range of 72 dB. So in practice, this DV camera is a little less good than the mono Nagra that it replaces when the move is made from film to DV as an original capture medium.

Recording Level Parallels to Early Cinematography

In the early days of the cinema industry, light meters did not exist. Cinematographers learned that with a certain amount of light on a subject, a certain f-stop, frame rate, and shutter angle would produce an exposure that contained a full tonal range from black to white, said to be exposed correctly. Light meters were not introduced until the late 1930s and have been in use ever since.

---

[2] For aficionados, the reason this is not 96 dB is because of the necessity for dither to linearize the medium. Dither is some deliberately added low-level noise used to smooth the steps of the medium.

[3] For experts, this was from the 1-kHz clip point to the weighted noise floor, weighting consisting of a 400-Hz high-pass and a 22-kHz low-pass filter. This seemed appropriate because the camera had a lot of low-frequency noise, which is usually acceptable because it is less audible than mid- to high-frequency noise.

Certainly one of the most famous still photographs of all time, *Moonrise over Hernandez* by Ansel Adams, was photographed without an exposure meter: there simply was no time to take a meter reading because of the fleeting weather conditions. What Adams knew was the f-stop and shutter speed for the full moon, and he exposed the negative for that.

Sound people today are like cinematographers before 1935, or like Ansel Adams in 1941, without meters and in such a hurry that we have to know what we're doing. We learn what sound levels are expected, and once we have a good feel for it, we can apply the methods of this section to help fit the real world into the recordable space—the dynamic range—on the medium. However, it does take time to learn what to expect. Table 5-1 gives some day-to-day sound levels so that you can calibrate your ear to know when you may be in trouble and have to resort to special measures. The table lists two different measurements: a type of average level called L_{eqA} and the peak level of various sources.

The first thing to notice about Table 5-1 is that the first and second columns of data are very different. Just watching television shows a difference of some 27 dB from the average level to the peak level, a huge variation.

The L_{eqA} method of measuring sound pressure level involves first frequency weighting; that is, modifying the frequency response rather like tone controls do, but in a specific way that better matches human perception (rolling off the bass and extreme treble because we don't respond to them as strongly as to mid-frequency sound). This process loses some level relative to the peak because content is taken away. Second, a type of AC-to-DC converter is used, called rms, with a 1/8th-second time constant, progressively under-reading shorter and shorter events. This process also loses level relative to the short-term peak, because short time events slip through this relatively sluggish device. Finally, the *eq* part of the term means equivalent; that is, a long-term running average of the thing being measured, with excursions in level both above and below the level measured. All three of these items cause the reading to be reduced compared to the instantaneous peak, and used together, they accumulate to a very large difference. The "flat, peak, impulse" method of measurement means no frequency weighting is employed (flat frequency response, i.e., tone controls set to neutral), the detector used captures the peak (highest) value, and the impulse time constant is used of 35 milliseconds (ms). While we can hear distortion in as little as 2 ms and thus must leave some headroom

Table 5-1 Sound levels encountered in various shooting situations.

Item	dB SPL*	
	L_{eqA}	Flat Response, Peak Detector, Impulse Time Response
Quiet room suitable for recording without extra precautions	20	68
Fairly quiet room but would require careful manipulation of background both in editing and mixing	28	62
Apple G5 measured at user's head, with computer on the floor below	36	60
Fairly quiet Hollywood street, peak represents car and truck passbys; suitable for shooting at least close-ups, especially if traffic could be controlled	48	65 (car by); 93 (truck by)
Quiet model dishwasher at 1 meter	51	63
Television news listening at 3 meter	55	82
Normal speech measured at typical close boom position at 0.5 meter	65	86
Noisy Hollywood street: 7900 Sunset Blvd. at Director's Guild of America on a Saturday afternoon, peak level caused by city bus driveby across the street	65	105
Interior Los Angeles delicatessen at lunchtime	70	104
Normal speech measured at lavaliere position	75	95
Urban street including bus passing observed from bench at side of street	82	107
Actor shouting at 0.5 m	na	128

*The reference level of 0 dB for SPL is a pressure of $20\,\mu N/m^2$.

for instances even above the level stated, it is the fastest setting of a professional sound level meter.

Note that average levels are often published widely, but the peak level causes us distortion problems and so must be observed for our purposes here. Also note that the difference between the two values is not fixed: it all depends on the situation. For instance, look at the first two items, both rooms that we could record in, although we would certainly prefer the former. Although the first is some 6 dB noisier on the flat, fast measurement, its weighted average level is 8 dB quieter! This wasn't even audible because the increase in noise in the quieter room was apparently at very low frequencies, where hearing is not nearly as good as in the midrange.

This is the stuff that makes people throw up their hands and say that measurements are meaningless and you can't quantify something like hearing, but that would be wrong. We can make great use of L_{eqA} to check the background noise level of a space, say while scouting locations, whereas we must use the faster measurement (and even leave some room above it for shorter-term events) to determine how much input level the microphone and recording system is going to see on peaks. The peaks require special care in handling because they can cause distortion. Having such a professional sound level meter available is rare, but coming to know what background levels and peak levels are like, even experientially, is useful.

Fortunately, the wide potential dynamic range of real life is not often encountered while recording many kinds of programs. Take an interview situation: it probably won't get loud, although having a low background noise is important because speech in a quiet setting leaves holes in the program material, silence on the part of the talker between the syllables—or more exactly, the phonemes, which are the fundamental molecules of speech—that can reveal noise. The noise in the silences may be either the acoustical noise in the space or the hiss caused by the electronics, and it is the latter about which we can do something discussed here. Acoustical noise has to be reduced by selection of the site, and directionality, location, and aiming of the microphone.

Just an actor or documentary subject talking normally measures an average of 65 dB SPL at a conventional boom location for close-ups, but we must leave headroom for occasionally louder brief sounds, measured to be

86 dB[4] peak.[5] And getting to the instantaneous peak value so as to prevent any audible clipping probably takes this up to something over 90 dB. With a lavaliere on the chest, the levels will be even higher. So will the camera remain undistorted at these levels? And how much room do we need to leave for an occasional over-the-top performance.

To know, we have to make a measurement. We set the Panasonic camera to its normal input sensitivity of −50 dB using the menu system. Then we connect a sine wave generator to the input and put in a single midrange frequency tone, such as 500 Hz. Starting at a low level, we increase the level of the generator until the input abruptly distorts while listening to the monitor. (We have to be sure that nothing else in the chain is distorting first, by setting the camera's main recording level control correctly so that the signal stays in bounds, in this case meaning it stays out of the red on the meter, and by setting the monitor level low enough so that the monitor output is not distorting.)

When we do this and measure the voltage where the input is just below the point of obviously distorting, we find a value of 48 mV (0.048 V). Thus, we have to keep the microphone's maximum output to 48 mV or we will distort the camera's microphone input. It will make no difference if we turn the camera's level control down: *If the sound is distorted at the input, no amount of level setting of subsequent controls will fix the problem.* This fact eludes many people, especially ENG crews, as stand-up reporters' audio is often grossly distorted, and we can presume that the operators have done their job and set the level. What's happening is that the radio mics they are using have relatively high output, and they are overloading the microphone-level input of the cameras, so no level setting of the main level controls of the camera can fix the problem. In fact, one popular ENG radio mic receiver puts out a nominal −20 dBu when mic inputs are intended for around −50 dBu!

So for our purposes, let's choose a microphone, a good one. (This is meant to be illustrative, and by filling in the numbers from your particular example of microphone and camera combination, the method can be made universal.) Take the Schoeps Mk41 hypercardioid capsule mounted

---

[4] dB is used colloquially here and at many places in the text. Strictly speaking, the term dB only specifies a ratio, and without further delineation is unclear. The term SPL is implied anytime we are speaking of acoustical levels.

[5] These numbers were measurements of me talking at 1 meter, measured L_{eq} (for the 72 dB SPL measurement) and impulse peak (35 ms) on a B&K 2230 sound level meter.

on their Collette Series electronics, a CMC6U, and let's look at its specifications (www.schoeps.de). The microphone's sensitivity is 13 mV/Pa, the maximum undistorted level is 132 dB SPL, and the noise floor is 16 dBA. A scene recorded with this microphone that has exemplary sound for dialogue is in *Almost Famous.*[6]

While these numbers with their strange units may at first glance seem impenetrable to all but engineers, figuring them out will help us prevent massive distortion on peaks, among other things, so it's a good idea to understand them. The easiest item to get from the numbers is the dynamic range of the mic. It is 132 dB minus 16 dB equals 116 dB dynamic range, from the input overload point to the weighted noise floor.[7] We can note immediately that 116 dB is a whole lot more than our selected camera can do, which we measured to be 69 dB. So anything we can do to adapt the "gallon" of the dynamic range of the world into the "half gallon" of the dynamic range of the mic, and thence into the "quart" of the dynamic range of the medium, is a good thing.

The sensitivity specification is 13 mV for 1 Pascal. One Pascal is a unit of pressure equivalent to a sound pressure level of 94 dB. With the microphone overload point at 132 dB SPL, that's 132 minus 94 equals 38 dB more. Now we have to figure out what 13 mV plus 38 dB is, a mixed bag of units. The term dB specifies only a ratio, so in this sense it is a multiplier times the voltage. There's an exact way to do this and a way to crib the result. Let's start with the crib, because that'll get us there faster: 38 dB is 40 dB less 2 dB. And 40 dB is 100 times, and 2 dB is 20 percent less (small numbers of dB are fairly linear). So 100 times 13 mV less 20 percent is 1.04 V. (If we'd been a little more observant, we would have found that the spec sheet tells us the overload is 1 V, and we wouldn't have had to calculate it!)

In order to generalize this, we need the real math solution. In order to reverse the logarithmic effect of decibels, we have to do the following:

1. Take the number of decibels and divide it by 20.
2. Raise the result of the division to a power of ten: 10^x.
3. The result is the ratio that corresponds to that number of decibels.

---

[6] Boom operator Don Coufal, production sound mixer Jeff Wexler, dialogue editor Laura Harris, re-recording mixers Rick Kline, Paul Massey, and Doug Hemphill. Dreamworks DVD 87818 Chapter 23, 3:30–5:52.

[7] Weighting the noise floor means adapting the noise measurement with a frequency-by-frequency response curve, like a tone control, that more or less accounts for the low-level characteristics of human hearing.

So to get the final answer, multiply the ratio by the starting point for the measurement. For our example:

1. 38 dB ÷ 20 = 1.9
2. $10^{1.9}$ = 79.4
3. 79.4 × 0.013 V = 1.0326 V

The microphone can put out a little over 1 V, but the camera's input overloads at 48 mV (0.048V). We've got a significant problem, at least potentially. First let's see what the maximum SPL is that we can record without mic preamp distortion. To do this, compare the sensitivity of the mic to the input overload:

1. 48 mV ÷ 13 mV = 3.692.

So the output of the mic can be 3.692 times that at standard SPL of 94 dB. What is that in decibels?

2. dB of a voltage ratio = $20 \log_{10} 3.692$ = 11.3 dB
3. 94 dB SPL, which is the level for 13 mV, plus 11.3 dB, which is the factor above 94 dB where the mic input distorts, is 105 dB SPL.

Many scenes fall under 105 dB SPL, and much of the time you'll get away with a setup that plugs this mic directly into this camera. For instance, the ordinary dialogue measured in the table is easily accommodated, with about 19 dB remaining as headroom, plenty to accommodate even short-term peaks. Conveniently, the Panasonic camera supplies phantom power to the microphone, so all you need is the mic and an XLR cable and you're in business. You'll also need accessories such as a boom pole, shock mount, and windscreen, but these are incidental to our purpose here. However, if the actor suddenly shouts, it is almost certain that gross distortion will result, even if the main level control is jerked down; to reiterate, the distortion is occurring *before* the opportunity to reduce the signal with the main level control.

Cries

With this simple connection you must beware sounds above 105 dB SPL—they will distort. Because the mic can handle 132 dB cleanly, and the camera input only 105 dB when the two are directly connected, what we need is a kind of neutral density filter for sound. A neutral density filter is a gray glass disc put in the light path of the lens that is used to reduce the intensity of bright scenes to the capability of the camera's light sensor. Likewise, a *pad*

Figure 5-2 The exterior of a custom-built pad.

is a device that knocks down the level of the output of the microphone so that louder scenes can be recorded without distortion.

What we need is simple: a 27 dB pad if we want to maximize the capability of the system, matching the maximum undistorted output of the microphone to the maximum undistorted input of the camera. However, unfortunately it's not a simple thing to just go to the store and buy such a device. Perhaps you could get a 20 dB pad premade, but not a 27 or even 30 dB one (most audio people have never heard of such large amounts of padding!). So we'll have to build one (Figures 5-2 through 5-4).

The first thing to understand is that by putting a pad between the output of the microphone and the input of the camera, we are giving up on the phantom power capability of the camera supplying the microphone, and we'll have to supply power externally. A battery-powered box in line will do the job; one example is the Professional Sound Corporation (PSC) 48 PH phantom power supply. Follow that with a 27 dB pad on the way to the camera and we will have achieved our purpose.

A pad for a balanced line such as a microphone line consists of three resistors (Figure 5-3).[8] Pin 1 of an XLR connector is ground and the

_____

[8] Today at least. Much older designs of pads had to take into account the source and load impedances in a matching type of impedance environment, such as 600 ohms. Nowadays we don't worry about such things because source impedances are so low and input impedances so high, although if we were to calculate the pad with the source and load impedances in place, we'd get a *very* slight difference in attenuation.

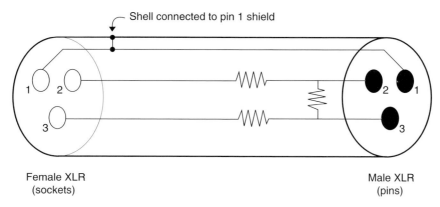

Figure 5-3 The schematic of a pad, showing the XLR pin numbers.

shield connection and is wired through (pin 1 female to pin 1 male) and connected to the body of the connector as well. Pin 2 is connected with a series resistor between input and output, as is pin 3. A parallel resistor goes across pins 2 and 3 of the male end of the connector. Together, the three resistors form a voltage divider. Here is how it is calculated:

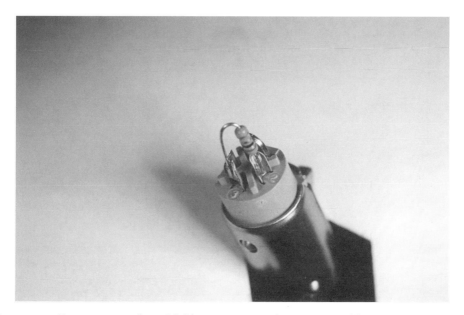

Figure 5-4a In our example, a 1 kOhm resistor is first mounted between XLR pins 2 and 3 of the male connector side of the barrel adapter.

Figure 5-4b Then, two 10.2 kOhm series resistors are added as shown. The free ends are then clipped and extended with hookup wire to the corresponding pins 2 and 3 of the female connector, as is the ground, pin 1.

We need a −27 dB pad. We select a 1k0 ohm resistor for the branch that is in parallel with the camera input,[9] and now we have to calculate the two series resistors (Figure 5-4). First think of them as one. The parallel branch represents the fraction of the voltage that we want delivered by this voltage divider. The equation for such a voltage divider is:

$$-27\mathrm{dB} = 1\mathrm{k}0/(x + 1\mathrm{k}0)$$

So undoing decibels to a ratio as before (27/20), the result raised to the power 10^x, then $1/x$ to get a negative decibel result (it's attenuating) gives:

$$0.04668 = 1\mathrm{k}0/(x + 1\mathrm{k}0)$$

Doing some high school algebra means rearranging terms to solve for x:

$$0.04668(x + 1\mathrm{k}0) = 1\mathrm{k}0$$

$$0.04668x + 46.68 = 1\mathrm{k}0$$

$$x = (1\mathrm{k}0 - 46.68)/0.04668 = 20.4 \text{ kOhms}$$

---

[9] Because that will provide a low enough source impedance to drive a reasonable amount of cable.

Dividing this in two to build our balanced pad makes it 10.2 kOhms. Looking up the closest 1 percent resistor from an E96 chart of values, we find 10.2 kOhms falls exactly on a 1 percent part value. (For the case of any arbitrary pad value, the closest 1 percent values have a negligible error for this purpose.)

So with this pad in our system, we can now record up to 132 dB SPL cleanly. Because this is a higher level than most people have heard of (after all, isn't 120 dB the threshold of pain?), aren't we being a little crazy? Well no, not really. An actor screaming measured 0.5 m away produces peaks of 128 dB SPL, and Lewis Fielder has recorded maximum peaks of 129 dB in the audience at 36 live music concerts.[10] This is close enough to 132 dB that having a method of recording to higher levels without distortion, for unusual situations, would be a good idea. For instance, I measured the peak level inside the bass drum head of REO Speedwagon in the early 1970s and got 138 dB!

There is a way to record with low distortion to higher levels than 132 dB with this and similar microphones: add an additional pre-electronics pad. This is one that is inserted between the microphone pickup capsule and the microphone's own electronics, and reduces the level before distortion can occur and raises the headroom correspondingly. For some models of microphones, these are built-in and switchable. For the Schoeps mic, they are screw-in devices made in two values: 10 and 20 dB, Schoeps models DZC 10 and DZC 20, respectively. For instance, I had to use the DZC 10 attenuators to record the University of Southern California marching band at homecoming because of the high peak levels that a marching band can produce. With these in place, we can record levels up to 142 or about 150 dB SPL for the two models, respectively. Note that levels above 140 dB cause instantaneous hearing damage and so should be approached with caution. For the loudest screams of an actor, the 27 dB pad described previously is perhaps just enough, but without much headroom for instantaneous peaks, and perhaps a 10 dB pad would be warranted if the boom mic is near the actor, as well as earplugs for the boom operator! Also, with these pads you could record gunfire cleanly at close range, but you'd better be wearing hearing protection, and in some extreme instances of close

---

[10] Fielder, L. D., "Pre- and Post-Emphasis Techniques as Applied to Audio Recording Systems," *J. Audio Eng. Soc.*, Vol. 33, pp. 649–658 (Sept. 1985).

gunfire, it is possible to stretch the diaphragm beyond its elastic limits and wreck it.

One reason that sound levels in the 135 to 140 dB range sound unusual to many knowledgeable people is that in many publications, tables of sound pressure levels for many everyday activities are given as average levels over a period of time. Louder sounds than speaking, when evaluated in the short term, can produce correspondingly higher levels. For instance, a bus passing by when viewed from a seat at the bus stop in an urban setting measured 107 dB peak. The combination of the Schoeps microphone and the Panasonic camera would distort on this combination without a pad for this rather ordinary scene.

Whispers

At the other end of the dynamic range is the very quiet. Some very quiet things to record include quiet room ambiences, Foley sound effects such as clothing rustle, and the ticking of a clock as used in Bergman's *Cries and Whispers* to indicate that the scene is quiet. This is not a sound design point to be overlooked: the *sound* of silence is not silence. Think of it this way: the picture equivalent of silence is going to black, not a view of an empty room. A quiet space might be represented by the sound of a fly, a single cricket, or some such, but it would rarely be represented as pure silence.

Recording such quiet sounds requires quiet microphones and quiet electronics. The Panasonic camera has 69 dB dynamic range below its input overload of 48 mV. If we plug the Schoeps mic into the microphone input directly (no pads) because we're recording quiet things, how quiet can they be? The simple way to calculate this is that it is 69 dB below the 105 dB SPL that we calculated previously. Why? Because that is the input overload point for no pad and the dynamic range with the microphone directly connected. The difference is the equivalent sound pressure level of the camera preamplifier noise, 36 dB SPL, subjectively about 16 times noisier than our hearing threshold. And it is 20 dB noisier than the microphone from its specifications, so the camera preamp noise *masks* or conceals the real noise floor of the microphone. The combination may do well enough shooting ordinary scenes, but in order to reach down to the quietest acoustic levels, a quieter external preamplifier is going to be needed.

A Shure FP-33 is a battery-powered field recorder with 117 dB dynamic range[11] on its microphone inputs—a number derived from its specifications. Comparing it to the camera shows an improvement of 117 dB minus 69 dB equals 48 dB. With each 10 dB representing subjectively twice the dynamic range, this dedicated mic mixer is about 32 times quieter than the camera's electronics. Furthermore, doing some more calculations shows that the mixer's equivalent input noise level is some 11 dB quieter than that of the microphone, thus making its noise negligible.

To use such a microphone mixer, its output, set to line level, should be sent to the camera's inputs, also set to line level. Be absolutely certain that both the output of the mixer and the input of the camera are switched to line level, because feeding a line-level signal into a microphone-level input, even if line up on tone can be done (described later), will cause serious distortion. The combination of the Schoeps mic and the Shure mixer will then be able to record sounds with far less noise than using the mic into the camera's microphone input.

If we are really going for the quietest sounds, we might want to pick a microphone with an even lower noise level, such as the Neumann TLM-103. By virtue of its large diaphragm, it can be quieter than the Schoeps, at the expense of having greater variation in the off-axis frequency response. Thus, we probably would not want to use the Neumann as a boom mic because, among other things, it is much larger and heavier, but as a specialized Foley it may excel, for instance. Its noise floor is equivalent to 7 dB SPL (A weighted), about the lowest among recording microphones, and its sensitivity is such that the output noise is still above the noise floor of the Shure mic mixer.

---

[11] This 117 dB of dynamic range may not be the actual performance because it may be measured at the two extremes: noise with the gain all the way up and referred back to the input, and headroom with the gain controls minimized for maximum headroom, two settings that can't be achieved simultaneously.

To come full circle, what about the other end of the dynamic range, the loud end, for these combinations: the Schoeps and the Neumann microphones into the Shure mixer? The Schoeps can produce about 1 V, but the Shure distorts at an input level 10 dB less, thus requiring a 10 dB pad in order to reach 132 dB SPL. Unfortunately, putting in such a pad will kill the phantom power available from this mixer, and we'll have to use an external power supply, just as described for the Panasonic camera. With the simple connection without an external power supply and pad, and the Shure providing the phantom power, the combination clips at 122 dB SPL, useful for many day-to-day purposes but not reaching the highest levels of a screaming actor without distortion.

The Neumann has a maximum output level of 3.5 V, so with the Shure mixer a 21 dB pad will take the undistorted equivalent level up to 138 dB SPL, or, looked at another way, with no pad, a level of 117 dB SPL can be handled.

Cries and Whispers

While we've discussed handling loud sounds and soft ones, what if they happen simultaneously within one scene? This might occur if an actor in a quiet space, murmuring to himself, suddenly shouts.

Digital overload, like microphone preamplifier clipping, comes on abruptly and generally sounds pretty horrible. It is most noticeable on voice content in the vowels. Consonants are sharper, harder, faster sounds, which means they take up a wider frequency range, thus tending to hide distortion. Vowels, on the other hand, have a more orderly waveform, repetitive from cycle to cycle, and a well-defined fundamental and harmonics at twice, three times, and so forth times the fundamental frequency. This spectrum means that distortion, which tends to spread the content across a wider frequency range, will not be masked or hidden. So the first thing to give an indication of distortion is typically distorted vowels.

The most common way to handle a scene with wide dynamic range is to ride the gain; that is, adjust the microphone channel level control to adapt such that the loud passages don't distort and the soft ones are well above the noise level of the electronics. Naturally, this is only effective if the potential distortion is caused by over-recording on the medium and not clipping the microphone input, as described earlier. Riding, or adjusting the gain constantly, does no good if the signal is already distorted or noisy because of the conditions at the microphone preamplifier *input*. The main recording level control on cameras or mixers is *after* the microphone preamplifier, so its use is to adapt the dynamic range presented at the output of the microphone preamplifier to the dynamic range of the medium.

There are two contravening factors at work here. Constantly adjusting the gain means that within a given take one is riding the gain so that the foreground sound, usually speech, is well recorded. A problem with this though is that then the background sound is constantly varying. This causes problems editorially, where a cut between two recorded sections could reveal a large change in the background sound. So there are two forces at work:

1. Keep the foreground sound undistorted in loud passages by turning the level down and not electronically noisy in quiet passages by turning the level up to keep the signal above the noise level of the medium.
2. Maintain one best level within a whole scene, including shot-to-shot setup variations, which will make the most cuttable sound by *not* riding the gain.

How does this dilemma get resolved? First, the degree of the dilemma depends on the dynamic range of the recorder. When early film sound optical tracks had little range, about all that could be done was that in order to have something sound loud, something quiet had to come before it—it was only through contrast with the quiet preceding passage that something could be made to sound loud. This was called "the cinema mixer's trick." There really wasn't any dynamic range to spare.

With modern high-capacity recording, less gain riding needs to be done because the range is larger. However, that doesn't mean that you cannot protect the loudest sounds from distortion—you should. What it does mean is that through training and experience, one comes to know what is acceptable in terms of gain riding. It is especially helpful if you edit your own sound recordings because the feedback that this produces makes you a better mixer. No one prescription can be given, except to consider the following:

- Human mixers, as opposed to limiters and automatic gain or volume controls called compressors, can anticipate the action, particularly if they are rehearsed for a fiction piece. One can sneak the gain riding in *before* it is needed and in an otherwise quiet place.

- Boom operators can be especially helpful in leveling out performances from various actors/subjects. This is particularly true if a hypercardioid and not a shotgun microphone is in use because the hypercardioid typically has much smoother response off-axis, mostly just attenuated on-axis sound, so a stronger actor can be put at a more off-axis angle, while a weaker one is favored with the on-axis. If this is tried with a shotgun, the off-axis sound coloration is too great to accept.

- Certain sounds can afford to be recorded with distortion, because they are distorted anyway. Gunshots come to mind: keeping them within the undistorted range in a scene containing other sounds to be recorded would probably require just too much change of the background sound to accommodate good recording. It is easier to simply let the system distort briefly, and then if needed, edit in cleaner gunshots in postproduction.

- Once a wide dynamic range is available—say by use of an external mixer and staggered levels between two channels discussed following—then riding the gain gives way to setting the level; that is, we set the level just once for the loudest part of the scene to be certain it's undistorted, then leave it alone. This produces the most editable sound. Any gain riding that will be necessary for intelligibility and performance can then be done in postproduction, when there is time to go over and over it as necessary.

Another specialized way to get a gallon of dynamic range into the half-gallon of the camera's dynamic range is to divide the gallon into two different half-gallons. You could, for example, following the microphone battery power supply, put in a Y-adapter and send one signal to both inputs of the camera, with one of them having a pad and the other having no pad. In this way, the padded version would capture the loudest part of the performance cleanly, but with noisy lower-level passages, while the second channel would have distorted high-level passages but be quieter in low-level ones. This requires a lot of coordination between production and postproduction sound—after all, one track *will* be distorted some of the time, but it is a way of capturing a wider range and using the second channel, when what is desired is monaural (single microphone) boom operation.

Using this tactic with the Schoeps mic and Panasonic camera, for instance, could theoretically extend the dynamic range of the recording from 69 dB to 69 plus 27 dB equals 96 dB range, a great improvement. That would be from an equivalent 36 dB to 132 dB SPL. We'll see how to set the levels on this combination in the next section.

Multiple Level Controls in the Chain

A chain consisting of a microphone and two potential places to pad its output has been described. Real-world situations with a camcorder using an external mixer have many more points in the system where the level may be affected. For instance, these are, in the order that the signal encounters them:

- Microphone pre-electronics pad, previously described

- Microphone level in-line pad, previously described, which may be a part of an external power supply or a separate device placed in the microphone line. If one is used, it does not pass phantom or T power, which must be supplied before the pad

- Mixer's input sensitivity switch, Mic/Line, or various Mic levels and Line. For instance, changing from 48 V phantom power (implying an electrostatic microphone) to a DYN input (for an electrodynamic microphone) may adjust the input sensitivity of the mixer because electrostatic mics are normally "hotter" than electrodynamic mics (more output for the same SPL) by something on the order of 20 dB

- Mixer's input trim control (pad). This replaces the need for external microphone-level pads with a variable input gain or pad on the mixer. This is only available on typically larger and more expensive mixers

- Mixer's channel level control

- Mixer's master level control

- Mixer's output level switch: Mic/Line. This switch is provided so that if the only input provided by the camera is at mic level, it will not be overloaded. If mic/line switching is available at both the mixer output and the camera input, line level is preferred because the higher level in the line is less susceptible to electrical interference

- Camera's input level switch: Mic/Line. Set to correspond to mixer's output

- Camera's input level control

- Camera's monitor level control. Also, there is often a switch that provides monitoring for channel 1, channel 2, or channel 1 plus channel 2

- Mixer's monitor return level control

- Mixer's headphone level control

- Headphone level control, such as in a distribution box for production sound operator and boom operator (potentially separate).

At first this can seem to be almost hopelessly complicated because there are so many places for the level to be set. One of the primary reasons for this is that each component part in the chain has to be prepared in the marketplace to face all kinds of conditions; thus, for instance, the mic-level output on a microphone mixer. That only exists because sometimes the only thing available on the next piece of gear in line is a microphone input, but there is a way to simplify the settings for this chain. First is to understand the signal flow through the chain so that troubleshooting can be done if the signal goes awry. Second is to know the nominal setting of all parts of the chain so you know when you are deviating from normal. Third is to calibrate the level for those parts of the chain that are metered so that the mixer and camera are adjusted to the same sensitivities, and what is read on the mixer will read on the camera, so that the mixer becomes an extension of the camera. Fourth is to understand the consequences of getting the levels wrong. Let's take each of these up in turn:

1. The signal flow is given in the aforementioned order. However, it is a fairly comprehensive list, and any single set of equipment may have fewer parts. It is worthwhile to draw a diagram of your particular system with all of the places that affect level so that you can follow the logic. A typical example with an external mixer and using single-

system recording is given in Figure 5-5. Single-system recording means recording audio and video to the same medium; double-system recording uses two separate media, such as videotape and DAT, and a means to synchronize them, such as a time code slate jam-synced with the camera.[12]

2. We've already had a discussion about the dynamic range at the mic and on the medium. Setting levels correctly helps the gallon into half-gallon into quart problem, and some of this has already been discussed in the context of the microphone input. For the whole system, nominal settings need to be applied. For instance, it is useful to know that level controls normally are run at 7 on a scale of 10, that headphone monitor controls on camera are often operated fully up, and so forth.

3. Calibration is used in the context of a separate mixer and recorder. Start with a tone generator from the mixer, set to a standard level such as 0 VU, and then set the mixer output switch to line level, the camera input sensitivity switch to line level, and adjust the camera input level control for a standard meter reading, such as −20 dBFS.

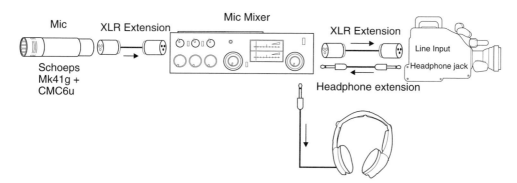

Figure 5-5 Block diagram of a single-system shooting setup with an external microphone mixer. The return of the headphone signal from the camera to the mixer, and monitoring by way of that path, ensures that the signal has made it to the camera.

---

[12] In the case that the camera and slate are jam-synced together, then disconnected, time of day time code has to be used so that the two stay in sync. Some motion-picture cameras rate the accuracy of their time code crystal oscillator in fractions of a frame over hours of operation, but this may not be true of camcorders. For good lip sync, jam-syncing may be needed more or less frequently, depending on the matching of the camera and slate oscillators.

Because two different types of meters are in use, VU and digital peak, the readings for the nominal setting are *not* the same.

4. The consequence of getting the level wrong at one point in the chain and making up for it at a later point can be added distortion or noise. This may be a small problem or an overwhelming one, depending on the degree of the mismatch. Say in one stage the level is down by 10 dB and is then subsequently restored to full level. Any noise that comes in stages between the two will be exaggerated by 10 dB. Worse is clipping distortion early in the chain, which we attempt to fix later in the chain. Once distorted, the signal is distorted, no matter what you do with subsequent levels.

Another Kind of Overload Distortion and How to Avoid It

So far we have described the overload distortion called clipping and how to use pads before and/or after the microphone's own electronics to maximize headroom. There is an invisible type of this overload possible too, and it plagues all directional microphones especially: infrasonic overload. Directional microphones of all types are much more susceptible to wind noise, boom panning noises and other very low-frequency noises compared to omnidirectional types. But directional mics are necessary in most film/video recording applications, just to emphasize the direct sound and suppress reverberation and noise occurring in most settings. The only exception to this rule is lavalieres, which are mostly omnidirectional, and through this property, less wind-susceptible than other types.

Infrasonic (formerly called subsonic) overload from wind or boom panning leads to bobbles in the audio—little moments of time where the sound seems to be compressed or even go away. Once you've heard it, you'll be able to recognize it. Electronic infrasonic overload may occur at two potential places in the chain: right in the microphone's internal preamplifier or in the camera or mixer's microphone preamplifier. Either of these may be prevented by putting a pre-electronics low-frequency filter (alternately called low-cut or high-pass) between the pickup capsule and the microphone body. In the case of the Schoeps, this is a screw-in device called a CUT-1, with adjustable low-frequency response above a steep cutoff frequency. In some other microphone models, the low-cut switch may be built in; however, then it is not clear as to whether the low-cut switch is before or after the electronics. Placing it before the microphone's own electronics most improves the headroom, whereas placing it after protects the rest of the chain—in particular, the microphone preamplifier in the camera or mixer—from infrasonic overload.

Generally speaking, for recording dialog, one can use a 60- or 80-Hz high-pass (low-cut) filter and do little or no damage to the voice and decrease the amount of wind and panning noises dramatically. This is especially true of steep filters, such as the Schoeps CUT-1, a 24-dB/octave filter below 60 Hz.[13]

Combining Features for Best Wind Performance

The combination of ingredients that produces the lowest wind suscepti-bility involves using an omni pickup capsule, protecting the capsule from wind, protecting the electronics from low-frequency and broad-frequency range overload, and protecting the camera or mixer microphone input from excessive amounts of signal (Figure 5-6). A system consisting of a Schoeps MK2 omni capsule plus DZC20 pad plus CUT-1 filter plus CMC electronics plus BBG windscreen with Windjammer should have the greatest attenuation of wind effects possible. The output level of the mic should be scaled to the input capability of the mixer, possibly with an additional pad, and an additional mixer high-pass filter might not be out of place (Tables 5-2 and 5-3). An omni capsule implies that one must use the closest possible working distance, but the advantage of low wind suscepti-bility may overcome the working distance problem.

---

[13] If this particular Schoeps CUT-1 is used, there are other considerations: its use increases sensitivity by 5 dB and decreases headroom by 5 dB. If an attenuator is also used, it is placed on the pickup capsule first, then the CUT-1 comes in the chain.

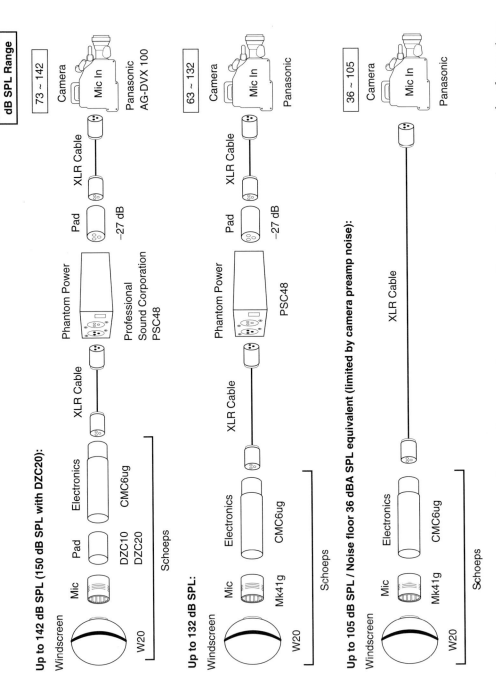

Figure 5-6 Various combinations of microphones, pads, power supplies, mixers, and cameras for the various sound pressure level and wind noise conditions encountered. Required shock mounts and booms are not shown. (Other useful combinations of microphones and windscreens are at www.schoeps.de/E-2004/windscreens-select.html.)

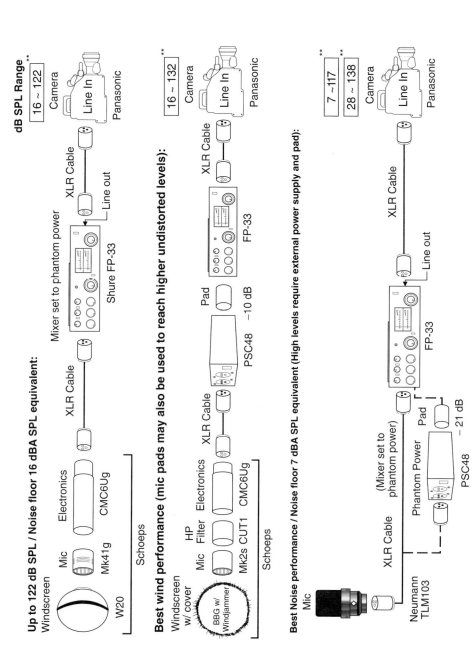

dB SPL Range **

Up to 122 dB SPL / Noise floor 16 dBA SPL equivalent:

16 ~ 122 **

Best wind performance (mic pads may also be used to reach higher undistorted levels):

16 ~ 132 **

Best Noise performance / Noise floor 7 dBA SPL equivalent (High levels require external power supply and pad):

7 ~117 **

28 ~ 138 **

** These extremes are not available simultaneously, but rather represent the range over which the mixer may be adjusted to work.

Figure 5-6 *Continued*

Table 5-2 Some common microphone specifications.

Model	Description/Where Used	Sensitivity at 94 dB SPL, mV	Max SPL	Noise Expressed as SPL* Equivalent	Dynamic Range, dB
Audio Technica AT835b	Shotgun/ inexpensive boom mic	12.5	130	24	106
Audio Technica 4053a	Hypercardioid/ inexpensive boom mic	22.4	146	19	121
Neumann TLM 103	Cardioid/very low noise studio mic, Foley	21	138	7	131
Neumann KMR 81 i	Short shotgun/ good-quality highest SPL shotgun, boom mic	18	128 (138 with pad)	12	116
Neumann KMR 82 i	Long shotgun/ good-quality outdoor boom mic	21	128	12	116

Continues

Table 5-2 *Continued*

Model	Description/Where Used	Sensitivity at 94 dB SPL, mV	Max SPL	Noise Expressed as SPL* Equivalent	Dynamic Range, dB
Schoeps CMC641Ug	Hypercardioid/good-quality, highest levels, an industry standard	13	132 (142 with pad)	16	116
Schoeps CMC68Ug	Bidirectional used with above for MS stereo	10	134 (144 with pad)	18	116
Sennheiser MKH60-1	Short shotgun boom mic	12.5	125–134	18–25	107
Sennheiser MKH416-P48U3	Short shotgun/industry standard boom mic	25	130	13	117
Sennheiser MKH 70-1	Long shotgun boom mic	50	124 (132 with pad)	5 (13 with pad)	119
Tram TR50	Standard lavaliere	16	134	26	108

*A weighted

Table 5-3 Input overload and pad values needed for selected microphones with selected audio inputs to match the microphone maximum output to the electronics microphone input maximum undistorted level.

		Beachtek DXA-4C	Sony DSR-PD170	Panasonic AG-DVX100A	Shure FP 33
	Mic input overload, mV	880	141	48	316
	Mic input overload, dBV	-1	-17	-26	-10
Microphone Make, Model		**Required pad value, dB**			
Audio Technica AT835b		None	−15	−24	−8
Audio Technica 4053a		−20	−36	−45	−29
Neumann TLM103		−12	−28	−37	−21
Neumann KMR 81i		None	−16	−25	−9
Neumann KMR 82i		−2	−18	−27	−11
Sanken CSS-5		None	−13	−22	−6
Schoeps CMC641Ug		−2	−18	−27	−11
Sennheiser ME66		−4	−22	−31	−15
Sennheiser MKH60-1		None	−10	−19	−3
Sennheiser MKH416-P48U3		−5	−21	−30	−14
Sennheiser MKH70-1		−5	−21	−30	−14
Tram TR50		−5	−21	−30	−14

The Director's Cut

- Microphone electrical outputs have a potentially very wide dynamic range, from very small to rather large voltages depending on the scene they face. The range can be tamed through the use of pads, which work like neutral density filters.
- If the microphone output voltage exceeds the input capability of the microphone preamp, the sound will be distorted *no matter where the level control is set*. Pads are necessary to keep the maximum output of the mic from exceeding the input capability of the preamp.
- Setting the record level is the most important act of a recordist. Because digital recording distorts abruptly when overloaded, it is better to under-record somewhat than risk ever over-recording.
- To record very soft sounds, such as Foley and some ambiences, a camera mic preamplifier may be too noisy, and use of an outboard better one is necessary to avoid hearing hiss.
- Multiple level controls in the chain can be confusing, and the best way to work through the confusion is to know the nominal settings of all the controls and switches affecting level in the chain and to set them there to start.
- Wind noise can be avoided by use of omnidirectional microphones, high-pass filters, and efficient windscreens.

CHAPTER 6

Connecting Up, Reference Levels

The world of video production today is at once simpler and more complex than ever before. Simpler because innovations such as FireWire[1] carry both picture and synchronized sound at the same time in digital form on one cable. So we can shoot on a camera, transport the data at the full picture and sound resolution that was captured to an editing system,[2] edit and mix it, and transport it out to a record deck, all without ever leaving the digital domain.

There are useful variations on this setup too, such as accompanying a tape-based camcorder with an external hard disc recorder. The recorder may be controlled by the transmitted time code over FireWire so that it goes into record mode each time the camera is rolled. The two advantages of this setup are that you have a backup by recording to two media at once, at precisely the same quality, and the fact that you can detach the hard disc recorder from the camera and connect it to an editing system, again by FireWire. This connection may operate at greater than real-time speed because moving audio and video from the hard disc drive into the editor becomes a file transfer, rather than a conventional audio/video capture transfer, which occurs in real time. So a part of the workflow is speeded up by a significant factor.

In a somewhat more sophisticated postproduction setup, differentiation can also be made between a picture-based editing system with sound capability and a sound-specific editing system, and the content may be transferred in digital form back and forth between the two editing systems (see Figure 6-1). The sound may be transparent through this process or it

---

[1] Also known as IEEE Standard 1394 and iLink.

[2] Some editing systems may first capture at lower resolution to have greater playing time capacity and then once an edit has been made, recapture the original at full quality for the ultimate output.

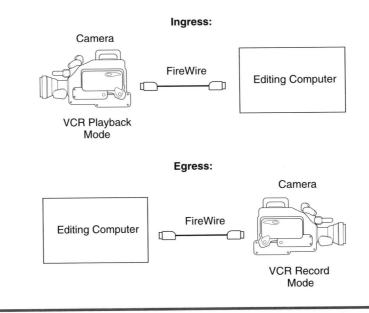

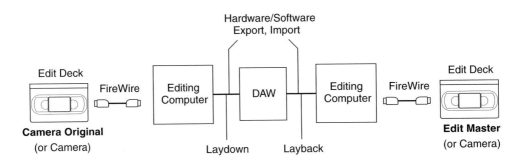

DAW may be a separate computer or software running on the same computer. If on the same machine, the audio software will need to know how to locate the sound files used by the picture editing software

Figure 6-1 Several block diagrams of workflow.

may be acted on by a number of plug-ins, processes that deliberately modify it, but nonetheless there is little the user needs to do to get the electrical interfaces to work perfectly. This is a great advance in simplicity of use because many problems in audio occur at electrical interfaces that are greatly simplified using a workflow path that uses FireWire for its interconnections. Among the advantages are that you don't have to worry about level, channel assignments, and so forth. The signal is transmitted fully as it was captured to tape or disc with no degradation, so if the levels are proper on the original, they will still be on import into the editing system.

A large variety of interfaces are possible beyond the FireWire one, and they are easily confused with one another: analog, digital, +4, −10, AES, S/PDIF, impedance, and so on are all terms that may be involved. The cost of confusion could range from blown loudspeakers to highly distorted or noisy sound, even when the original recording is perfectly clean. The purpose of this chapter is to eliminate these problems by providing an understanding of what is going on. Table 6-3 gives information about a variety of audio connectors.

The first item to notice about an interface is whether it is carrying digital data or carrying audio in analog form. Unfortunately, the problem of distinguishing the two is made more difficult by the fact that the same type of connectors are often used for both, even on the same piece of equipment! To get back and forth between analog and digital sound requires an analog-to-digital (A/D) converter in one direction or a digital-to-analog converter (DAC) in the other. Usually these converters are incorporated into other pieces of equipment, such as cameras, and remain unseen by the user, but sometimes in high-end applications they may be stand-alone boxes just for this purpose. A camcorder contains both (Figure 6-2): the microphone or line-level analog inputs are converted to digital for storage on the medium, and converted back to analog for monitoring, while also being available digitally from the medium or even in real time over FireWire or Serial Digital Interface (SDI). Many camcorders only perform conversion on their own source signals, such as the output of the picture's CCD array, whereas other models provide A/D conversion of picture and sound for external inputs.

In one form of the digital professional audio interface, AES-3, XLR connectors (Figure 6–3) are used, whereas professional analog audio routinely uses XLR connectors too. So the only way to know whether a given XLR port on a piece of equipment is analog or digital is by labeling. The consequence of connecting a digital output to an analog input could be blown tweeters in monitor loudspeakers and/or power amplifier failure. This is because the digital signal is composed of a wide range of frequencies extending very far above the audio range, and this is seen as very strong ultrasonic levels by subsequent audio equipment to which it is

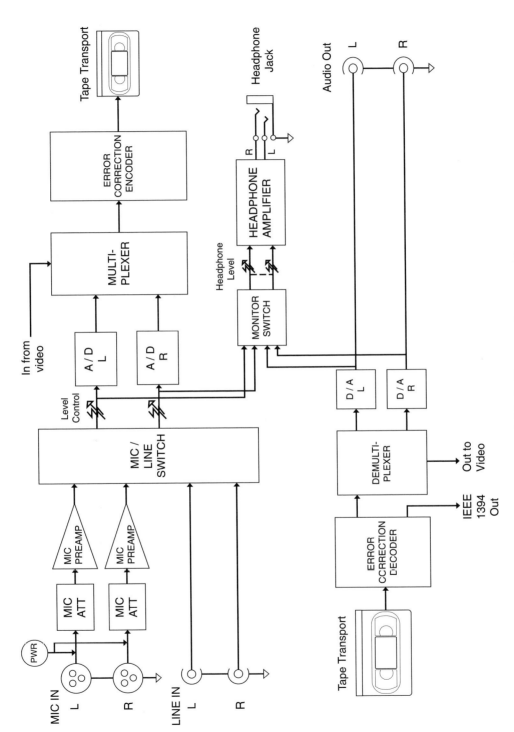

Figure 6-2 A block diagram of a camcorder.

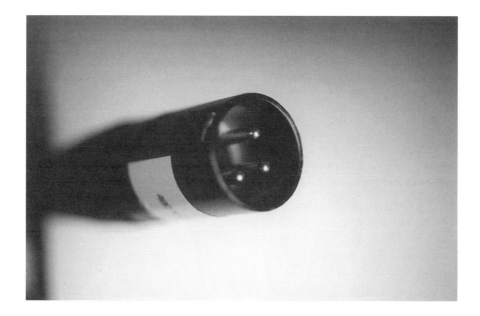

Figure 6-3 An XLR connector pair that may be used for both analog and professional digital connections.

directly connected without first being converted to analog, which may cause damage. Conversely, connecting an analog signal to an input intended for a digital signal will normally result in there being no sound, although damage is unlikely.

In professional audio studios, for digital audio connections, the XLR connector carrying AES3 (available at www.aes.org) format signals is the most common. XLR connectors have a gender assignment: males, those with exposed pins, are today always outputs, whereas females having sockets are always inputs. Each three-pin connector carries two audio channels interleaved in time as one signal, and the wiring is balanced; that is, each of the two primary conductors carries a signal that is the same as the other, except that the two are upside-down mirror images of one another. The third conductor is a shield for the other two and sometimes may not be used. The two primary conductor signals are said to be out of phase or in opposite polarity from each other. The reason for using balanced wiring is that it is less susceptible to outside interference, particularly from magnetic fields, although these digital audio signals are already rather impervious to outside disturbances.

This system also has what is called *characteristic impedance*, a measure of the ratio of voltage and current found on the interface, and uses matched impedance, so the inputs are said to terminate the outputs. This means that it is bad practice to use a Y-adapter to distribute an output signal to more than one input because each output is expected to see just one input in a one-to-one relationship. The impedance is 110 ohms, and this makes the use of Cat 5 unshielded twisted pair computer cable practical for studio-length runs, which should all be unshielded, including both installed and flexible leads (equipment cords). For such runs it is commonplace to use the accompanying telephone-style RJ-45 connectors instead of XLRs. Current practice favors the use of pins 4 and 5 of RJ-45 connectors for the first AES3 pair signal, and pins 3 and 6 for a second AES3 pair signal. For runs in harsher environments, such as near transmitters where many interfering signals are present, specific AES3 shielded cable with 110-ohm characteristic impedance is available.

In video studios with lots of video wiring and switchers to consider, another form of the professional interface is available, called AES3id, so that digital audio signals may be cabled and routed using standard video techniques. Television stations use this 75-ohm unbalanced version of AES3, for instance. In this case, the same cable (RG-59/U) and connectors (BNC) that are used for video are also used. There is no way to distinguish input from output connectors because both are the same gender, so you have to make certain by observation that outputs are connected to inputs.

For both AES3 and AES3id wiring, each cable carries a pair of audio signals, such as a left-right pair. The two signals are interleaved in time and decoded by receiving equipment into the original pair with the correct timing.

On consumer equipment, a different version of the digital audio interface is used, called S/PDIF. The signals are similar but not identical to AES3 ones, and this can lead to difficulties, and the electrical interface is different too. Because the connectors for both inputs and outputs are the same gender, there is also potential labeling confusion over what constitutes an output and what an input. Does "Tape Out" on a unit mean connect this signal to the output of the tape machine, which would be easy to think but would be wrong? Better labeling is, for example, "Out to Tape," meaning connect this output to the input of the tape machine, but this is infrequently found.

There are several ways for S/PDIF signals to be transported. With a wired electrical connection, the interface uses RCA or Cinch phono pin plugs[3] (Figure 6-4). Phono jacks are found on CD players, for example, on both left and right analog outputs, and for the single digital output that carries two channels on one wire. There are two ways to distinguish between the analog and digital connectors. Usually the insulator of the left channel analog connector will be white and the right channel analog connector will be red, with the digital connector's insulator some other color. Yellow is typically reserved for composite video signals. The other means of distinguishing analog from digital is the labeling: "Left" used alone as a designator implies analog because the digital interface carries two signals on one conductor.

Another way that S/PDIF format data may be conveyed is by optical fiber connection, and these are commonplace today (Figure 6-5). The most common of them is called TOSLINK, and it has associated cables and connectors available. They have the advantage of using light as

---

[3] Called each of these four in turn somewhere, so all of the terms have been used. Just one of them is usually sufficient to specify the connector in most cases. Hereinafter they will be called phono plugs or jacks.

Figure 6-4 An RCA connector pair that may be used for consumer analog or digital audio.

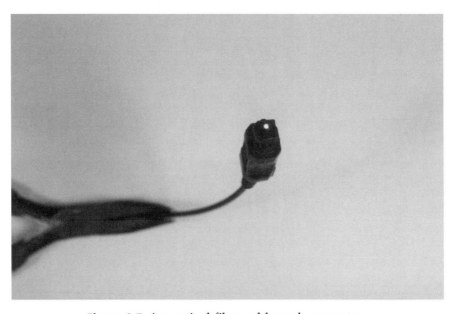

Figure 6-5 An optical fiber cable and connector.

the medium over a strand of glass inside the cable, thus requiring no electrical interconnection and preventing certain problems arising on the interfaces because of grounding difficulties, the ground loops that can lead to hum.

One nice thing about digital audio connections is that if you have the same connector type on both ends of the cable, you just need to plug them in, and in all likelihood the interface will work. The audio levels are represented within the digits transmitted, not by the electrical voltage on the interface. Thus, you merely need to make the connection and the audio levels will be right, which is one advantage of digital interconnections over analog ones.

If you face translating from one type to another, AES3 to S/PDIF or vice versa, it is possible to translate the electrical interface's level and impedance by means of transformers. However, even after correct electrical interconnection, AES3 signals often are not recognized as valid by S/PDIF inputs. If this connection does not work, you need a format converter from AES3 to S/PDIF.[4] It is more likely that an S/PDIF signal will be recognized by an AES3 input, but this is also not guaranteed. There is no harm in trying to connect the signals, once the level and impedance issues are out of the way, by means of an appropriate transformer.

There is another way you can get into trouble on a purely digital interface. Clicks or "snats" (loud, sharp, short clicks) can arise from clocking problems. Clocks for audio are like the quartz crystal oscillator in many watches, setting a pace for the internals of 'machines, and for the audio on their ports. But just like different quartz watches, the clock in a DAT machine might be slightly different in speed than one in an editing system. When they are connected together, you can hardly notice the difference, and the small difference in rate that occurs can be mostly overcome by buffering—placing the incoming stream in a memory at the speed of the source machine and removing it from the memory for use at the speed of the receiving machine.

---

[4] The following company makes transformers and format converters of between AES and S/PIF and vice versa:

    c4-AUDIO-SYSTEME GmbH

    Elmring 11

    38154 Koenigslutter

    Germany

    Telephone 0 53 53 94100 0 (From U.S. 011 49 53 53 94100 0)

    Fax 0 53 53 94100 88 (From U.S. 011 49 53 53 94100 88)

The problem comes when that memory becomes either under- or overfilled. At this point, the memory will have to jump to refill or remove data, and a snat results. This can be as often as more than once a second (rarely) or as infrequent as once in, say, 20 minutes, and thus be hard to track down.

There are two ways to cure this problem: (1) Operate the receiving equipment so that its clock is derived from the transmitted data, which means that it can't simultaneously be synchronized to the rest of the studio—for receiving data it must be operating as an island, divorced from the other studio equipment; or (2) Lock up the source equipment to a studio master clock by connecting its word clock input to the same word clock that the editing system is using. A studio master clock is a piece of gear having a high-precision clock. Although it may have many types of outputs to cover both audio and video cases, the one most prominent for audio is called word clock, a reference signal that is at the sampling rate, in most cases 48.000 kHz. Distributing it to all equipment that will accept a word clock input, and switching that equipment through hardware and/or software switches to sync to their word clock input, overcomes the snat problem among these pieces of equipment. By the way, it does not matter what type of digital audio connection—S/PDIF or AES3 on copper wire or optical—is used; snats may still be a problem.

The remaining problem is with equipment that has no word clock input, such as almost all CD players[5] and inexpensive DAT machines. There are two possible solutions. First is to make the receiving equipment follow the incoming signal as its clock source; this can be a hardware and/or software switch. The receiving equipment, say an editing system, can't then simultaneously be producing a digital output that is in sync with the rest of the facility, but this may not be important. For instance, you would have to monitor the output sound by way of the editing system's analog out, rather than its digital out to other equipment, because this would then involve the other equipment in operating at the original sending equipment's rate, and so forth. The second solution is to use the converted analog output of the source machine into an analog-to-digital converter of the receiving machine.

There is one more way that digital audio interfaces can be problematic, and it is even more fundamental: the source machine and the receiver must be

---

[5] The Denon DV-C680 with the optional ACD-25SC sample rate converter and ACD-27CS time code boards has a word clock input and converts 44.1-kHz sampled CDs into a 48-kHz AES3 output.

operating at the same nominal sample frequency. If they are not, several consequences may occur. The first would be no sound at all as the receiver fails to lock up to the source. The second is that the receiver might be tricked into operating so far off speed that it accepts 44.1-kHz samples from a CD player, for instance, on a 48-kHz input, in which case when the sound is subsequently played back at the normal rate for the editing system, the pitch will be raised by 8.8 percent, a large amount, and the time shortened by a corresponding amount. In some cases this may not matter, but it usually would be an obvious distortion of the original.

The third possibility is for the system to transfer the audio at 44.1 kHz, but tag it with that information, and then perform a sample rate conversion upon playback to get it to play at the correct pitch and speed in 48-kHz files (the sample rate always used for accompanying a picture). The problem is that very good sample rate conversion is taxing on computer hardware, limiting at the very least how many tracks this can be done on simultaneously. This is the method that Final Cut Pro 4 uses in order to accommodate mixed sample rate files, such as 48-kHz DV files and 44.1-kHz CD files intermixed within one editing session, but it at the very least uses up considerable computer horsepower to do it well.

Reviewing the requirements for digital audio interconnections to work well leads to the following recommendations:

- For FireWire interconnects, the first issue is that you need the correct connector and cable to the correct standard as shown for the task in the following table:

  Note that FireWire 400 ports may also be called iLink.

  For FireWire interconnects, the main software issue is that the source tapes or files for a given program all are at the same sample rate and word length, with a strong preference for two-channel, 48-kHz, 16-bit audio. Violating this recommendation leads to additional work either by you (in transferring files to a common format) or the workstation (which may slow it down and cause audio quality problems), at least.

  Otherwise this is the most straightforward of the interfaces, containing as it does both picture and sound. However, there are synchronization issues to consider because of the use of unlocked audio in DV (explained in Chapter 2).

- For AES-3 interconnects on XLR connectors on both ends, the sample rate and word length issues apply to make inputs consistent with other files used within the editing system (48 kHz strongly preferred),

Table 6-1 Firewire Interconnects.

1st Cable End	2nd Cable End	Used To	
FireWire 400 IEEE 1394a standard 4 pin	FireWire 400 IEEE 1394a standard 4 pin	Connect two DV camcorders together for copying or for continuous recording using certain models	
FireWire 400 IEEE 1394a standard 6 pin	FireWire 400 IEEE 1394a standard 4 pin	Connect DV camcorders to computers or to DV recorders, either having IEEE-1394 FireWire ports	
FireWire 400 IEEE 1394a standard 6 pin	FireWire 400 IEEE 1394a standard 6 pin	Connect FireWire hard drives to computer IEEE-1394a FireWire 400 ports	
FireWire 800 IEEE 1394b standard 9 pin	FireWire 400 IEEE 1394a standard 6 pin	Also known as a bilingual cable, it connects either a 6-pin FireWire 400 device to a 9-pin Firewire 800 port on a computer, or it connects the	

Continues

Table 6-1 *Continued*

1st Cable End	2nd Cable End	Used To	
		6-pin FireWire 400 port on a computer to a 9-pin FireWire 800 device	
FireWire 800 IEEE 1394b standard 9 pin	FireWire 400 IEEE 1394a standard 4 pin	Connects a DV camcorder to a FireWire 800 port on a computer	

but if only a 44.1-kHz source is available, such as from a CD, acknowledge this and provide for it within the editing environment or by other means. Snats occurring on this interface usually mean that there are clocking issues. If they are occurring, see if the source machine has a word clock input, and provide one from the same source used by the editing machine. If not, then set the editing import software so that it clocks from the input source, such as saying "Clock derived from AES input" or some such language in a clock menu.

For AES-3 interconnects on BNC connectors on both ends, the same considerations apply as for those on XLR connectors.

For connections between AES-3 balanced 110-ohm connectors (XLRs) and unbalanced 75-ohm connectors (BNCs), a transformer adapter needs to be used.

- For S/PDIF interconnects with phono connectors on both ends, the same issues as for AES-3 interfaces occur. For DAT machines, their native sample rate and word length is 48 kHz and 16 bits, compatible with DV editing systems. For CD players, the sample rate is on the 44.1-kHz standard, and thus sample rate conversion considerations apply, as explained previously. However, CDs are more quickly imported by file copying rather than by playing them on a player, so the need for this interconnection decreases as time goes by.

- For mixed AES and S/PDIF systems, an appropriate transformer may be used. You must confirm that the software will accept the relatively few bit differences between the two systems.

Analog Interconnection

Analog interconnections have many variations, which can get you into trouble if they are mixed within one system. The first notion is the level regime. Three basic level domains are encountered:

1. *Mic level.* Typically rather small in the millivolt range (thousandths of volts), although at very high acoustical levels these signals can approach a volt or more.
2. *Line level.* There are two common standards for line level, called, colloquially, −10 and +4. The −10 level is found as a reference on consumer-level equipment, often on phono connectors or mini phone connectors (3.5 mm). The +4 level is found as a reference on professional-level equipment, most often on XLR connectors. The meaning of these levels is described in the following text and can be seen in Figure 6-6.
3. *Speaker level.* This is a nominally higher level than line level but is also backed by a lower impedance power amplifier output. The voltage depends on the loudness, and a typical one is 2.83 V for 85–95 dB SPL, depending on the loudspeaker.

Among these three the first item to note is the difference between mic level and line level, because the connectors for these may be the same, and it would be highly unusual to find speaker-level connections on the same connector. The consequence of connecting a line-level output of a unit, such as a microphone mixer, into a mic-level input, such as that of a camera, is almost certainly great distortion. That's because you are connecting something putting out around a volt or so for normal signals into an input intended for millivolt levels: the much higher line-level overloads the mic-level input, and the input clips the signal, usually badly. The corresponding consequence of connecting a mic-level signal into a line-level input is having a weak signal. If you turn the level up enough to hear it, then it may be noisy because this millivolt range signal is being connected to an input capable of in the range of volts, and raising the gain will also raise the noise.

The mic/line problem is a common one in video production, and solving it is not difficult. It occurs because each piece of equipment is designed to face a harsh world in which it has to adapt to all possible conditions. Thus, a microphone mixer will have both line-level and microphone-level outputs because there is no a priori knowledge on the part of the designer as to what it might be connected to next in the chain, and there may only be one or the other type of input available. Many, if not most, professional cameras have input XLR connectors that can be switched between mic and line levels. So because both ends of a single cable between a mic mixer and a camera are switchable, several bad combinations can occur. It is simply necessary to set both to the same level, preferably line level.

Line Levels

There are two prominent electrical reference levels in use to exchange signals between pieces of equipment, called +4 and −10, which are normally professional and consumer-grade, respectively. You might wonder where prosumer equipment falls in this area, and in fact it is ambiguous. For instance, a piece of prosumer gear might be equipped with XLR connectors, implying a +4 reference, but then use consumer-type levels. CD players and DAT machines are on yet a third standard, which will be explained later.

The first thing to understand about these reference levels is that they don't represent any particular piece of program material very well. They are the levels of line-up tones that are sent between pieces of equipment so that interchange can be performed without adding noise or distortion, but relying only on them may cause trouble. The reason is that the program material doesn't bear much of a relationship to the reference, in many cases. What is actually important is that the highest peak level of the program should never exceed the highest-level capability of the recording medium. The meter scale for most digital audio metering has a maximum of 0 dBFS. All other levels are below that, such as −6, −10, −20 dB, and so forth (even if there is not enough room for the minus sign and it is implied). The standard is set this way because the maximum level recordable without distortion is the most unambiguous point of all, and various items of program material use headroom in different ways, implying different reference levels; thus, while a case can be made for a variety of lower reference levels, 0 dBFS is the most obvious one.

However, for interchange between digital and analog systems, a reference in the analog domain that is at the top of the permissible levels is never used. The primary reason for this is that VU meters are commonplace in the United States. VU meters are sluggish devices, taking some 300 ms, nearly one-third of a second, to reach full reading with a suddenly applied signal. This means that for shorter signals, the meter does not read their full value and they are underestimated. Because we can hear distortion in as little as 2 ms, the VU meter could easily miss content that is audibly distorted. This fact was accommodated in years of analog recording by setting the reference level for 0 VU some number of decibels below the maximum capability of the medium and allowing the medium's headroom to accommodate the peaks. In film sound using conventional magnetic film, this amount grew over the years as film got better and better to being as much as 23 dB!

So for exchange between digital and analog media, a reference level that is some number of decibels below 0 dBFS is useful. How many decibels below depends on who you are and what you are doing, because there is no complete agreement on digital reference level. SMPTE specifies −20 dBFS, and many professional digital video recorders observe this reference. It was developed so that most of the content of existing analog film masters could be transferred without adjustment, although the fact that the analog media actually has about 23 dB headroom makes life a little difficult. One Hollywood studio transfers from the film reference level tone[6] to −24 dBFS and then turns the level up in the digital domain by 4 dB to get back on the reference, encountering potential distortion in the process that is then tamed by using audio limiting, described in Chapter 9.

At the other extreme are those users who have little headroom in the analog path they are driving, and they may use a reference level as high as −12 dBFS, assuming that the analog equipment they are driving only has 12 dB headroom. Examples are audio for VHS tape delivery and certain analog satellite and microwave transmission systems. A third reference level of −18 dBFS is used by broadcasters in Europe for digital recordings.

---

[6] Which is at the analog magnetic reference level of 185 nW/m.

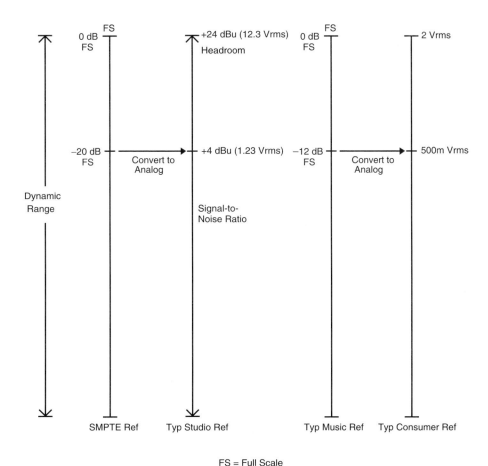

Figure 6-6 Diagram of various digital level references.

While tones at these levels are used for line up, particularly accompanying color bars at the heads of program tapes, what is most important is that the maximum peak of the program material be known and accommodated in transfers.

Whatever digital reference level is chosen between −12 dBFS and −20 dBFS, a digital-to-analog converter will convert that digital level to an analog voltage level at its output. This is where the notion of +4 or −10 comes into play. The terms +4 and −10 are shorthand for the following:

+4 dBu, which is a voltage of 1.23V. The *u* refers to that voltage which corresponds to 1 mW of power dissipated in a 600-ohm resistor, namely 0.775 V, and +4 dB above that voltage is 1.23 V.[7]
−10 dBV is a voltage of 0.316 V. The *V* refers to a voltage referenced to 1 Volt. −10 dB below 1 V is 0.316 V.

Each of these may be used to correspond to digital reference levels between −20 and −12 dBFS. Note that because the references are different (*u* means that voltage which corresponds to 1 mW in 600 ohms, namely 0 dBu equals 0.775 V; *V* means dB relative to 1 V), these two levels are 12.2 dB apart, not 14.

With −20 dBFS digital reference set to correspond to +4 dBu, then 0 dBFS will be +24 dBu equals 12.3 V, a quite high voltage level. This high voltage level is why it is found only on professional equipment, and not all of that!

With −12 dBFS digital reference set to correspond to −10 dBV, the other extreme from the last case, then 0 dBFS will be +2 dBV equals 1.26 V, nearly 20 dB below the pro reference, and a level easy to obtain, even on most battery-operated portable equipment. See Table 6-2.

The 20 dB range discovered previously is the reason why there are sometimes interface problems with so-called line-level signals, and these problems are compounded when CD players, computer sound cards, and other sources are added to the mix. For CD players, the rather loosely applied standard is 0 dBFS equals 2V (± 3 dB, or from 1.42 to 2.83V). For computer sound cards, all bets are off because there are so many potential level controls between a track being played back and the output of the DAC. These include potentially the gain setting in the track within the editing system, the gain control of the sound card software, and a gain control in the operating system. With three level controls between the track and the outside world, it is easy to see why there is little standardization of the output.

Fortunately, in most cases, these differences can be calibrated out. Let's say that we have a professional DAC, a CD player, an S-VHS tape machine, and a computer sound card, all as sources for our monitoring system. We

----

[7] The *u* is a more modern usage than the *m* that preceded it, which was dBm for 1 mW reference. Because actual 600-ohm loads are not used nowadays, and milliwatts are not actually dissipated, the updating of the term from *m* to *u* makes sense.

Table 6-2 Reference Levels

Source Device	Reference Level on Medium	Reference Output Voltage	Reference Level dBu	Maximum Level dBu
Pro DAC	−20 dBFS	1.23 V	+4	+24
CD Player	−12 dBFS (example only; there is no one widely observed standard)	0.5 V	−3.8	+8.2
S-VHS	International Tape Association reference level	0.316 V	−7.8	+8.2
Computer Sound Card	−20 dBFS (example only; there are wide variations among cards, and their output is influenced by multiple software level controls)	Varies	Varies	Varies

put each pair of source channels into pairs of input channels of a small monitor mixer, such as a Mackie 1202. We could manipulate the various levels with the main faders, but this is not the best way to operate because they will have very different settings. The best way to perform gain staging is to set the channel level faders to a standard, often marked 0 dB or "U" for unity gain, that level at which what is presented at the input is reproduced at the output. Then set the main faders also for 0 dB. Observing the LED-style VU meter, set the input trim control for each source playing a standard level tone so that the meter reads 0 VU. The input trim controls do the work of adjusting for the variety of reference voltage levels to be found with these various sources.

To connect all of these up, it may be necessary to use some audio adapters. Besides XLR and phono plugs described previously, phone plugs or mini (3.5 mm diameter) phone plugs may be used. Stereo phone or mini phone plugs—those having a distinctive tip, ring, and sleeve conductors—may be used in one of two ways (Figure 6-7). In the most common form, they are used for stereo with the tip carrying the left channel signal, the ring the right channel signal, and the sleeve being a common ground for the two channels. In a variation, only one signal is carried, but in a balanced mode, with the tip being the positive signal, the ring is the negative signal and the sleeve is ground.

Mixing Balanced and Unbalanced Connections

In the olden days of audio, life was easy. Professional equipment was equipped with input and output transformers, and these produced a balanced, usually floating (no ground reference on the lines) system.

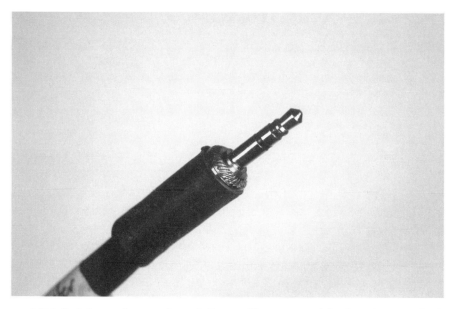

Figure 6-7 Miniature phone plug, 3.5 mm diameter, with tip, ring, and sleeve connections permitting balanced microphone or unbalanced stereo headphone connections.

Impedances were matched so every output expected to be looking into a 600-ohm load provided by every input. No fan out was possible without a distribution amplifier; that is, each output was only capable of feeding one input. If you wanted to drive more than one input, an extra distribution amplifier was necessary. All of this was derived from telephone company practice, which had to be of very high quality for its day to deliver the goods across long telephone lines, and depending on the quality of the (rather expensive) transformers, hum was low, frequency response and distortion were good, headroom was high, and so on.

Professional and consumer worlds were quite different and at opposite ends of the spectrum when it came to signal distribution. Consumer-grade equipment used the unbalanced system, with outputs represented on one conductor plus ground connectors wired to similarly equipped inputs. Impedances were bridging; that is, they worked just like your electrical outlets: you plug in as many bulbs as you want to one circuit, and the system does not care how many bulbs are plugged in until you reach a maximum determined by how much current you are drawing. Thus audio signals could be applied to a Y-adapter to distribution to multiple inputs.

Although unbalanced audio was not as bulletproof for hum as the professional system—something that its lower reference voltage levels also did not help—the unbalanced system was good enough for small, stand-alone systems in general, but integrating consumer equipment into larger professional systems required additional interface equipment. Thus, the IHF Match Box and +4/−10 box came on the scene. A way to use cheaper consumer equipment in a professional studio, these made the level and balanced/unbalanced transition necessary to enable the use of such equipment.

So far the distinction between professional balanced lines and consumer unbalanced ones has been straightforward. If you needed to go in between the two domains, then a match box would do the job. However, this is where things get more complicated. Good transformers are expensive, leading electronic designers to try to emulate their isolation properties with circuits, attempting to achieve the same end more cheaply. The salient thing about a transformer is that the two sets of wires around the core, called primary and secondary, are not connected to each other electrically—they are said to be galvanically isolated. This is how transformers provide isolation: the electrical voltage input to the primary wiring is turned into a magnetic field, which is then relayed to the secondary magnetically, and in its wiring produces the output voltage.

Unfortunately, circuits to provide such isolation range across a very wide span of quality, and some of them can be downright bad in some circumstances, clipping prematurely for instance, so if you should happen to have a signal peak at 0 dBFS in the digital domain, it may well clip electronically some 6 dB sooner, at −6 dBFS, depending on what the output circuit is driving. And this electronic gimmickry is used across many levels of equipment, with more expensive professional gear sometimes worse than less expensive. Unfortunate too is the fact that you can rarely tell anything about this situation from the specifications of the unit. One DTRS-format eight-track digital tape machine, an "upgrade" from a former model, performs much worse than the earlier model when confronted with an unbalanced input connected to its output, as it would be in many semi-professional environments. Even higher-end equipment is not immune: Dolby's SP frame racks for SR noise reduction, which no one would call semi-pro gear, employ a similar technique.

One way to test for this is the following: use a battery-powered voltmeter to measure the voltage at reference level out of a piece of equipment. Then connect it to the input of the following piece of equipment, keeping the voltmeter in parallel with the input. If the level doesn't change, it is likely that the interface port will be all right. If it changes by −6 dB (half the voltage), it is likely you are in trouble.

File Transfers

By far the more efficient means of moving audio around between media and systems is by means of file transfers rather than streaming transfers. That's because whole sound files can be imported into an editing system, say, in one action, and it takes place at much greater than real time. Among the considerations are that the imported file format matches that of the system into which it is being imported. Let's say that you have DV format files and you wish to import music from CDs. The problem is the mixed sample rates: 48 kHz for DV and 44.1 kHz for CD. Several things may occur: one is that the session plays back the samples of the CD, but at the new sample rate, thus raising the pitch and shortening the duration. This may be all right for some sound effects, but it will make voices thinner and music in

Table 6-3 Audio Connectors

Name	Uses	Notes
RCA, Cinch, Phono, Pin Plug	Analog audio, digital audio, analog video	Most ubiquitous consumer plug found on most nonportable consumer equipment
3.5 mm Mini plug, mono and stereo versions	Headphones, some consumer microphones	Mono version has a tip and a sleeve; stereo version has a tip, a ring, and a sleeve
2.5 mm Micro plug, mono and stereo versions	Microphone inputs of microcassette recorders	Be careful not to confuse with 3.5 mm plugs/sockets
BNC	Analog and digital video, digital audio (especially to AES3id standard)	Locking connector
XLR	Analog audio, digital audio	3-pin for balanced connections
Banana plugs	Loudspeakers, test equipment, Nagra line inputs/outputs	

the wrong key, so the other possibility is sample rate conversion upon import, as described formerly.

The other concern in making file transfers is whether the system doing the importing understands the syntax of what is being delivered. There are many different file formats in use. Some contain only audio with minimal other information about how it was recorded, whereas other file formats contain a great deal of information about where a given sound is to be used in a time line, what fade files are to act on it, and so forth. One primary difference among the file types is whether the audio format represents the least sensitive information first (called little endian, such as .wav files) or the most significant information first (called big endian, such as AIFF files). Some file formats for exchange are listed in the following table.

Audio File Formats

Today's audio file formats are the result of years of development, with many systems owing quite a lot to older ones. In many lineages, each new format is really an extension of older formats, accomplished by placing new wrappers around the file recorded in older formats to add new information. In this way, some audio file formats today bear a strong resemblance to Russian concatenated (or nesting) dolls—opening each one reveals a new, smaller doll within. Some newer formats that wrap around older ones restrict the range of choices of the older ones. For instance, .WAV files may contain low-bit-rate coded audio (see Chapter 10), but when used as an AES 31 file, the coding is restricted to linear pulse code modulation (PCM).

One of the first of these formats was called IFF, developed for the Amiga computer. It begat WAV, which begat BWF, which begat AES 31, each one adding a layer of additional information to the basic audio. Basic digital audio files in widespread interchange use are the formats AIFF-C, BWF, WAV, and SDII. There are also numerous file formats used for given proprietary systems. Some of the proprietary system file formats may be interchanged with each other (e.g., Akai machines can read Fairlight files).

The second type of file contains the audio media and editing instructions and additional metadata, or data about the data. These formats include OMF1, OMF2, AAF, and AES 31. Audio file formats that may be embedded within OMF, for instance, include AIFF-C, SDII, and WAV. However, OMF files may also be just edit decision lists with pointers to the actual audio; such OMF files are called composition only files.

Digital audio with a sample rate of 48 kHz using 16-bit linear PCM coding requires 5.76 MBytes per track minute (48,000 samples per second times 16 bits per sample times 60 seconds per minute divided by 8 bits per Byte equals 5,760,000 Bytes). So 1 GB of digital audio storage holds 173 minutes of monaural 48 kHz sampled 16-bit audio. Other sample rates, word lengths, or number of channels can be scaled from this number.

Media are filled to various degrees depending on their use. For instance, whereas media for exchange can be filled rather fully, media for editorial purposes must leave room for editing changes to the audio, additional editing files, and operational overhead. For editing purposes, 50 percent full is probably normal operation.

Name	Where Used	Limitations	Endian	Handling of More Than One Channel	Metadata
Sound Designer II (SDII), on PC with .sd2 file extension	Editing systems; very popular but with some limitations due to its age	Sample rate up to 48 kHz; 2 GB file limit; produces length limitation	Big, due to Motorola roots	Channels interleaved	Mono/stereo, bit depth, sample rate
AIFF (Apple Interchange File Format) (.aif, .aiff)	Editing systems; very popular but with some limitations due to its age		Big, due to Motorola roots, although variants in little	Channels interleaved	Number of channels* (mono/stereo are the only interesting ones), bit depth, sample rate, application-specific data area
AIFF-C (Apple Interchange Film Format for Compression) (.aifc)	Not widely used in post.		Big	Channels interleaved	Mono/stereo, bit depth, sample rate, application-specific data area; -C indicates potential for bit-rate-reduced (compressed) audio

Continues

Continued

Name	Where Used	Limitations	Endian	Handling of More Than One Channel	Metadata
WAV (.wav) for Waveform Data	Started on Windows but widely used today, even on Apple, for interchange		Little, due to Intel roots	Tracks interleaved	Number of channels, bit depth, sample rate; may contain bit-rate-reduced (compressed) audio
Broadcast WAV (.wav); despite being another format, .wav is the correct file extension	Broadcasting; edit WAV with extensions developed by broadcasters	No specific hooks for accompanying a picture	Little, due to WAV roots		WAV format file with added metadata about production and timing

Continues

Continued

Name	Where Used	Limitations	Endian	Handling of More Than One Channel	Metadata
OMF 1					First attempt at producing interchange-ability with audio and EDL, particularly between picture and sound editing stations
OMF 2					Second attempt
AAF					Third attempt
AES-31					An extension of Broadcast WAV; an attempt at workstation interchange

*But the number of channels jumps from four to six, with the six being other than the standard 5.1, so AIFF is not useful for 5.1 channel files.

Common Problems in Digital Audio File Transfers for Sound Accompanying Picture

Here are some of the common problems found with digital audio file exchanges, in particular those that come from picture editing systems:

File operations:

- Different software version of the system that generates the export data than expected between source and destination, or among source, translator software, and destination

- Changing software version partway through a project

- File naming conventions unintelligible or illogical. A file named "tempdub" conveys hardly any information because there are a great many of these in a production

- Leaving file extensions off the end of file names, such as .wav

- Improper formatting of export media, including fragmentation caused by not starting from an empty file structure on such media

- OMF files transferred between different editions of an editor before export to the audio system.

Editorial operations:

- Illogical track layout, like sounds jumping among tracks such as interchanging boom and lavaliere tracks at random. Consistency in naming and logging of tracks is necessary.

- Audio not in hard sync before export; it is difficult to see sync on low-resolution video. To check sync, it is useful to have a production A track that has been carefully checked as a reference. Dialog may then be split across other tracks and their sync checked by listening and sliding the split tracks, playing the edited track and the A track simultaneously, and listening for phasing, a swishy sound resulting from the comb filter that occurs when sound is nearly in perfect sync.

There is software on the market that helps to autoconform sound to sound, such as Vocalign from Synchro Arts.

- Insertion of wild sounds without a means of tracing sync back to the source. This means the sound department has to do the work all over again if the same source is to be used. For instance, laying in music from a CD in the picture editor provides no means to trace back to the source. Instead, copying the CD to a time code DAT machine before insertion into the picture edit, then importing from the DAT with time code, provides a means to get precisely the same sync in sound editing. Note that such sound is exported, but the sound editor may need, for instance, a longer length of it, and this is where it is valuable to be able to repeat the picture editor's work in the sound editing room.

- Over-reliance on exporting systems has led to less accurate production of human-readable EDLs, but these are the only backup if the export fails

- Text information on a sound clip

- Subclips/group clips in multicamera shooting

- Start times for a session do not match sequence time

- Noisy editing rooms with bad monitoring lead to the picture department saying "it sounded all right on the Avid" in explaining a bad transfer. Picture editing suites are notorious for having bad monitoring conditions, and thus they are usually no place to judge audio quality. The story is told of completely distorted audio being received by a sound department that, when they went to check how it sounded in the editing room, found that the tweeters in the monitor speakers were burned out.

Digital audio problems:

- Different sample rates between source and destination. This is particularly a problem when music interests are involved because they would prefer 44.1-kHz sample rate of the CD, yet most film and television operates at 48 kHz. Just importing CDs as sound effects into projects necessitates a sample rate conversion if they are to be imported with the same pitch and duration.

- Audio digitized in draft mode at 22.050 kHz

- Sample rate conflicts caused by pulldown, when film or genuine 24 P video is in use. Shot with 48-kHz standard sample rate at 29.97 fps, then pulled down on the telecine results in a nonstandard rate. If audio has been inserted without pulldown, it will drift in sync by 0.1 percent, with the sound being longer than the picture. This can be checked by measuring the length and calculating the difference. If it is 0.1 percent, which is one frame in a thousand with the sound being longer, the likely source is the lack of a required pulldown.

Ordinary audio production items caused problems:

- Level too low or high

- Channels mixed together or interchanged.

Improper setup for export:

- Incorrect consolidation: in the case of Avid, leaving Audio Suite plug-ins activated: group information, pitch change, time compression/expansion, fades, levels

- The sound editor needs *handles*; that is, sound for each region of audio used in the picture edit before the beginning and after the ending, providing the ability to make smoother changes than are usually done by the picture department. Handle lengths range from a few frames to the full length of the take depending on the material, the density of edits on the tracks, and the desires of the sound editor. For long-form work,[8] handles are provided that are the length of the take, so the maximum chance is available to find presence that intercuts.

Improper or no labeling of the media:

- The Multichannel Postproduciton Media Label in Chapter 10 suggests content for a label for interchange.

---

[8] This is the industry term for feature films and television miniseries.

One frame or more sync errors in exported files (probably originate in software mathematics) are common:

- It is useful to have a sync check such as a clapperboard slate once in an export file so that hard sync can be checked after import.

- It is highly useful not to rely on a crucial transfer, but rather to test the transfer path ahead of the time when a transfer will be essential.

The Director's Cut

- Do not confuse analog and digital connections; they may appear on the same connector types but cannot be interchanged.
- Connecting up digitally is usually fairly straightforward, but clicks and snats can result from certain conditions. FireWire interconnect is probably the simplest connection method, although you must get the right cable type and the software must accommodate the particular device being controlled.
- Never confuse mic and line level. Camcorders routinely have a switch to turn their input jacks from one mode to the other, but they cannot work properly with the alternate type of signal level.
- Analog connections are more difficult because there are both professional and consumer levels and methods of wiring. Using a balance box is the best way to interface between the two.
- Digital reference level for sound accompanying a picture is −20 dBFS. Most music people don't believe in this and use higher reference levels.
- Music-oriented people tend to deliver product at 44.1-kHz sampling rate, the CD rate. This is not compatible with sound accompanying pictures, which samples at 48 kHz. Thus, CDs have to be sample rate converted to fit into video editing systems.
- Audio file formats have to be set correctly on export for interchange. For instance, OMF files must include audio files as well as how to use them.

CHAPTER 7
Sound Design

Sound design is the art of getting the right sound in the right place at the right time. This chapter concentrates on defining what is the right sound. The right place can be defined as placement of a sound into the right one of multiple tracks, an organizational skill exercised during editing that anticipates and strongly affects mixing. The right time defines the placement of sounds in a time line, often with a synchronous relationship to the picture or to other sound effects. The right place and time have to do with the details of editing and are covered in the next chapter.

A concept that filmmaking borrowed from theater is *mise en scene*, defining what the director puts into the scene. This is the frame that we see—what is in it and what is excluded, the lighting, costumes, and blocking of the actors—that is, their massing and movement. When first applied to cinema, the concept meant everything in front of the camera: the set, costumes, composition of the shots, patterns of light and dark, and so forth. More recently, the term has been broadened within its use in film studies to include cinematography and its effects, such as depth of field, editing, and sound. Thus, sound stands today in critical thinking as one principal ingredient of the film art, and reading a film means understanding the role that each of these ingredients plays in perception, including sound.

The first notion of film sound influenced by the *mise en scene* idea is that somebody somewhere has decided what you hear, moment by moment, within a movie—the fact that there is an author, and what you hear is not accidental but planned. What you hear could be just the sound of what the camera sees in documentary fashion, but it is often a more constructed sound, built out of bits and pieces by professionals to simulate a desired overall sound impression. Sometimes just to portray reality, sound may have to be changed from that which was captured during production. Off-screen sound recorded during production may include inappropriate noise, and substituted sound is more appropriate. At other times, various film sound styles may dominate even within one film, from the real to surreal to montage across a range representing increasing levels of abstraction, for instance.

Certain film sound conventions prevail that are perhaps stereotypical, but that also have the advantage of transmitting emotional information quickly. At the end of the climactic scene after the Ark of the Covenant has been closed in *Raiders of the Lost Ark*, Indy and Karen are left exhausted but happy. The ambient sound that we hear is that of crickets, a quiet and peaceful sound that ends a remarkable sound sequence: the fact that we are at peace is transmitted to us quickly by the use of such stereotypical sound.

We come to understand the conventions of film sound through exposure to a great many examples; we are all trained through listening to films, whether we know it consciously or not. Thus, a scene with a particular piquancy for us is that of lovers gazing into one another's eyes accompanied by orchestral score. The camera dollies back to reveal—an orchestra playing in the foreground. What could be more likely? The literalness of this sound joke is funny, and the confusion between what is source music and what is score. It is a play on film sound conventions.[1] Another example is at the beginning of *Diva*, when we hear score over the titles, but the mail carrier shutting off the radio on his motorcycle kills the score. The fact that music is going to play a major role in this film is highlighted by this act in the opening seconds.

One of those conventions is that keeping sound constant across a picture cut implies that although we may have changed point of view, we are nonetheless still in the same space. This job of improving overall continuity is most often handled by presence (also called *room tone* or, in England, *atmosphere*). Presence is defined as sound that matches the sound captured during production so well that it may be intercut with production dialogue tracks without discontinuity. It is the sound of relative quiet for the space being portrayed. Note that it is not silence, because cutting to silence leaves us nowhere. It may well be very, very quiet though, and hopefully often this will be the case because we want the best dialogue intelligibility possible most of the time, and the fact that the background is quiet rather

---

[1] Good jokes have a way of being recycled. Mel Brooks used this joke in *Blazing Saddles* when the sheriff rides to his new job across the Western landscape, only to reveal in a pan the Count Basie Orchestra playing the score.

than loud helps intelligibility. Sometimes it is impossible to get precisely matching presence, and the result is a bump at an edit. Dialog editors smooth dialogue using such tactics as cross-fading and delaying of the sound edit compared to the picture one until the beginning of the next utterance after the cut to hide it.

If dialogue tracks can't be perfectly smoothed, or if you need to create a new sonic space other than the one on the set for the scene to exist in, ambience tracks, also known as backgrounds, play a similar function as presence (Figure 7-1). They provide continuity across picture cuts, as well as substitution of a new space for the original. If presence is low enough in level, despite its having discontinuities at edits, backgrounds may be used to cover up or mask the discontinuity, as well as providing a storytelling element of their own. Think of *Star Trek:* each part of the ship has its own background sound, and part of cutting from Engineering to the Bridge, or to 10 Forward, is the change in ambience that accompanies the cut. We as the audience are taught by the filmmakers what each space sounds like, as well as looks like, so we can orient ourselves quickly in a scene change.

With dialogue and its intercut presence, and potentially one or more ambience tracks, a real-sounding dialogue scene may be constructed. The next element that is often used to help sell the reality of what is seen is Foley. Named for the person who invented it at Universal,[2] Jack Foley, it is a series of sound effects made while watching the cut picture in a quiet, dead, recording stage.[3] The mic is typically used close to the sound source. Recordings of footsteps, chair squeaks, clothing rustle, and small physical effects like pouring a drink, or large ones like a body hit, or those of a dinosaur brushing up against foliage, may be Foley effects. Given the close mic perspective in the quiet dead room used for it, Foley is most often exaggerated reality. The technique tends to hype the effects so that heard alone they seem bigger than life, but this is made necessary by the masking effect of having many other sound tracks running simultaneously. For Foley to read through the clutter of all those other sounds, it has to be recorded in this way. Even the lowest-budget films can afford Foley today because the requirements for doing it well are fairly minimal: find a quiet absorbing space, such as a high-school stage with all the curtains down surrounding you. Then play the cut video over a picture monitor, possibly

---

[2] www.npr.org/programs/lnfsound/stories/000324.stories.html
[3] The term *stage* comes from Hollywood practice: shooting stage, Foley stage, dubbing stage. In the outside world, this might be called a studio or recording studio.

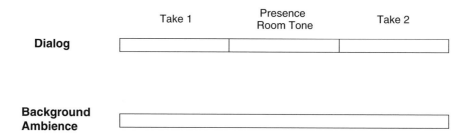

Figure 7-1 The difference between presence, which is intercut with dialogue tracks, and ambience, which has its own track(s).

with headphones so you can listen to the production sound, although this is optional. With a microphone close to your feet, for example, record the sounds of walking, placing them on another medium such as a simple hard-disc recording system, a DAT machine, or even a separate camcorder.

One principal notion that applies to all types of sound effects is well illustrated by Foley, and that is layering. If you have a crowd walking, you can get a crowd to walk and use multiple microphones on them and record them all at once, a technique I found in use at Bejing Film Studios, but if you are only one person, you can record sound that corresponds to one person in the shot, and do this repeatedly on various recordings, building up the whole scene. To accomplish this, it is useful to record each one to a separate track of a hard-disc editing system, and thus each can be recorded in sync as you go. If you use a DAT, then every track has to be transferred to an editing system and "sunk" up. Even for the multitrack recording where each has been recorded in sync to the picture, getting hard sync often means moving Foley effects forward or backward in time somewhat, but with this system, one large step of the process is relatively automated.

So far we have discussed dialog, and with it intercut presence, ambience or backgrounds, and Foley effects. The next major category is cut or hard effects. These are sound effects drawn from production sound, sound effects libraries, and original recordings made for the individual film of sound effects that typically bear a one-to-one relationship to picture. An anecdote illustrates this best. Some years ago on the particularly tight postproduction schedule for *Tucker*, the re-recording mixers were spending long, long hours at work. The son of one of them had written his father a postcard that was promptly posted on the meter bridge at the top of the mixing console in the dubbing stage. It said, "Gee Dad, I get it—see a car, hear a car." There could be no better definition of Hollywood postproduction sound cutting than that made by the young kid who missed his father. The Hollywood craft tradition says that anything we see that can make a sound will.

Some directors accept the craft tradition that says that everything that can make sound will at face value, whereas others question it. A process often found in Hollywood is for sound editors to cut a large amount of effects, basically everything they can think of, and then for the director to strip out what he or she finds unnecessary on the dub stage. This approach is exactly what sound design means to replace—the idea that decisions should be left for the end of the process and for the director to make. In *The Sum of All Fears*, for instance, an early scene in the film is a tension-ridden bomb shelter scene of the President of the United States commanding forces during a crisis. The phone rings and it's his wife calling with trivialities, and we realize that this is not the real thing: it's a rehearsal. The spell is broken by the call. Sound editors provided all kinds of sounds, intended for use in both the screen channels and the surround ones, to embed the viewer in the scene and raise its tension level through engaging the listener. The director, on the other hand, found all of these communication chirps and whizzes distracting, particularly in the surrounds, so stripped them out, and the scene played without most of them. Just enough ambience of a similarly composed scene was used to set the stage, but most of the effects that were cut were not used in this case.

For other types of filmmaking, especially when this process is carried out by just one person or by a very small crew, the selection of just what effects to use can take place even before one gets to the mix. There is always some kind of limitation on the number of tracks. The number of tracks that is desirable seems always to be $n + 1$, where n is the number of tracks available. This begins with the simplest mixes with only a few tracks, and it continues through the largest mixes I have seen, with hundreds of tracks: "but if we could just have one more" is often heard. This is also a factor in sound design: keeping the cut tracks to the available range of equipment and software, and this problem is increasing today as editing processes take on what traditionally have been mixing ones. Plug-ins or filters that run on editing workstations take up some of the computer horsepower available, and it is often difficult to know when limits are being approached and what will happen once those limits are exceeded. This is a level of abstraction that is new to the industry: it used to be that the limitation was on the number of dubbers that could run sound tracks, but today it is how many plug-ins per channel are allowed before the editing system can no longer run in real time.

Hard effects help illustrate and highlight certain items. For instance, although supposedly realistic, those face punches in action films are anything but real for sound. I remember visiting a Hollywood recording stage some years ago on a studio tour. A large-fisted man was hitting a ham as hard as he could to get face punches. While this rather literal recording was better than the real thing, especially for the recipient, it's really not enough for the larger-than-life ones of action-adventure movies. One thing to do is to slow down the original recording, making it appear bigger than life. Another is to layer together a whole parcel of sounds to make one enormous splat out of several merely exaggerated ones. Ingredients might be throwing an old leather jacket onto the metal hood of a fire truck,[4] dropping overly ripe fruit onto concrete and slowing the recording down, or breaking a stalk of celery over one's knee.

One factor that layering produces and that is useful is concealment of the original sound source. Recognition is less likely when sounds are heard together simultaneously in time and panned to the same location. Also, concealment occurs with the pitch and time shifting that accompanies off-speed playback, which is often used with such effects to make them seem larger than life. By the way, it is interesting to note that off-speed playback, particularly of an extreme nature, is much easier to accomplish with analog recorders than with digital ones—it is a reason in itself to keep one analog recorder around equipped with a wide-range varispeed in an otherwise all-digital studio.

What differentiates these kinds of sounds recorded for hard effects from Foley is that no attempt is made during recording to match a previously recorded picture in sync, but rather the object is to gather separately a whole set of ingredient parts that when blended together through editing and mixing take on a life of their own, becoming one auditory object, whether composed of a single ingredient or many layered together.

Walter Murch has stated an important concept in comparing sound design to a three-ring circus. Through evolution in time, big circuses settled on

---

[4] Ben Burtt at Skywalker Ranch for *Raiders of the Lost Ark*.

three rings, not two or five. How did they get there? It has to do with how much information can be processed by the brain at any one time. More than a certain amount of information leads to disconnection as the senses are overwhelmed. Yet the whole idea is to fully engage you, so growing to the point of diminishing returns is valuable too. Circuses evolved to the point where three things at once could be featured. Note that each of these three rings could contain many performers acting in concert, so there are many more molecular elements than three, but the molecular components are clustered into three groups, for which we can pay adequate, albeit potentially shifting, attention.

In our case the analogy has to do with being able to pay attention to what are called auditory streams. While we can only pay attention to three things at once, our attention may shift among more, because we can only hold so many in our heads at one time, but we can also shift gears among streams. Note that this means we definitely need more than three individual sound tracks, because a single auditory event may be built up from many different elements, but for any given point in time all of the elements clustered together into blocks form no more than three items we can typically follow or pay attention to.

Taking this idea a bit further, we might say that the three elements we can pay attention to are more easily delineated if they are of different types. Three dialogue tracks operating in overlapping fashion would be like three lion tamers in the three rings: confusing. But dialog, Foley, sound effects, and music tracks, being rather thoroughly differentiated, are more likely to form separate auditory streams that we can follow.

Film Sound Styles

There is a range of sound styles used in film, and the style may shift within one film across the range through time. The most literal is the realistic style, which may wind up sounding as though it is just what occurred in front of the camera, but which may have to have been built from multiple elements to sound that way. Surrealism breaks with realism by concentrating on unconscious, subjective sound, often associated with a character's point of view. Montage goes even further in being the most abstract, with often a wide schism occurring between picture and sound.

Realism

For an ordinary dialogue scene, the sources are:

- *Dialog from the original production sound.* Sound editors use both circled takes (the ones examined at dailies and that have the potential of their picture winding up in the finished film) and outtakes (those that are likely never to have been seen by the picture editors) to find material from which to construct the dialogue tracks

- *Wild lines.* Recorded typically the same day on the set, using the same microphone setup and so forth, but optimizing for noise in particular. For instance, if wind machines are necessary for a visual effect, they will be shut off and the dialogue repeated. Or if the boom mic cannot get close enough during shooting, the scene can be repeated for sound only

- *Presence/room tone for above.* This is intercut as needed to remove unwanted utterances and otherwise smooth the track into sounding like a continuous whole. Today it is often captured from between utterances of the actors and looped to fill out the required length. However, it is also useful for the director to take a beat before saying "action," allowing the sound editor a moment where everything matches the shot and all is quiet

- *Automated dialogue replacement (ADR).* Generally performed in quiet, dead spaces. Thus, it is typically used with an accompanying ambience track to produce a complete-sounding picture. It is used also for voice-over, which may have a tighter mic perspective (closer) to sound as though the narrator is directly speaking to us from inside his head; occasionally this method of distinguishing a narrator from production sound (the narrator is less reverberant) is reversed, as in the soap opera when the camera sits on the unmoving face of a character and we hear them speak in a reverberant space: we know that we are inside their (big, empty) head. One benefit of ADR is being able to start with a clean slate for sound effects, ambiences, and music. Gary Rydstrom, who has done his share of them, says this is what makes animation so fun, and difficult, because no production sound exists

- *Production effects (PFX)*. This includes sound effects recorded using sync sound on location, which may need separation editorially from dialogue because the processes employed during mixing may well be different between dialogue and effects

- *Ambience/backgrounds*. These sounds form a space for the movie to live in. They may be used to set locale, period, threat level, and other exposition and emotional story-enhancing items. While presence serves to fill out production sound tracks, interspersing sound so that the result sounds completely continuous, in the best of all possible worlds, the presence will be rather quiet compared to the foreground dialogue and production effects because production has taken place in a controlled environment. If this is so, then the sound designer has greater freedom because dialogue intelligibility is already good. Then the sound designer can add ambience elements that enhance the story.

The specific track layout for these will be considered in the editing chapter. When cut and mixed, the attempt is to stick to the reality portrayed by the camera. As has been mentioned, in some instances, use of sound from the location may be impossible, and ADR plus ambience might be substituted, but the point is the same—it is to sound as though it occurred in real time, in front of the camera.

A term used in video production (but not routine in film production) to enhance this real sound is *sweetening*. To add sweetness, other cut effects or music may be added to the smoothed track by virtue of being filled correctly with presence dialogue tracks.

Music that is to appear as though it is present in the scene is nearly impossibly difficult to shoot in real time on location because if it is heard at all it will proscribe many sound edits that might otherwise be made. Whenever possible, such source music, like playing from a radio within the scene, is faked and added in postproduction as a sweetener. About the only case where it cannot be faked is if a band shows up live in a shot, for instance, and even this can be controlled so that you collect all of the bits and pieces that make up the whole on location. You might wish to record:

- The band in a natural, moderately close perspective for the entire tune

- The band in a distant perspective for the entire tune. This can be faked in postproduction as needed if sufficient postproduction tools such as reverberators are available, but if they aren't, the easy way to over-come their lack of availability is to make a separate recording, at the same tempo, energy level, and so forth, but from a distant perspective, to be available for intercutting or even cross-blending with the closer perspective sound.

- The foreground action, with the actors speaking their lines loudly enough to be heard over the band playing in the background

- The foreground action, with the actors speaking their lines at the same level as when the band is playing, but with the band miming their performance in the background

- Of course, if the band doesn't show in a shot, then you don't need it, but be certain the actors are delivering their lines with sufficient energy that their timbre sounds as though it is being spoken over the loud background that will be built in postproduction.

Another common reality situation that needs careful consideration is shooting in a busy restaurant. In fiction filmmaking, the idea is to get the extras to *look* as though they are talking, but to keep them silent, or at least very, very quiet, so that the foreground dialogue (directed to have an appropriate energy level for the scene portrayed) is well recorded. In documentary situations, Table 5-1 in Chapter 5 shows that the general background noise level is just about the same as the dialogue level in a busy deli, so recording here is much more of a problem. Radio mics help a little by being so close to the actor, but there are still large requirements imposed on intelligibility and editing that are difficult or impossible to overcome. For instance, a quiet, secret communication in a busy deli is just about impossible to record in situ. It would have to be faked on some level, either by controlling the original shooting or by constructing the sound from ADR and deli ambience tracks, possibly with some of the original sync tracks in instances where it can help sell the reality of the shot.

In order to construct a reality from parts, there are some principles used in recording and editing for sound effects. For moving objects such as cars, supervising sound editors ask sound effects recordists for several perspectives. Fundamentally, these are:

- Start up from a stop

- Stop from running

- A steady. This is a constant perspective of a car running, for example. The microphone is "running" along with the car. It would be used when the camera follows along with the action, such as with a trailer shot. A steady could use either an interior or an exterior perspective.

- A pass-by. This is a drive past a fixed microphone position. It is an exterior perspective. Among the factors that constitute a pass-by is Doppler shift, the crowding together of sound waves that makes the apparent pitch go up as a sound is approaching you and spread apart as the object recedes into the distance, lowering the pitch. The most obvious of all of these is on European police cars with their distinctive two-pitch sirens passing an observer's location. If you hear such a sound on a sound track, you associate with Europeans capitals quickly.

While this list describes four states of sound effects for one object, each of these could have many variations, with different speeds, squeals on various materials, and so on. Nonetheless, this is one way to think about what the microphone hears and how it will be used.

One factor in realism is the interaction between actors and sound effects. In the opening scene of *Raiders of the Lost Ark*, Indy collects the idol from the cave but has also set the ancient mechanism to protect it into motion. On his chase through the cave to get away from the machinery, at one point he looks up over his shoulder. At what? There is about to be a giant rolling boulder bearing down on him, but he doesn't know this yet. What he looks at is a sound effect of the latch mechanism releasing the boulder, provided in postproduction. Steven Spielberg and Harrison Ford knew that this was about to happen, and anticipation heightens the tension, so looking back over your shoulder makes sense, and then the question arises "what is he looking at?" and sound effects provide the answer.

Sometimes reality is just too strong for picture, and sound carries the day. This works in the sense that a radio play does, stimulating the imagination. *Fahrenheit 9/11* uses this technique for the airplane crashes into the twin towers. Because the pictures are very, very familiar, it is useful to go to black picture and tell the story only with sound for a period of time. This use of sound only can be compared to the picture technique of watching the reaction that people have to a horrible event rather than seeing the event itself, picturing the event in the mind's eye. In fact this is what *Fahrenheit 9/11* follows the black sound-effects-only scene with, continuing and extending the thought.

It is always amazing how different a track sounds without picture; we pay a different kind of attention to it. *Fahrenheit 9/11* took advantage of this, but it is a fairly rare instance. On the other hand, an easy experiment is to listen to a section of a film with the picture off, which can reveal a universe of sound that most people don't notice with the picture present.

The goal of using dialogue plus presence, ambience, and hard effects including potentially source music[5] is usually to portray reality, but as can be seen, this is actually a lot more complicated than it first looks. I remember doing lighting for a play in which the director asked for just one spotlight on the single actor for the whole play. I thought about what the director was saying, and it was that there was not to be a lot of self-conscious lighting, with light cues varying, and so forth, to detract from the intensity of the one-actor experience. I lit the scene with three basic sources, a spotlight on the actor, a strong backlight that set him off from the background, and several soft background lights. I got the effect of one light as you would perceive it if you weren't consciously thinking about it, but it actually took several lights to do it. These were ganged together for dimming, so they went up at the beginning and down at the end together, and most of the audience was probably never the wiser that there was more than one light source, but the actor's head was separated from the background better and the set illuminated dimly, all through the use of more lights than the director had called for: one light might have been literally what he asked for, but the effect of a single light source and simplicity was his goal, and that was better achieved with more than one light.

Sound tracks are a bit like this: sound editors may well produce a lot of tracks that when finally perceived add up to a whole that we take in as one. The idea that multiple sound tracks treated similarly tend to cluster together as one, such as all fading together, also proves to be useful to form auditory streams from ingredient parts. The island part of *Castaway* is a good example of creating the illusion of reality, how hard it can be, and how effective.

Stretched Reality

Sometimes it is necessary in an otherwise realistic presentation to hear things that we could never hear if we were present at the camera in real

---

[5] Called *diegetic* in critical studies.

life. In particular, this applies to dialog. An outrageous example is the opening of *American Pie 2*, which shows the exterior of the protagonist's frat house. As the camera dollies in, indicating we are being taken inside, we hear the conversation inside, and then we cut inside in continuous time. It is physically absurd to hear this in the same perspective outside that we will once we are inside, but it is an accepted convention to hear dialog that we couldn't in ordinary circumstance. This is movie reality.

Another example comes from the history of telephone calls in the movies. In the earliest sound films, when an actor talked on a telephone we couldn't hear the other end of the call. So the dialogue had to be forced, with the recipient repeating all of the important content for the audience to hear. Soon the telephone filter was developed, and we could hear both ends of the call, with the end off-camera portrayed through the bandwidth-limiting filter that made it sound as though it was coming through a telephone. Already by the early 1930s, such conventions were accepted as being realistic, when in fact you couldn't hear the other end of the conversation in real life. The reason was to prevent the clumsiness of having to repeat what the other person said. This convention ruled for many years, and it grew a bit more complicated as editing got quicker; whenever a caller was off-screen they had to be filtered, but then you have to cut the filter in and out corresponding to what you are seeing, and, if you should just happen to go to a split screen in the middle of the call to show both ends, no filter is appropriate.

In more recent times, the convention of filtering the opposite end of phone calls has been changing. Filtering takes away the presence of an actor, and if, for instance, a threat is being issued, then somehow it is lessened through filtering. While we need the filter to establish that it is a phone call in the beginning, gradually over the call or multiple calls, the filter can be made less significant (by extending the frequency range). This applies to the threatening phone calls of the black mailer played by Goran Visnjic as he speaks in multiple calls to the character played by Tilda Swinton in *The Deep End*, for instance.[6]

Another example is in *Vertical Limit*. Here, mountain climbers have gone beyond their limits, and they know they are going to die because help cannot arrive in time. One has a conversation on a walkie-talkie with her

---

[6] Supervising re-recording mixer Mark Berger.

brother, and she knows her fate.[7] At the beginning of the conversation, the sound is filtered, or possibly re-recorded through an actual walkie-talkie, but as time progresses this effect is gradually lifted. The camera also becomes more intimate with the protagonists. We come to a point where the brother is right there in the cave with the doomed climber despite being miles away, because the voice is heard full range. The full-frequency range voice is much more intimate sounding, especially than the low-fi walkie-talkie. We are hearing the reconstruction of the voice of the brother from the point of view of the other, rather than the real thing. It is an interesting effect and the imposition of a kind of hyper-reality that works emotionally at this climax of the picture.

What Is Seen Versus What Is Heard: On-Screen Versus Off-Screen

Sometimes the effect of not seeing something is more horrible than expressly seeing it. Colonel Turner, the traitor who is exposed on the flight of the assault team away from the castle at the end of *Where Eagles Dare*, is given the chance by the lead of the assault team, played by Richard Burton, to commit suicide by jumping out of the plane, without benefit of parachute. The scene is played out such that Turner stands up to go to the door, and we cut to Richard Burton and Clint Eastwood. What we hear is the sound effect of the door latch opening. We don't need to see the body tumbling from the plane and landing splat on the ground; that's for rougher pictures. It is the sound effect that is so horrible in context. And one could say that this sound effect is the climax of the film because the whole point of the raid was to expose leaks from the British side (which, by the way, didn't happen, but this wasn't known when the picture was written).

There are doubtlessly many such citations. Two that spring to mind are the sound of the dragoons attacking the marchers in *Dr. Zhivago*, as played out in Omar Sharif's (Zhivago's) reaction to the event, rather than seeing the event itself. Another is that Jimmy Stewart alerts the city to the fact that a murder has been committed at the end of Hitchcock's *Rope* by firing a gun out the window, and we hear the off-stage sounds grow as people react to the shots, call the police, and then we hear the police arriving as the world of the killers collapses around them.

---

[7] Columbia Pictures DVD 05066, Chapter 23.

Hyper-Reality

If stretched reality can be said to be pushing the limits of the real, Hollywood sound tracks for blockbuster action films go even further, beyond all possibility of the real to the hyper-real. There are a great many examples of this concept, available especially every summer in the local multiplex. Perhaps one way to describe these effects is with an inverse example. Gary Rydstrom recounts a conversation with Steven Spielberg about the sound for *Saving Private Ryan*. Spielberg said he didn't want a "Hollywood sound job," and Rydstrom knew exactly what that meant: he strove not for hyper-realism but for realism tempered with psychological sound. That is, although we hear the pitched battle realistically, including from an underwater as well as a more normal perspective, we also hear some of the sound from the point of view of the characters on the Normandy beaches, whose hearing has been affected by the extraordinarily loud sound around them. In speaking to veterans, Rydstrom learned that it was the particular sound that the German tanks made that they remember to this day, and because no working Panzer tanks could be found, he relied on the memory of the veterans to make a German tank sound that was realistic for them.

Surrealism

The next style to consider is the surreal, emphasizing the unconscious. Surreal sound might represent the point of view (hearing?) of a character as we slip from a realistic presentation into a more subjective one. There are several ways to do this: one is to strip out much of the sound and concentrate on just one or a few elements. We know the scene is noisier than this, but we also know we are making a transition to a more internal view of the world as sound disappears. It becomes more like our perception, following just a particular auditory stream. A good example is the opening scene of script reading in *All That Jazz*. The director is about to have a heart attack, and we cross over from a realistic presentation to a subjective one by stripping away most of the sync sound progressively and hearing just one or two Foley sounds, such as drumming his fingers on the desktop. To get back out of this state, the ambience corresponding to the reality sound is brought back in.

Dream states may be portrayed similarly, characterized generally by simplicity. We don't perceive ambience in dreams, and the sounds that we do hear may undergo transformations such as being in a different pitch range, made more or less reverberant, or changed timbre. Any of these used singly or together is an indicator that we have left reality behind. When we subsequently cut to the face of our protagonist in bed and we hear distant city ambience, we know through the reintroduction of the ambience that we've been jerked back into reality, and what preceded is just a dream.

Another way to lessen the reality and go toward a more outright filmic viewpoint is to add music. Here the big question is "what is the balance between music and realistic sound?" For instance, in the sequence of the biplane flying through flamingoes in *Out of Africa*, music is dominant. What makes the scene not all-out montage is the fact that we still hear the biplane, albeit nearly buried in music. The small sound of the distant biplane anchors us with the image and keeps it real.

In *Bourne Supremacy*, the title character suffers from amnesia. To get into his head—his subjective reality—a different type of surreal sound effect with more tonal sounds than normal is used in particular scenes, and one of its accompanying methods is to place more sound in the surrounds than would be there for a realistic presentation.

An example of manipulating realism versus surrealism or objective versus subjective sound is in the 2002 version of *Solaris*.[8] When "Chris Kelvin," played by George Clooney, makes preparations for going to sleep for the first time, we hear the Foley of him climbing into bed and music. As he goes to sleep, we see a shot of him in close-up, and the music comes to dominate. Interestingly, there is no ambience of the space ship at this point. Then the music is continuous over flashbacks of his life on Earth. This music, and the subjective handheld camera used as opposed to the more formal tripod-mounted one that has dominated in the previous scenes, tells us this is his dream. Also, the Earth scenes are warmly lit, while the space ship scenes are cold. Then, while remaining in subjective space, Chris meets his wife at a cocktail party. The reason we know this is still his dream is that the music dominates until the middle of a warm, handheld shot, and ambience and his clearing his throat breaks the music and causes it to fade out. The continuity that the music has provided over these preceding shots has let us know that it is all a dream, and the fact that the music remains over a shot and then is broken by an utterance of an actor helps us know we are still in his dream.

---

[8] Twentieth Century Fox Widescreen Edition DVD, Supervising Sound Editor and Re-Recording Mixer Larry Blake. Sequence starts at 20:48 in Chapter 8.

He has a conversation with a colleague, and we hear it and cocktail crowd ambience (interestingly, only in center-channel mono). Along with some exposition, the colleague tells him to go ahead and deal with the woman who is to become his wife, and who he has met earlier as he saw her on a train. He does, and during their conversation we cut back to him sleeping in the cool color of the space ship, in order to reinforce the fact that it is a dream. The conversation continues unchecked underneath this cutaway. Music begins under their continuous conversation, but an elevator shot of them together is shown for the first time, clearly just after the conversation has taken place. Thus, at this moment there are three intermixed time frames at work, and yet they remain quite clear: the sleeping Chris in the space ship, the flashback to Chris and Rheya's first meeting conversation as what is heard, and the flashback to their first touch as what is seen.

The music then comes to dominate once again, as they make love, intercut between the cool-color space ship (but wait a minute, where did *this* Rheya come from?) and the warm flashback, the past and the present. Finally, to come out of the dream state, we see a shot of Chris alone in close-up, and the music fades under the ambience, as though the music has been masking the ambience all along and we are just becoming aware of it, much like waking up from a dream. Interestingly, the music just disappears as her hand enters the shot: the abstraction is broken; we are back to reality. He is startled by her presence (after all, she's dead in real reality—it's just this particular reality that she's alive for), and this is a doppleganger. The sound is ambience, Foley of him moving rapidly, and his dialogue "God damn it" accompanied by heavy breathing: he's had a shock. Next he slaps himself awake. The surrealistic dream mood is thoroughly broken.

Interesting is that this new reality has more prominent ambience than the world left behind at the beginning of the sequence. The function of the ambience is to tell us that we are in the here and now. When he first goes into the bedroom and shuts—and, on the advice of a crew member, locks— the door, the music starts immediately and dominates the ambience right away.

Montage

If music completely overwhelms the other tracks, we move into the region of pure montage, typically represented by multiple picture cuts over continuous music. Here we are in the land of the most abstract. Montage can provide a little relief from the dialogue that delivers the ongoing story—it is the pause that refreshes. It often has a narrative role, moving the story forward by giving us information that otherwise would take yet more dialogue to convey. An example is that of Susan Alexander singing, Kane's love interest in *Citizen Kane*, as the camera cranes up to the top of the opera house and comes to rest on the skeptical stage crew. This is good storytelling because it shows us directly and through companion shots that she's on the road and always reviewed well by Kane newspapers, but she really can't sing, all in one brilliant sequence.

However, it is usually difficult to make a montage sequence as emotionally involving as those scenes where we have more direct connection to characters. This is because the nature of the abstraction of montage usually distances us from having empathy for the plight of the characters. There are always exceptions to the rule, such as one of the most famous of montage scenes, the Odessa steps sequence from Eisenstein's *Battleship Potemkin*, where the baby carriage gets loose and bounces down the steps. Here we have a universal emotion built into our species of protecting babies that makes it work.

Sound montage, as opposed to filmic montage, although more frequently performed in other forms such as radio plays, is nonetheless useful for certain film sequences too. Sound montage is characterized by multiple sound tracks and threads coming and going, usually cross-fading among them. A technique to distinguish the multiple tracks of montage besides simply level is to change the relative balance between direct sound and reverberation, with a higher level of reverberation implying a greater distance, so that sound can seem to approach and then recede from the listener. Two examples of the use of sound montage occur in *THX 1138* and *The Conversation*.

A remarkable thing about montage is how often you find that picture and sound mutually reinforce each other, sometimes without actually doing anything to manipulate them together. Music has a beat, a downbeat, and other items regarding its phrasing. When a downbeat occurs on a picture cut, when a walker just happens to synchronize with the beat, when a key change accompanies a scene change, these are all items that resonate with viewers/listeners because they just seem to make sense of the abstraction in front of them.

In *The Wonderful Horrible Life of Leni Riefenstahl,* we see her at the editing table looking at the picture and listening to the sound of music during the Nuremberg Nazi rally. She glorifies in the sync that she produced between the waving of hundreds of Nazi flags and the music. She as the filmmaker knew very well that such things, which remain subconscious to most viewers, nonetheless help move the viewer emotionally.

Shifting Levels of Reality

A common opening for a movie is to start with scored music over titles, a montage. Such sequences function at a high level of abstraction, with a kind of psychic distance maintained from the audience—we are *reading* titles, not particularly following the background action, which can nonetheless serve to set the period, locale, and perhaps something about the characters, but on a rather abstract level. *Days of Heaven* starts this way, with old photos that set the era—Woodrow Wilson is President—and the setting of an Eastern industrial city with which the West of the movie will be contrasted. After all, the filmmakers want us to be engaged, but at the same time, read the titles. When the main narrative starts, we are signaled this by the music ending, and usually ambience of the first scene takes over on the sound track. A not infrequent alternative is for the music to fade under a voice-over, which also helps set the stage, such as used in *Love Actually*. By either means we are eased into the story. Then we hear the real narrative begin, and the signal for this is production dialog. In hearing this we have moved from a greater level of abstraction—montage and voice-over—to a greater level of reality.

Likewise, at the end of a movie rounding out the final denouement, typically the music score swells as the camera cranes up, a signal that the narrative is over. *Road to Perdition* has multiple endings, and the entrance of score on the first ending created the deliberate false impression that "okay, okay, thaaaaaat's all folks," and some audience members in the audience that I was in had been cued by the score that the movie was over and got up and left! Of course they weren't remembering that the bad guy had not been called off the trail, and that this is a tragedy and shouldn't have a happy ending. Those who left when the score told them to missed the real ending.

A movie opening sometimes used is to start with score and then modulate the score from sounding like score to sounding like source music originating from within the scene. This may be accomplished by worldizing the score and cutting it into different tracks in sync with itself. To make the transition, all the re-recording mixer has to do is to cross-fade from the score track(s) to the source track(s).

Worldizing is the process of bringing the world to the sound, by re-recording it through an acoustic space that deliberately modifies the sound. The idea is that clean sound is not always desirable; sometimes we want the sound dirtied up to make it sound more like the real thing. For *American Graffiti*, Walter Murch wanted the pop songs to sound as though they originated in a gym, not like needle-drop score. To do this, a loudspeaker and microphone were arranged to re-record the songs in a gym. Normally this would just add reverberation and move the perspective farther away. However, the difference in this case was that the loudspeaker and microphone were moved around continuously while the music was playing. This constantly changing path between loudspeaker and microphone made the sort of swirling sound that was right to accompany dances at a high school gym. Interestingly, worldizing only became necessary when the channel from microphone to listener became so clear that sometimes it was too clear. The restored opening of Orson Welles' *Touch of Evil* as recut following Welles' instructions by Walter Murch employs worldizing. This was a major point of contention with the studio, which wanted a conventional score over opening titles. What Welles fights for in his memo is the following:

> As the camera roves through the streets of the Mexican bordertown, the plan was to feature a succession of different and contrasting Latin American musical numbers— the effect, that is, of our passing one cabaret orchestra after another. In honky-tonk districts on the border, loudspeakers are over the entrance of every joint, large or small, each blasting out it's [sic] own tune by way of a "come-on" or "pitch" for the tourists. The fact that the streets are invariably loud with this music was planned as a basic device throughout the entire picture. The special use of contrasting "mambo-type" rhythm numbers with rock 'n' roll will be developed in some detail at the end of this memo, when I'll take up details of the "beat" and also specifics of musical color and instrumentation on a scene-by-scene and transition-by-transition basis.

> In the version I was shown yesterday, it's not clear where you have decided to place the credits. A brief report on this will determine whether or not my old ideas for sound and music patterns in this opening reel are still of some potential value.[9] . . .

---

[9] Orson Welles' memo to the studio, as seen on the bonus section of the widescreen DVD disc of *Touch of Evil*. There is further sound information in the memo, showing just how important Welles considered it. At this writing it is at http://wellesnet.com/touch_me-mo1.htm as well.

A process parallel to worldizing is futzing. To futz a sound is to deliberately screw up its frequency range, response, and distortion so that it sounds as though it is coming through a particularly bad channel. In early days of film sound, a telephone filter restricted the frequency range for telephonic voices, and this was enough. In today's world, with much higher fidelity, somehow just restricting the frequency range to the bandwidth of a telephone is not enough; it's got to be more screwed up to sound right. Here, a box lined with absorption has a particularly bad small loudspeaker hung in it, and the output of it is picked up with a microphone. By overdriving the loudspeaker, or its amplifier, and by manipulating the signal path between speaker and microphone (direct, off-axis, around a barrier, muffled, and so forth), a variety of futz effects can be accomplished. An example of dialogue futzing is in the trench run at the end of *Star Wars*. In this case, side-band processing (i.e., transmitting and receiving the signal over a somewhat mistuned radio system) was also used.

Sound Design as an Art

There can be no one prescription for what the sound elements should be and the interaction among them, because if there were, we could quantify art and then a computer could practice it. Instead, it is the funny juxtapositions and experiments that lead to a great sound track. There are some ideas that are fairly universal though:

- *Emotional memory plays a role.* Here, the most obvious is certain pieces of existing music. Music carries with it emotional weight, as for instance nostalgia for an era plays a part. However, it is dangerous too because it imposes its own order: beat, downbeat, key changes, and so forth. And the riskiest part of using existing music, especially of the pop and certain other genres, is that people have associations with it that are not under the control of the filmmaker: not everyone feels that "Leavin' on a Jet Plane" means the same thing to them, and it may trigger unexpected emotions among a part of your audience, which means they are not paying attention to your story

- *Sound effects with lots of low-frequency content tend to be threatening.* This can be said to be primordial for humans, as a thunderstorm or an earthquake are the natural events that contain a lot of low-frequency content. An early example of sound design like this is for *Butch Cassidy and the Sundance Kid*, where the off-screen and distant pounding hoofs of the horses on their trail provides an intermittent threat to our rascally heroes.[10] It is worth pointing out that this subjective equation has been enhanced in recent years as 5.1 channel sound, with its dedicated low-frequency enhancement (0.1) channel, permits greater levels of low frequencies

- *Exaggerating reality may prove useful.* In the jungle scene in *Apocalypse Now*, the sound of insects is exaggerated and powerful, forming almost a musical score, as the threat level increases throughout the scene with the extreme, processed buzzing of mosquitoes before the characters come across the tiger. The particular sound raises tension simultaneously through its familiarity and its exaggeration—it's like having a mosquito in your ear.

If anything can be said about how sound design is practiced at the highest levels, it should be pointed out that it is the result of a lot of experimentation. This idea overarches recording, editing, and mixing. Hundreds of everyday objects are found by sound designers to make useful noises that, when synchronized to particular things on screen, sell the reality of a shot, even if that reality is far-fetched. The inventiveness of sound people in this search is remarkable, and good ones are always on the alert for interesting sounds. For instance, Ben Burtt went on a trip to an airbase to record jet takeoffs and landings. The most interesting sound encountered on the trip was that of the stalled air-conditioner motor in a cheap motel that, pitched down, got used for the Star Destroyer in *Star Wars*. You never know.

The motor sounds for the robots in *I, Robot* were the result of a lot of experimentation on the part of sound designer Erik Aadahl and of feedback from the director in diagnosing what he did and didn't like. During the months of recording, processing, and presenting sounds to the director, some of the rejected options included pitched-down hummingbird vocals, steel sheet wobbles, processed pneumatic air hisses, and cable "zuzz" sounds. "The final NS-5 robot sound was a combination of varispeed underwater bubbles, completely synthetic sounds designed on a 'Kyma' system, and telephone cord squeezes for closeups of the fibrous robot muscles moving," says Aadahl.[11]

---

[10] As edited by Don Hall.
[11] Erik Aadahl, private communication, 2004.

The dinosaurs in *Jurassic Park* came about by experimenting with many different animal sounds, layering them together and matching them to the screen action. One principal ingredient was that of a baby elephant trumpeting. The elephant did it only once despite multiple visits to record him, and one recording was extended into making this signature sound for multiple uses in the film by placing other sounds around it, editing it judiciously, and pitch shifting it through off-speed playback so that it could be reused without such strong recognition that it was in fact the same effect used over and over.

Spotting

Spotting refers to the director, the person in charge of the sound, and possibly the composer and/or others working their way through the edited piece and exchanging information and notes about what the meaning of each scene is in a film, and how to best supplement, or even directly tell, the story with sound. The term *spotting* may also refer to meetings in which the requirements are passed out to each subspeciality, such as at a meeting between the supervising sound editor and the Foley person.

A well-known sound designer tells the story of working with a famous director on several pictures. As they were spotting their first work together, the director would say "oh, there's a car by," and the sound designer would respond "okay." After the literalness of this wore off, and they came to know each other better, the sound designer said to the director, "I can see the obvious—tell me what emotion you want the audience to feel?" On their next picture, the director asked, "could you provide a morality tone here?"

The Director's Cut

- Sound design means, among other things, that what you hear moment-by-moment is chosen deliberately by an agent, even for a nonfiction piece.
- Certain sound stereotypes transmit information quickly, such as low frequencies equalling a threat or a soft cricket indicating sound peace.
- Smoothing tracks, especially dialogue ones, helps overall continuity. Inter-cut presence and separate ambience or background tracks help provide continuity.
- Things that we see that we associate with making sound will normally make that sound. The source for this may be production sound or deliberately added sound effects, called hard effects.
- Film sound styles range from realism through stretched reality, from hyper-reality to surrealism. These are each portrayed using certain types of sound effects and/or music, and even more rarely, processed dialog.
- Off-screen sound may have a strong storytelling utility.
- Sound effects of moving objects include start-ups, stops, steadies, and pass-bys.

CHAPTER 8
Editing

Computer-based workstations, either those based on picture editing with a sound component or those specifically designed for audio editing called digital audio workstations (DAWs), have revolutionized sound editing for movies and videos over the last decade. Compared to razor-blade editing of audio tape or film, there are several differences between the analog and digital approaches that make the productivity of digital audio editing much higher.

Nonlinear Editing

The first of these is the nonlinear nature of computer-based editing. The term *nonlinear* in this case refers to the way that the main storage mechanism, the hard-disc drive, combined with the editing system software, basically works. It works rather like a phonograph record with a tone arm that you can pick up and place at the beginning of a groove anywhere on the record, quickly, as each piece of sound is needed. The editing system keeps track of where each portion of audio exists on the disc. It then plays them back in real time, by skipping the "tone arm" around as necessary, filling up the immediate storage mechanism, the random access memory (RAM) of the computer, from the bulk storage mechanism, the hard drive, before the sound is needed. Then the edit system pulls the digital audio from the RAM, processes and routes it appropriately, and presents it to a digital-to-analog converter (DAC) for output conversion to analog, at the right moment. This is in contrast to linear-access media, such as a cassette tape, where you have to fast forward, potentially past lots of intermediate tape, to reach a random position on the tape. Older conventional analog systems were linear access; computer-based ones where the audio is stored on disc drives are nonlinear.

This description that involves hard-disc drives and RAM shows both the advantage of fast, random access and also gives a feel for some of the potential limitations of the process. The size of the hard-disc drive(s) available on the machine will determine the amount of program material available, considering too its format (mono, stereo, or multichannel; sample rate; and word length). Roughly speaking, the size of RAM will determine how many tracks can be played simultaneously. Another potential bottleneck is how fast the computer can move content from the hard drives to the RAM and from the RAM to the processor and out to the DAC. Moving a project from one computer system to another can reveal such problems, as edit sessions that will play on one system will not play on another, for instance, because the resources available on one system may be so much greater than those on another that the processes bog down on the lesser system.

Standard DV format picture and sound is recorded at 25 Mbps, which is 3.125 MBps. (Note the capitalization difference: the abbreviation Mbps is millions of bits per second; MBps is megabytes per second, and the two are related by dividing the number of bits by eight to get the number of bytes.) That's 11.25 GB per hour. While storing this amount of data seemed impractical just a few years ago, today it's easy; at this writing, more than 13 hours can be stored for $115, and this number has improved dramatically over the years. Sound without picture requires much less space, with the two sound channels of 48 kHz sampled audio on DV tape only requiring about 6 percent of the data space. Two-channel, 48-kHz sample rate, 16-bit bit-depth audio uses 691.2 MB per hour, which at current rates can be stored for about $0.53. Thus, a large 2,000-hour stereo sound effects library at this resolution having 1.4 TB[1] of data can be stored for just over $1,000, and the real problems become acquiring and cataloging the content, not the cost of storage. In fact, the cost has come down by a ratio of about 16,000 to 1 in dollars over the last 20 years, not even including the effects of inflation.

Random-Access Editing

A particular set of editing features grows out of the random-access-based nature of editing on a nonlinear editing system. It is another benefit,

---

[1] Today a terabyte is considered to be a thousand gigabytes. An older method of counting that has largely been subsumed through time is to count from megabytes to gigabytes, and from gigabytes to terabytes, each by a factor of 1,024.

although sometimes it can get you into trouble. The sync relationship of a given sound to the picture is easily adjustable—you just grab and move a clip or region of sound along the time line, unless perhaps it has been locked, in which case you would have to unlock it first. Depending on the particular mode of the editing software, it may move only in whole frame increments or down to single samples at a time. Nudge edit controls let you move a sound back and forth in time at a specified amount per nudge and sync up the sound to the picture as desired. A potential problem is that you may move more sound than you intend, given particular modes of the editing software, so you must be alert as to how various editing modes work. For instance, you may move one region but affect all others coming after it in some editing modes.

Nondestructive Editing

With audio files stored on disc, and another file organized to control the playing of the audio files out in real time, comes another benefit: nondestructive editing. In cutting mag film, a sound editor would trim the film from the head of the individual transfer to the position where he or she just wanted the sound to start, then find the tail of the usable sound and cut off the excess. Thus, there are three pieces of film: the head trim, the utilized sound, and the tail trim. In order to be able to extend the sound should that become necessary—say to accommodate a picture change—an assistant editor managed the trims and had to be able to find them if a scene had to be extended; that's the way to ensure that matching sound at the edit was available.

With computer-based editing, all of the sound exists for the full length of the sound files all of the time.[2] In an edit, nothing is really cut. The controlling software points to where it needs to go to play back the sound at the right time, and it is merely a matter of editorial adjustment to add something to the heads or tails of a sound. This is much simpler than having to store and locate trims. On the other hand, for particular cases of exporting—for instance, if just a small sound clip is exported from a long sound file—it is overly burdening to export the big file just for the purposes of getting a small clip from it. In this case, export software may be

---

[2] This is true most of the time. There are circumstance where to save space on disc the portion of the audio file not used in a particular edit is discarded.

used that specifies handles, an amount of sound occurring before the first fade of a utilized sound clip to after the last fade-out. Then in subsequent work, if the file parts not used for the export are needed, they may be reimported.

Visual Waveform Editing

The earliest form of sound editing for film occurred on optical sound tracks. The modulation was visible, so most edit points were easily found, both by listening with a reader, and ultimately for the finest editing, by observing the waveform directly from the film. In the 1950s, magnetic recording became the standard, for several reasons: it could be immediately listened to and did not need laboratory processing, and it could be erased and reused, which made it cheaper. However, the recording was invisible, and magnetic sound readers had to be used along with scrubbing to perform fine editing. Scrubbing consists of moving the film back and forth over a reading head to find the start of modulation, a typical place to cut because an incoming loud sound tends to cover up the discontinuity that occurs at the edit (even though the edit is just before the loud sound: it's called backwards masking, meaning that it works backwards in time). A system was developed to write a squiggly line down the back of the film with a marker pen to show the modulation, but this was abandoned as editors got used to editing an invisible medium.

Digital audio workstation editing brings us full circle, back to the early days of sound editing, with its visible waveform, where editing can be performed using both senses, sight and sound. However, it is a rather high burden on the computer to draw the waveform of each of a number of tracks in real time, and it is a testament to the increases in computing power and dropping costs over time that it works as well as it does. Editing systems typically provide a means to turn on and off the visual waveform display on a track-by-track basis, to reduce the computer overhead. The detailed waveform display is replaced with blocks that are much easier for the computer to draw. It might, for instance, mean that more processing plug-ins could be accommodated operating in real time if the computer doesn't also have to be drawing the waveforms, although how these tasks are parceled out to the various parts of the computer, whether done by dedicated hardware or by the host computer, varies.

Edits and Fade Files

Most audio edits involve something more than just an instantaneous cut. To make such a cut while any sound is playing at all will typically lead to a click, as the waveform jumps at the edit to the new vertical position, cutting together the two instantaneous amplitudes of the waveforms before and after the edit. This applies to a new sound starting in a track, where before the edit the waveform will be flat and at zero amplitude, and to two sounds edited together, where the amplitude of the two waveforms before and after the edit are not identical. Only if the instantaneous level and the direction and slope of the waveforms before and after an edit match can an instantaneous cut be performed without producing a click. Clearly, such a condition does not occur very often. Such an instantaneous cut is called a butt splice, and it is useful in some specific cases, but most edits are a little more complicated. They involve a brief fade. In cutting magnetic film, this is usually restricted by the diagonal splicers used to one-quarter frame, and this is a good rule of thumb for digital editing—in the absence of any reason to do anything else, perform a 10-ms fade.

That 10 ms applies to both a new sound coming out of silence and to the end of that sound going back to silence. It also applies to cross-fades between two active sounds. However, it is just a rule of thumb. Digital audio editing systems give much more flexibility than was ever available from magnetic film splicers in length of a fade or cross-fade and shape of the fade (whether the incoming and outgoing sounds are abrupt or more slowly rising or falling during the length of the fade). In fact, to get longer fades with magnetic film, chemicals were applied to the oxide of the film to selectively remove the oxide coating containing the recording along the length. Some kinds of music editing of smooth string sections, for instance, use long cross-fade times. Two magnetic tracks were necessary, running in sync, with one fading out while the other fades in. This is another advantage of digital audio editing: you need not use up two tracks for two sounds that smoothly cross-fade because they can fit on one track. However, this can lead to some editing peculiarities because the underlying file must be long enough to complete a desired cross-fade, and this fact may be unclear.

In order to make a fade, or half of a cross-fade, the DAW has to multiply each sample during the fade time by a factor that increases over time for a fade-in or decreases for a fade-out. If such a fade-in is performed on several tracks at the same time, it has the potential to overwhelm the processing power available. Thus, some DAWs use a separate file, called a fade file, wherein the fade has been precalculated[3] and is stored. In terms used for pictures, it has been rendered. To play a complete region, the DAW first plays the fade-in file, then the audio file (which can be cut to instantaneously in this case because at the end of the fade-in all of the conditions are met for making an audibly seamless edit), then the fade-out file. The DAW jumps to fade files as necessary, an easier act for the computer than actually calculating the fades on-the-fly. This is why the structure of some editing systems contains audio files, and fade files, and explains why fade files can be reconstructed if they are lost—because all of the information to reperform the fade exists in the audio files and the one controlling the playback of the files. The controlling file is often called a project or a session file. This file is similar to an Edit Decision List of a picture editing system. It doesn't store the actual audio, but rather tells the DAW how to play back the audio files.

File Management

Three types of files have been discussed: project/session files, audio files, and fade files. It is crucially important to understand what these multiple types do, because many hours of postproduction time have been lost by exporting just a project/session file without the underlying required audio files, for instance. The DAW software must understand where to find the audio and fade files, and if their relationship is changed by moving them around on discs, for instance, the software can lose track of where it is supposed to get the audio. At the least if files are moved, you may have to relink the broken connections. Of the three, the project/session files and audio files are essential, whereas the fade files are a little less important because some systems such as Pro Tools can reconstruct missing fade files, although it takes time.

Exporting audio from Avid workstations may use Consolidation. In this process, just the utilized portions of the audio files (perhaps with handles, additional content attached to the heads and tails of a clip to promote the sound editor's ability to smooth edits) are exported. Long segments that

---

[3] That is, the audio has been acted on by the varying fade factor over the length of the fade, producing a new, specialized audio file called a fade file.

are not used are not exported, so the total export may be in some cases greatly reduced, thus speeding up operations.

Plug-ins/Processes

Traditionally, editing personnel have performed edits and mixing personnel have done virtually all of the signal processing necessary to ensure a good result. The only exception to this rule was one where the transfer room that made the mag film transfer might operate on the original sound, such as making an off-speed transfer, or one reversed in time, often performed to conceal its source. Editors were restricted to editing by the practicalities of the medium. Today DAWs have many processes available to alter the sound, and these range from the straightforward to the complex. Some of these are extensions to basic editing:

- *Time compression-expansion.* A complete sound may not fit within a given track length of time. By spreading out or shrinking the area concerned, a sound may be made to fit into a time sequence. This process is not perfectly transparent in digital audio, because small clips are being removed or inserted, so the more the process is stretched, the higher the likelihood of hearing artifacts. Also, time compression-expansion may be performed with or without accompanying pitch shifting.

- *Pitch shifting.* A related process to time compression-expansion, pitch shifting often proves to be particularly useful with sound effects. Lowering their pitch makes them seem bigger and more impressive than the original sound on which they were based. Pitch shifting may be performed with or without accompanying time stretching. Pitch shifting can be useful to dialogue editors in order to insert words from a different take or part of a documentary that don't quite match in pitch.

Note that a combination of both pitch shifting and time changing may be accomplished with an analog tape machine equipped with a varispeed control, and this can be much more effective for large speed changes than using digital techniques because analog doesn't suffer from the artifacts of splicing. However, the speed change and pitch shift are by necessity locked together in a one-to-one relationship. In an extreme example, Gary Rydstrom reports he used a U-Matic recorder set to move only at the rate necessary to prevent excessive tape wear—its nominal pause mode—and recorded it onto another machine overnight for odd sounds used in point-of-view sequences in *Strange Days*.

- *Reverse*. This takes an audio segment and reverses it heads for tails. It is useful in making sounds less recognizable, although if they have recorded reverberation, that can prove unnatural as the reverberation occurs before the event that caused it.

  Reversing sound segments can be alternated with the same sound segment playing forward to improve the discontinuity at edits. Say that a sound effect contains an element with a rising pitch over its length. If it were looped, with the tail of one segment spliced to the head of the next repetition, the jerk in pitch at the edit is likely to be noticeable. By alternating segments heads-to-tails, tails-to-heads, then heads-to-tails, and so on, there is no abrupt change in pitch at the edits.

- *VocALign*. This is a plug-in from Synchro Arts that uses a production track as a guide and slips an ADR performance on another track into sync. It does this by automatic microediting of the ADR track to match the original track in time.

- *Subharmonic synthesis*. Normally used with sound effects, such plug-ins find the lowest tonal frequency in a particular frequency range, such as 50 to 100 Hz, and produce an added output at half of the frequency, thus adding a new fundamental. The effect is to make larger and more impressive specific sounds, particularly explosions, canon fire, and the like. One example of the use of such a device is on the giant voice of the tomb near the beginning of *Aladdin*. Subharmonic synthesis may be combined with slowing down the original recording, and equalization, to make prodigious amounts of bass.

These processes are performed on the clip/region of an audio file that is used by the project/session. A new audio file is generated and inserted in place of the existing one. The original file can be called back if the process is to be reversed for some reason. Some years ago, Lucasfilm produced a made-for-television movie, *The Ewok Adventure*. Randy Thom was the sound designer for the film, and he time-reversed an effect for an ogre that stuck out of a tree and uttered a screech. He thought it sounded better that way. Then he found out that a sound editor had already reversed the screech and that he had put it back the way it was recorded!

Editors also employ some processes that were traditionally done by mixers, or in transfer suites before they received the sound. In this sense, however, these are used editorially, not as a mixing function, as explained following:

- *Normalize.* This is a level-setting process that examines the audio clip/ region and increases the gain until the highest instantaneous peak recorded level just reaches 0 dBFS. It is useful for under-recorded content, although working on peak level as it does, does not guarantee that loudness has been normalized. Normalization is typically done on an audio region-by-region basis and not on a whole track because it is used to get an overall smoother performance, before mixing is applied.

- *Gain.* This is a level control applied uniformly throughout a specific clip/region. The segment is replaced by one with the altered level. This is especially useful in matching a particular word, for instance, from a different take, that might be different in level to those before and after it. Another reason to apply gain is to increase the level of under-recorded material, without pushing it to the top of the range as normalization does, which could be too far for aesthetic purposes. Some DAW editors in mixing mode only have 6 dB of gain available above unity—defined as the point where the input and output levels are equal—and thus it is likely that more gain will be necessary at some point because of low-level recording.

- *Volume graphing.* This is an automation function that allows the editor to specify points in time for particular playback levels and to graph those over time. A mixer-like interface may be provided with automation so that a person can ride the gain to smooth out a performance, or an editor can take a view of a track that shows the level over time, which may be edited graphically. In this way, volume graphing is different from gain because it is dynamic, changeable throughout a region and from region-to-region. Whereas volume graphing performs the same act as the mixer does when facing the console faders, there are reasons to volume graph certain kinds of events while leaving others to the overall mix. One reason to volume graph would be to match a region inserted with those surrounding it in level, similar to using the gain function and accomplishing the same thing. Another primary reason is to tame certain features of dialogue recordings, such as a cough. An editor can volume graph around a cough more effectively than a mixer can mix around it because the editing process takes place out of real time, whereas the mixer has to hit the cough exactly, or the duck of gain in front of it may be audible, for instance.

- *Noise gate*. This is switch controlled by the signal that allows sound through when the level is above a specific, adjustable level, and otherwise mutes it. A noise gate might be used to clean up dialogue that has some background noise. With a cleaned track and an additional background track, bumps in the dialogue track caused by uneven presence across the edits may be concealed.

- *Noise reduction*. More sophisticated than a noise gate, a range of plug-ins are available that attempt to separate foreground sound such as dialogue from background noise and suppress the background, using a variety of strategies and at a variety of prices. Some of these learn the noise floor, frequency- by-frequency, and provide a multiband noise gating function at just above the ongoing noise floor.

- *DC offset removal*. Cutting together sound clips from different sources may produce clicks because the DC level of the two different converters in the two paths are different. In fact, this is a fairly common problem because with 16-bit audio, the smallest step is about 1/65,000th of full scale, and keeping the DC content to this small level is difficult. Thus, if there are clicks or thumps (if cross-fading has been done) at edits, a DC removal filter is indicated.

- *Clip removal*. (Note that this is not the same use of the word *clip* as in a segment in an audio bin of DAW audio region list.) This is software device to find clipping distortion and draw in an appropriate peak. Because clipping of original sources is usually the worst type of distortion that occurs, using this plug-in can save problematic clips.

These processes are used to smooth out bumps editorially as, say, the level varies for a sound insertion that otherwise matches. In this sense, what is being done at the editing stage is relative, clip-to-clip, not necessarily the absolute final choice of level that will be applied in mixing. Any of these processes might be used on dialog, sound effects, or music fairly early in the editing process, as they are useful to match regions. Other processes might be used too, but they are more generally thought of as mixing ones, such as filtering, equalization, compression/limiting, and reverberation, and so will be covered in the next chapter. Many plug-ins are available on the market, both from the original developers of DAWs and from a whole industry that has grown up to write specialized software. Plug-ins are written for particular sets of hardware/DAW software systems, as shown in Table 8-1.

Table 8-1 Audio Plug-Ins

Name	For Environment	Notes
Audio Units (AU)	Apple OS X	Real-time native processing*
AudioSuite	Mac OS, Windows 98, and NT Pro Tools or Pro Tools LE	Non-real-time; operates on clips/regions to create new ones that replace the originals; not automatable
MOTU Audio Systems (MAS)	MAC OS host software synthesizer programs	
Premiere	Mac programs such as BIAS Peak, BIAS Deck, Emagic Logic Audio, Opcode's Studio Vision Pro	Non-real-time process performed by host CPU
Real Time Audio Suite (RTAS)	Pro Tools LE	Performed in real time by host CPU; automatable. limitations include being only one in, one out and where they can fall in the chain

Continues

Table 8-1 *Continued*

Name	For Environment	Notes
Time Division Multiplex (TDM)	Pro Tools with particular hardware	Performed in real time by DSP; automatable
Virtual Studio Technology (VST)	Mac or PC, dependent on the host program	Real-time native plug-in format

*Native means that the software runs on the host CPU, in this case, as a part of the operating system.

Tracks and Channels

The organization of multiple, simultaneous tracks has its own descriptive language, developed from the analog case. Tracks are what you see on the screen, individual time lines that contain the audio clips/regions. These tracks are analogous to the 24 tracks of a two-inch multitrack analog tape machine or to the various strands of cut magnetic film interleaved with fill leader to make each strand match all of the others in length, interspersing the sound where it belongs in the footage to match the picture. Tracks may be assigned directly to channels. Channels may be thought of as electronic pathways that may deliver particular input A/D converters to particular tracks or, conversely, tracks to output D/A converters.

Tracks may also be routed to busses instead of directly to input/output channels. Busses get signals from one place to another, and they also mix them together. Once mixed together, only hearing separates dialog, music, and effects, so if you need separation for workflow reasons, separate busses for the various parts must be used.

Busses

The number of busses available on a given system determines how complex a mix can be accommodated by it. For instance, we need six busses to accommodate 5.1-channel mixing, but if we wish to perform the same mix but keep its component parts still separated, we need 18 busses, six each for dialog, music, and effects. Such complex mixing is probably beyond the scope of what many people want to do, but it has a primary advantage: the preparation of music and effects (M&E) mixes is easy, for foreign distribution in a dubbed language. This style of mixing is called *stem mixing* for keeping the ingredient parts of a complete mix separated.

There are three items that require the services of a buss:

1. *Mix busses.* These represent the final mix of all the elements together, or in stems. Typical mix busses would be Left, Right, Center, LFE, Left Surround, and Right Surround, connected directly to output channels labeled the same way.
2. *Track busses.* In multitracking of instruments in a scoring session, one keeps the various instruments separate and records them onto separate tracks, for which these busses are used.
3. *Aux busses.* The idea here is to pass a signal from a track to another device or process, and then back to the main signal flow. It is a detour from the normal signal flow. Such a process might be reverberation, for instance, where the high complexity and quality of a reverberator may require a piece of outboard gear to perform it. You might, for instance, assign multiple tracks to a bus, which then could deliver the signal to an added track that may contain some common processing for all of the tracks assigned to it, before being passed on to an output channel.

Pan Pots

The outputs of tracks may have pan pots (panoramic potentiometers) invoked so that a single input, the track, may be panned among multiple output channels, such as 5.1. Thus, tracks can be hard assigned to specific output channels, or they can be sent through a panner to a variety of output channels.

Solo/Mute

Solo and mute are functions associated with individual tracks as well. Solo means that the output is muted of all other than soloed channels. Mute kills the output of a channel. These are arranged as buttons to activate in most DAWs. In addition, the mute function may be one that is automated through the length of a track. This is useful in the case where some sound is thought useful but not necessary at the moment. It is still there, available in sync, but it is muted. Automation systems can often record mutes from a mixing screen or an editing screen.

Grouping Tracks

Tracks may be ganged together, called grouping, for common editing or setting of processing parameters such as level, and the grouping may be switched on and off. In addition to ganging whole tracks from head to tail, in some modes of editing software, clips/regions may be ganged for editorial functions. Most systems permit grouping contiguous clips together and moving them as a block, and some systems perform the grouping even when the selected clips are discontinuous.

Differences Between Picture and Sound Editing Systems

Many picture editing systems are frame based, extending their picture thinking (only whole frames count) to sound, with edits taking place on frame boundaries, and the minimum nudge being one frame. This may be acceptable for a lot of work, but film sound editors prefer somewhat greater editorial resolution. One reason is that there is a phase issue between the start of a sound and edge boundaries of a frame. That is, a sound may start three-quarters of the way through a frame, and it becomes unclear where to cut. If you cut on the leading frame boundary, you have the potential of hearing a burst of undesired noise before the desired sound cuts in (which you may be able to cover up with a fade file), or if you cut at the trailing frame boundary, you have cut off the impact of the beginning of the sound.

Many digital audio workstations perform work with a time resolution down to just one sample, which we might think of at first glance as an embarrassment of riches. While single-sample resolution is never necessary for picture-sound sync, it is useful in certain instances. For example, if two tracks that have associated stereo content have a one-sample sync slip between them, this will be audible in the position of a phantom between two speakers. Don't believe me; try it yourself. You can hear a one-sample offset, which is about 21 μs, in its effect on the position of a phantom image formed between stereo channels because the minimum that can be heard is in the 2 to 10 μs range.

Another potential problem solved by having single-sample editing and nudging resolution is that if two associated tracks become out of sync by even one sample, then are mixed together, the result is a frequency response dip, a part of the frequency range that is carved out. This is one reason that some sound editors like to work most of the time in a frame-based mode, so that all moves in time are in one-frame increments, on all tracks, unless otherwise needed.

Other differences between the mostly-picture oriented and the sound-oriented workstations are that the sound systems typically offer more tracks, greater flexibility with plug-ins, more provisions to handle multichannel surround formats, more sophistication in bussing for auxiliary purposes, and so forth. This means that some kinds of shows can be fully postproduced on current editions of picture editing systems, whereas those requiring a little more of sound postproduction probably require a specific step on a sound workstation, at least.

Picture-Sound Sync Resolution

Although the tolerance of many pieces of video equipment is ± 1 frame of picture-sound sync, in fact one frame of out-of-sync sound is noticeable to sound editors, and two frames is quite noticeable to virtually everyone. So if two pieces of video gear with a ± 1 frame tolerance are put in series, and both happen to be at the end of the tolerance, say both at +1 frame, the resulting two-frame error will be very noticeable.

Sound designers observe that having sound appear up to a frame early is better than if it is a frame late. This is curious, because in real life, sound is out of sync often because the speed of sound is so much slower than the speed of light. Watch a soccer match from the stands closely, and you will observe that the sound is out of sync, because at 1,130 feet per second, sound is pretty slow. Interestingly, motion-picture prints routinely compensate for the speed of sound by printing the sound on the print one frame earlier than expected for dead sync, thus arriving in sync at about 50 feet from the screen.

How to Edit

The foregoing discussion is background for the real problem confronting us: how to edit. Of course there is no one way to do everything, as we're discussing an art here. But there are some time-tested methods that can help clarify the process and thinking of sound editors. Not every program will fall into a neat category, but many will, and examples from them are important in illustrating what the task involves.

An overall workflow diagram of the postproduction process starts with editing the picture and corresponding sound for content. Typically at this stage, the sound edits follow the picture ones in a one-to-one relationship. Once the story has been blocked out this way, the picture editor continues to edit the sound a little more fully, such as adding in voice-overs, providing some simple sound effects, and adding some temp music. At this stage, they are not worried about smoothing the sound transitions from shot to shot and the like, but rather getting the story across most effectively. They may employ some of the techniques to make scene changes that are discussed as follows, for instance, but they will probably not use all of the dialogue smoothing skills that are the province of the sound editor.

Where do you make a picture cut? Walter Murch explains in his book *In the Blink of an Eye* that picture editors watch the scene over and over and punch the edit key at just the right editorial moment, in real time—they feel it. Then they look at the cut they've made, again in real time, and perhaps adjust it a frame at a time until it works. Sometimes a clue is in when an actor blinks. This is analogous to switching cameras in live television work. So at this point the raw sound is cut synchronously with the picture by grouping the picture and sound together and making one cut across both. This discussion applies to dialog-driven editing, but another possibility at an early stage for cutting montage is to bring in preexisting music and to cut the picture to the music rather than the other way around.

To do this work, editors usually use two to four production sound tracks. If monaural camera sound is all that is available, then one or two tracks will do, with two tracks permitting overlaps to be constructed without dealing with cross-fades. Cross-fades at this point wrap things together too much, which just may have to be taken apart later. Four production sound tracks permit two stereo elements to be edited and cross-faded. The next addition to this might be, if the style required it, some added tracks for hard effects. Let us say that the sound effects have to drive the story, like providing motivation for action by the actors. In this case, deliberate effects tracks (which might get replaced) are needed in an early stage of sound editing, just to tell the story.

The next element to be added is score. Early in the process this may take the form of temp music, sources drawn from libraries of prerecorded music for which the rights may not be attainable or the familiarity may distract from the story. Temp music is intended to be replaced with score composed for the show once one is written. However, music is needed to get the right pacing of the edit. Watch the main title crawl of *Star Wars* silently, and you will see that the presence of the music greatly affects the apparent speed of the picture—it speeds up with music present. Likewise, there is a large difference between editing on a small monitor and seeing a picture cut on the large screen. Presented on the big screen, edits seems faster, even frenetic, compared to a sequence of cuts on the small one.

This buildup of tracks, from production sound through hard effects to score, is enough to make early temp mixes to show the producer to get the gist of what is going on. It is always best to lock the picture at a particular point before the export of sound to another system, or for detailed sound work to begin on the same system. The sound work is so meticulous that coming along and making picture changes while sound editorial is occurring is often frustrating to sound editors, who have to work twice as hard in a constantly shifting environment. Some forms, like episodic television shows, do not have the luxury of permitting picture changes after lock. The workflow is pretty straightforward, from picture editing to sound editing to mixing. Feature films, on the other hand, often have many loops among these parts, as, for example, when test screenings reveal that changes to the picture are necessary, which ripple through sound editorial and mixing. The parts of sound editing that are often left to after picture lock are dialogue smoothing, ambience/backgrounds development, hard effects in greater detail than required for picture lock, and cutting in the score.

So far, the layout of tracks is pretty obvious because of the way they have been built up over the edit: Production A track(s), as the principal ones are called, possible Production B track(s) to produce overlapping tracks, effects, and music. In detailed sound cutting, however, expansion to a greater number of tracks is useful to gain greater editorial control over the elements and because more elements will be added. Given all the tracks in the world, one might assign each sound to a track and let that be that. Adjustments could be made globally, from head to tail of each track, because an adjustment such as equalization would then apply only to that one clip. However, this is impractical on a hardware basis, and furthermore, automation has greatly influenced what can be done, even automation microediting, with fine adjustments possible throughout a track. So multiple sounds occupy each track, and the question becomes how to disperse the sound clips among the tracks. The principles are:

- *Keep like sounds in the same track.* It is disconcerting to a mixer to confront tracks that are randomly laid out, with first a loud dog bark, followed by an exterior ambience, on the same track. These two sounds are at cross purposes and don't even match conceptually except to say they are both sound effects. One is a hard effect, adding tension to the scene, because the start of a dog bark raises the question "what is he barking at?" The ambience provides continuity, the connective tissue used over picture edits to assure the audience subliminally that although we've changed points of view, we are still in the same scene. Thus, they should be on different tracks.

- *If there is scene coverage of production sound, and all the characters are well covered, then keep it in one track* (or, in the case of Canon XL-series cameras with stereo original production sound, two tracks), as the equalization and so forth called for in mixing only needs to be applied to that track. In the words of Randy Thom, "if it sounds good, it is good," meaning in this context, that given no obvious reason to split tracks, don't split them.

  The alternative is track splitting by character, but this is done only in the case where one character's voice may need to be replaced, because he or she is off-mic or for performance reasons. It is usually difficult to match ADR with production sound exactly, so common practice would be not to even attempt replacing just one line of an actor within a scene, but the whole actor's performance for the entire scene. This would then call for splitting out the track of that particular actor, for use as a guide track, which would then be replaced with ADR.

- *One split of the production track that may be useful is to split out production effects.* This could be any sound-effect-like sound that occurs in the production track. The reason to split it could be its replacement by other, hard effects, which would simplify the operation later. Another reason might be getting the right mix balance between dialogue and the production effect, which is often wrong in the original recording because the effect is in the wrong scale. Another reason could be that the production effect may be enhanced by cutting hard effects in sync with it, layering the sound to make it bigger, and it simplifies getting the balance among the parts of the layered sound correct if the production effect is split off from the production track.

- *The corollary to keeping like sound together is to separate disparate sounds.* If it is to be a shock cut, with a bang, you probably want to split the tracks before and after the edit, to provide the mixer with an easy way to adjust the degree of the bang. If you cut the clips before and after the cut into one track, the mixer won't have the luxury of being able to anticipate the cut with a preadjusted fader, but instead will have to jerk the fader at just the right instance to get the effect desired. This can also be handled by microediting of the volume graph of an individual track, but the point is to leave the mix decisions to the mix stage of things rather than painting a mixer into a corner.

Fine Editing of Production Sound

By the time it comes to fine sound editing, we expect that the actors or subjects are saying the desired thing and that the best performance has been selected to use. On the other hand, sound editors for fiction films have a variety of sources on which to draw to make sound seem smooth and continuous, and to fix small slips of the lip and so forth, so the details may not be finished. The sources for constructing dialogue performances are as follows:

- *The take from when the camera is looking at the actor, despite whether he or she is on-camera at the time.* Only on-camera performances require hard sync, so long as the over-the-shoulder shots don't show the lips. So a continuous performance can be created in several ways. The simplest is to use the close-up sound of an actor over both the shot of him and the over-the-shoulder reaction shot of an opposing actor. Virtually no one ever complains that the sound perspective doesn't match, despite being alternatively on- and off-camera. Here sometimes it can be more important to provide ongoing continuity rather than verisimilitude of matching perspective.

- *Alternate takes.* This includes outtakes that no one thought were any good at the time, because perhaps just the syllable that's needed to fix a hesitation is present in the outtakes.

- *Wild lines*. If the production has looked forward to postproduction requirements, it will have planned for times when too much noise or reverberation exists to get clean sound and will have recorded wild lines for this eventuality. If the noise is under the control of the filmmaker, such as a wind machine, then it can be shut off and the actors can perform their lines with the same level of intensity as with the noise source on and as close as possible to the same performance as when the principal photography was shot.

- *ADR*. A necessity in some circumstances, such as shooting in a working Brooklyn used car dealer on a busy street. Editors work in preparation for ADR sessions by preparing cue sheets for each actor, who usually work alone, and attending the recording session to be sure that all bases are covered. A good ADR stage/recordist will match the perspective of the shot so that the ADR sounds a great deal like the production sound, only not polluted with the background noise.

  ADR requires a fairly quiet and dead space in which to record, a microphone and mic preamp connected to an input on an edit system, and the ability to play back the existing production sound track to actor/performer through headphones while simultaneously recording to new tracks. This is not too difficult to arrange with a conventional editing system, although professional ADR stages will have such matters as arming tracks, communications via headphones, and a three-beep system for delivering beeps to the actor's headphones just before the start of the line. Digital picture greatly speeds things up with the ability to loop within the edit software.

Another issue with a straightforward two-actor scene is dialogue overlaps. If we are on an over-the-shoulder shot and the actors overlap their lines, then we will likely have captured one of them off-mic and one on-mic. This makes it difficult to cut the picture to the one off-mic because the sound perspective will jump at the cut. One way to handle this problem is to make the actors clear each other's lines in production and to construct the overlaps in postproduction. Another is to be clever about the mic perspective while shooting, so that major bumps don't occur when cutting picture around to various views.

After potentially improving performances by selective use of dialogue from the sources mentioned previously, editors listen past the foreground dialogue to the presence, the sound behind the dialogue, because the evenness of edits that occur between pieces of presence before and after the cut determines whether the cut is successful in concealing the change. Hiding edits is what the work is about, because to hear them takes the listener out of the narrative. There are some alternatives if things don't match, as illustrated on the CD accompanying this book:

- A slow cross-fade will hide a presence change better than an abrupt cut.

- Delaying the sound cut compared to the picture one to just one-quarter frame before the entrance of the incoming dialogue line can conceal the edit. Backwards masking (in time) works to conceal the cut. The incoming dialogue masks the presence for a moment, and when it emerges from behind the dialog, the fact that it is a different level and timbre than before the cut is not very noticeable. Of course, this is all a matter of degree; massive change of presence cannot be hidden in this way.

- If the leading sound before an edit has significantly less presence than the one after the cut, it may very well be worthwhile to dirty up the former rather than trying to clean the latter. The example given is of crickets with shooting during Golden Hour, wherein one close-up has a lot more cricket activity than one shot earlier in the hour. The principle is to make the scene smooth and continuous, so attention is not drawn to the edits, even at the expense of sound quality over some cuts.

Stealing Presence

Where to go to get presence includes from the heads or tails of the take in use, in between words, among outtakes of the scene, and from deliberately recorded room tone. Most presentations call presence *room tone*, or in England, *atmosphere*, or *atmos*. We use the term *presence* here because it covers both interiors and exteriors, both of which need the treatment that having continuous presence provides.

If a short, neutral-sounding presence can be found, it can be looped and used to fill a longer time. By the way, editors spend a significant amount of time and listening to find neutral presence, without small noises in it that if it were to be used in a loop would be revealed through repetition. If the section found contains a tonal sound, then the loop can be done with tight editing, matching the waveform at the cut of the loop. If this is done carefully, no cross-fade may be needed. Otherwise, if a head-tail match cannot be made perfectly, or if the sound is more noise-like in character, cross-fades will be necessary between each clip. If the selection should have a tonal character with a rising pitch, then alternating heads-to-tails and reversed tails-to-heads clips permits there to be no abrupt change at the edits. Presence loops can also use different lengths for each insertion, a method to conceal the loopy nature of the sound. The idea behind all of these techniques is to hide the fact that it is a loop.

Where Presence Is Used

When a single track or a stereo pair of tracks is involved, presence usage is fairly clear: you want it to be continuous within a scene. If the scene involves moving from one location to another, then the presence will naturally change throughout the scene, and you can't use a bit from the first part of the scene to work over a later part where the scene has effectively changed. However, when characters are split between tracks, then things get a little complicated. If we add presence between lines of a character on their track, and between those of a second character on a second track, we've just increased the amount of noise (actually it typically goes up by 3 dB). However, if each has presence behind their performance, and it is cut out between the lines of one of them and filled in the other, we may hear the presence bumping up under the one's lines that wasn't filled. These two extremes represent the conundrum presented to the sound editor and demonstrate why you may not want to split tracks in the first place.

It may, however, become necessary to split tracks. Say one actor is well off-camera in a noisy location in a wide shot. We may find that the recording of foreground characters is adequate with respect to the noise, but using the off-mic character is just too much of a stretch. What is done to cover this situation is to cut the off-camera lines out of the production track and fill it with presence. Now record and cut the line in from an ADR session on a second track. With good ADR, no presence will be necessary because the production sound presence will cover any small background noise in the ADR track. Good microphone perspective on the part of the ADR recordist will also improve the verisimilitude of the shot.

Documentary Considerations

Documentary films often draw on interviews to provide the narrative thread throughout them. However, seeing a person sitting down in an interview situation is often not very exciting, and at the least, supplementary visual material is shot to provide a means to cut away to some other activity as a way of compressing time. Really what's being done is to use the picture in support of the sound, rather than the other way around. Sound collected from multiple interviews, and at different times within one interview, will be cut together to form a cogent narrative thread for a character. However, there can be sound editing difficulties involved in this process. One usual method in documentary production, given there is so much footage shot to collect enough to make the finished work, is to type transcripts with accompanying time codes for locating parts and then to edit what the character says with scissors on paper. Almost no interviewee gives a straightforward, linear presentation that is what is needed by the filmmakers without help. So editors will intercut material from different interviews and times in order to make the story hold up and be told well. Although there can be an ethical debate over constructing performances in documentary, in fact it is done every day, and we hope that by cleaning up people's interviews that we serve them, and the video, well.

Editing by transcript causes sound difficulties. The matching from one shooting situation to another is particularly a troublesome case. Editors, while concentrating on story, seem to listen through the equalization, reverberation, level, and other imbalances to what is said, even though there may be strong audio mismatches, and edit for story first, then sound matching. This can leave sound editing a bumpy task to smooth the dialog.

Fixing Bumps

Some of the differences between clips in either fiction or documentary videos may be ameliorated by the picture editor, such as level differences, but for the more subtle differences, that is left to sound editors. This may be the same person wearing a different hat, because fine sound editing usually proceeds only after picture editing has been done so that the story works. It is actually remarkable how much can be achieved by the application of appropriate, potentially small, changes to make the bumpy ride whole. These are applied on a clip-by-clip basis, and thus may use non-real-time plug-ins, such as Audio Suite in Pro Tools. Using such a plug-in, whole clips are processed at a time, out of real time. A graphics person would call such clips *rendered*. They have the advantage of being precomputed once overall playback is attempted, and thus do not add to the burden of signal processing in real time. The postprocessed clip is automatically substituted for the initial clip, which remains available if the process needs to be removed. The processes that are useful in dialogue editing are as follows:

- *Level matching*. May be accomplished with normalization or gain plug-ins, or volume graphing the clip, all of which are equal in their result but may be more or less clumsy or faster to do one way rather than another in a given situation.

- *Timbre matching*. This involves the use of equalization and/or filtering, described in the next chapter. Overall equalization is usually left to mixing, but it may well prove useful to have a different equalizer on a single inserted sound clip to better match those around it.

- *Pitch shifting*. Sometimes pitch shifting, usually by small amounts, fixes the fact that a sound clip has been moved from its position in one sentence into another, because of inflection differences in the two uses.

- *Reverberation or worldizing*. Sometimes a sound insertion is noticeably less reverberant than the sound around it. In this case, a reverberation plug-in may do, or worldizing the sound by re-recording it through a loudspeaker and microphone in a room will do.

Figure 8-1 shows the sequence usually employed to edit dialog.

Sound Effects

Next conceptually, once the dialogue tracks played together sound smooth and continuous, comes the editing of the hard effects. That's because such

Figure 8-1a Sequence of editing dialog: a sequence of tracks as delivered from picture editing.

effects provide motivation for the actors to take certain actions, and they are necessary in storytelling, even at an early stage, to prevent viewers from wondering, for instance, "what is he looking at?" By providing a sound effect, we can tell what he's looking at.

The basic principle of laying out tracks for sound effects follows the thinking discussed before: keep like sounds in the same track and disparate ones in separate tracks. Remember that at this stage you are working in bits and pieces that are only part of a whole; trying to put all of your eggs in one basket, such as all sound effects in one track, only organizes them minimally. You want to separate types of effects and keep the various types on separate tracks.

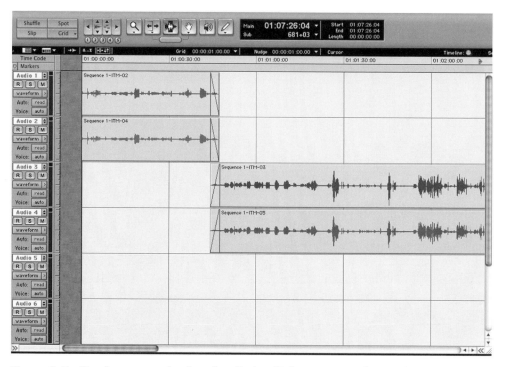

Figure 8-1b Tracks reorganized and split for dialogue smoothing; if a track with a cut in it matches across a picture cut, it is simply cross-faded; if it does not match, then it is split out into multiple tracks.

In recording and selecting hard effects, you generally want them free of background sound. That's so you can cut in just the effect, and the presence of the production sound, or the ambience track to be provided, will cover up any small discontinuity that occurs when the sound is cut in—just the effect will be heard through masking of its inherent low background noise.

An example of what kind of tracks to keep separate is hard effects versus ambience or "BGs" (backgrounds), as they are called. Ambience is like artificial presence or room tone: it is sound that is imposed by the editor as containing the storytelling threads of the environment. It is like what the set dresser does, providing an environment for the movie to live in.

Hard sound effects may be described as being of two basic types: those that come from sources that more or less emulate what you see and those that are drawn from a much wider range of recordings to fit the picture, but in a more oblique manner. An example of the first case is the sound for the

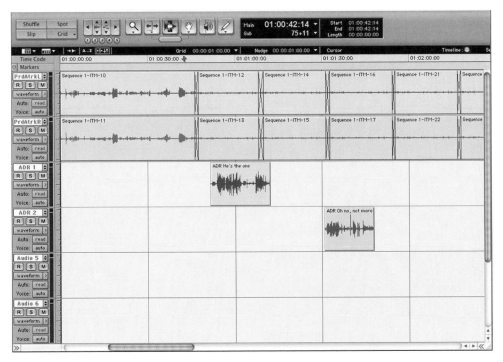

Figure 8-1c Tracks are interspersed with presence (room tone) and cross-faded as needed to sound smooth; ADR tracks typically do not need presence.

propellers of the flying wing in *Raiders of the Lost Ark*. This aircraft was designed by the production designers and never flew. It had electric motors to turn the propellers, so it sounded wrong. Substituted for them was the sound of a helicopter's blades rotating, recorded from below (with a strong windscreen), and layered together and cut into sync by making the propellers appear at the correct position for each picture shot. This meant cutting the tracks at the picture cuts into different sound tracks, so that the clips could be assigned by pan pot to different channels, because it is too difficult for a mixer to jerk the pan pots to new locations for each shot. This is an interesting example where the usual smoothness of keeping sound constant across picture cuts is deliberately broken to make the sound effect seem more real. With a catalog of sound recorded at different speeds of the helicopter blades, and different recording angles and distances to the original blades, a full set of effects is useful in matching the perspectives of the various shots. This illustrates the more literal kind of effect, substituting a helicopter's blades for the propellers of the flying wing.

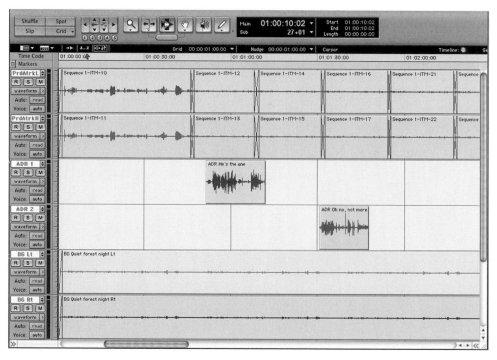

Figure 8-1d Dialogue tracks 1 and 2 have been filled with presence, ADR has been added in tracks 3 and 4, and background tracks, 5 and 6 have also been added.

Other hard effects, though, bear little resemblance to what is seen on screen. There are thousands of examples of these effects, but the basic method of finding them is to try out various effects and see how they work, one after another, laboriously, until something clicks. An example is the dinosaurs in *Jurassic Park*. Gary Rydstrom meticulously constructed these from existing animal sounds because he couldn't go to the zoo and record a brontosaurus. Even experts disagree about what sounds dinosaurs could make because the fossil record is only of bones, not the soft tissue that creates the vocalization capabilities of an animal. By layering, pitch shifting, and surrounding the basic animal vocalizations with ambience, footfalls composed of tree crashes, and sounds of the dinosaurs moving through the forest, a real-sounding world was constructed.

There are times too when the goal is not to construct a real world, but rather to leave it behind and enter the scene along with the characters, a more point-of-view driven or subjective reality. One method of doing this is processing sound effects, such as the insect sounds in the jungle scene in *Apolcalypse Now*, portraying a kind of hyper-reality. By far the most common method is using music to take us out of the more linear thread of the narrative and into montage, as described in Chapter 7.

There are CD sound effects libraries such as The Hollywood Edge and Sound Ideas, along with many others, containing many thousands of effects. Searching is made more rapid today with centralized sound servers containing sound effects libraries located in editing facilities, and even sources on the Web, such as www.sounddogs.com, www.findsounds.com, and many more. The biggest issue is perhaps that these libraries get so large that finding sounds in them by a written description is difficult, and one must just poke around. Attempting to catalog this by sound-alike means is www.comparisonics.com, who also have color enhancements to screen drawing to illustrate the frequency range of a sound, along with its dynamics displayed by height of the waveform as usual. As of this writing, Google returns more than 25,000 hits when asked for "sound effects library." One such library shows more than 300 "body hits." Amazon.com has more than 300 sound effects discs. So there are a great many sources for effects, including the originals for the "Star Trek" television show, for instance.

Despite all of the sound effects libraries, which are quite effective, nevertheless for certain films, crews record sound effects specific to that film. If you are doing *Top Gun* and you look in libraries, you probably don't find enough F-14 Tomcat takeoffs and landings to cover all of the possible variations you see in the movie; no effects library is that big. So a crew is fielded to record not only the planes but also everything else in the environment of the aircraft carrier. The attempt by this crew is to get sounds in isolation because ambience interrupted by other sounds is not necessarily useful. If neutral-sounding moments can be found, however, then they can be looped to form a long ambience of, say, the bridge.

Other event sounds, like the piston in the takeoff enhancement mechanism cocking, loading, and firing, may be recorded as a sequence. Then it can be taken apart into pieces and used separately, so long as the pervasive ambience underneath it is either low enough in level that the individual events take enough precedence that they overwhelm the bumps that might exist (by providing masking of the cuts from additional ambience tracks, for instance), or the ambience under it can be extended by looping to make a complete-sounding event.

Although sound effects are often kept constant across picture cuts, bridging the cut with effects, especially ambience, the function in doing this is to root the listener in the scene and prevent discontinuities when none are meant, excepting the point of view of the camera. There are other times when subtle changes are used in timbre across picture cuts to help the audience know where the scene is taking place. For example, in *Black Hawk Down,* which won the Academy Award for Sound,[4] the sequence on the DVD in Chapter 1 from 10:07 to 10:56 is a conversation between two helicopter pilots closing in on and then passing each other. There are exterior and interior shots. The timbre of the two helicopters is subtly different, and this probably subliminally helps us out in recognizing where we are from shot to shot.

Ambience/Backgrounds

Backgrounds provide the connective tissue for sound tracks. They provide perspective on the scene, interior versus exterior, and more explicitly interior with traffic close by versus a quiet farmhouse interior, and so forth. Generally speaking, they are picked for neutrality, not drawing attention to themselves through any specific sound events. While removing them makes a scene unreal, most people don't explicitly notice them. However, they are a storytelling mechanism in and of themselves. In *Boys 'N the Hood,* John Singleton employed the interior perspective of a grade-school classroom with nearby aircraft flying overhead, as this is the fate of South Central Los Angeles, to be located directly in the flight path of Los Angeles International Airport, when the planes are at a low altitude. Actually shooting in such a classroom would cause problems, because the sound of the plane passing over has to be used in total. Cutting it in the middle of a pass-over, in order to get the foreground words right, leads to trouble. So the way to do this is to shoot the scene in an ordinary quiet classroom and then add the plane flyovers on a background track, separately recorded.

Weather events such as thunder or rain play a part in backgrounds, foreshadowing that things aren't quite what they necessarily seem, as seen by what's in the picture. Special consideration is given to the spatial nature of background effects today, although even the oldest mono sound movies had respect for how space was portrayed. By adding reverberation

---

[4] To Michael Minkler, Chris Munro, and Myron Nettinga.

when desired, the space behind the screen was extended from the flat two-dimensional world represented to a space having perspective. In picture, converging lines produce an illusion called vanishing point perspective, where three dimensions are represented in two by suggesting the third. Likewise with sound, one primary way to represent space, at least interior space, and many exteriors as well, is through added reverberation. Backgrounds are more likely to use at least stereo original recording, if not multichannel, and to be spatialized than are hard effects. One byproduct of using the matrix encoder/decoder technology described in Chapter 10 is that two-channel stereo recordings, depending on how they are made, can appear spread out among screen and surround channels. Sometimes unintentional things will happen with stereo recordings and the matrix, and therefore it is useful to listen to the stereo originals through a surround decoder while laying them in to understand the eventual effect. You can do this by monitoring through a simple consumer surround receiver set for ProLogic decoding.

Foley Effects

The small sounds of real life are often re-recorded for movies on a Foley stage, as described in Chapter 7. Operating much like an ADR recording session, picture is available to the Foley artist, along with many props collected based on what is to be done. Foley is usually hyper-real, recorded closely on-mic in a quiet, dead space. It has to be exaggerated because with all the other sounds present, it would not read otherwise.

Cutting Music

Scored music is recorded to fit the picture, so it should be easy to edit in. However, this is often not the case because *picture lock* is a term that might better be called *picture latch*. It takes time for the composer to write and record the music, and in this time frame, the picture edit has often moved, so music editing becomes a serious task. It is something of a specialty, with a good knowledge of music preferred. To perform a seamless edit, a lot of things have to match: tempo, orchestration, key, and so forth.

Needle-drop music, that which is copied into the time line from existing music sources, is also a possibility, although rights are difficult to obtain.

There are several sets of rights involved: the composer, the performer, the record company, and so forth. Existing contracts between broadcast organizations and those licensing rights to playing them on the air, such as ASCAP and BMI, do not include synchronization licenses in their basic agreements. Putting music to picture makes the product a whole new entity and invokes different licensing requirements. Some of the purveyors of sound effects libraries and others also have library music that can be used by buying a license with the recording to use it.

Scene Changes

The foregoing discussion is largely concerned with what happens within a single scene. Within a given scene, continuity is often the rule, whereas a scene change involves changing the continuity, from making an abrupt break ("there, take that, the scene has changed") to a gentle approach (music bridging a scene change, for instance). Also, the point at which the picture and the sound change may differ, with the principal sound for the new incoming scene entering before or after the picture change.

Scene change also permits a resetting of our hearing, so that if one recording method has worked in one scene, such as all on a boom mic, then when the scene change occurs, it is relatively easier to change to a different technique, say lavaliere microphones, so long as that stays constant within its own scene. When these methods, along with ADR, become mixed up within one scene, there's more trouble in maintaining continuity. A scene change is like erasing a blackboard—the lecturer gets to start over. This is not meant to say that a given character shouldn't be recorded in the same way and match across scene boundaries, it is just a tendency that there is less requirement to do so across scenes than within a scene.

There are several ways to get from scene to scene, and a great many of them are illustrated in the British comedy *Love Actually*. This film involves cross-cutting among several different characters' stories (which come together at the end). The scene change types are, with citations from the DVD of the film in Table 8-2, as follows:

- *The straight cut.* While ambience may change, it is at a normal level before and after the cut. The cut illustrating this is from one dialogue scene to another. Chapter 3, 15:07.

Table 8-2 *Love Actually* Scene Transitions

Scene Change or Event Chapter/Time	Sound Transition/ Technique Used	What Happens	Notes
1/0:50	Music, then voice-over	Montage: Heathrow airport greetings, then explanation "Love Actually Is All Around"	Montage reinforced by hearing music and voice-over only, no dialogue or ambience
1/2:03	Fade-out/fade-in, music (score) to music (source)	Go to music studio interior where singer and backup vocalists perform	Scene becomes more real, less montage-like because of sync sound, when manager speaks over talkback circuit, first we hear feedback, further establishing where we are
1/4:00	Music swells, vocal drops—source music transitions to a score-like cue	Cut to exterior establishing shot, then title "5 Weeks to Christmas"	Continuity provided across multiple montage shots, establishing period
1/4:18	Music continues but we start to hear sync sound	Cut to interior	Music fades under dialogue but keeps playing
1/4:53	Same music continues but now we hear sync sound too	Cut to exterior establishing shot, new residence	Music with sync sound has a way of sounding more immediate and less like a montage than music only

Continues

Table 8-2 *Continued*

Scene Change or Event Chapter/Time	Sound Transition/ Technique Used	What Happens	Notes
1/4:57	Music continues over cut and phone conversation	Cut to interior, Liam Neeson at his computer	
1/5:15	Music continues under conversation	Cut to recipient of phone call	
1/5:33	Music continues under dialog	After cutting back and forth, we wind up on a scene with Emma Thompson in her kitchen	Scene transition wasn't all at once but rather back and forth, winding up on the far end of the initial phone call
1/5:50	Music continues	Exterior office establishing shot, blond guy enters door	
1/5:54	Music continues	Interior office, continuous time	Music continuity over these edits emphasizes continuous time
1/6:20	Music continues	Interior, porno set, day	
1/6:49	Music continues	Interior, church, day	

Continues

Table 8-2 *Continued*

Scene Change or Event Chapter/Time	Sound Transition/ Technique Used	What Happens	Notes
1/7:24	Music continues	Exterior, 10 Downing St., day, the Prime Minister arrives, camera follows him inside	
1/8:06	Music fades out under scene, not a scene change		This is the first time since the beginning that we are without music. It is a relief in a sense and shows how far we've come in getting into the story
1/9:10	Music cue fades in under scene		Music cue underscores the importance of what just happened
1/9:42	Prelap sync sound of next scene	Interior, church, day; back to marriage ceremony	"In the presence of God" is heard over the outgoing scene, yet belongs to the incoming scene
2/10:00	Source music wedding march pipe organ, transitions to Beatles "All You Need Is Love"	Singers, soloist, band members come out of nowhere	Note each part of building players is panned to the correct position

Continues

Table 8-2 *Continued*

Scene Change or Event Chapter/Time	Sound Transition/ Technique Used	What Happens	Notes
2/11:22	Source music continues unchanged across cut	Exterior establishing shot, wedding guest returns home to check on sick wife	Before the cut it is source music; after, it is score
2/11:25	Music continues across cut then fades out	Interior, day, continuous	She's not sick after all
2/12:06	Hard cut	Wedding reception, interior, day	
2/13:15	Hard cut	Wedding reception food prep area, day, moments later	Compresses time as Colin jumps from embarrassment to explanation with his buddy
2/13:55	Hard cut	Establishing wide shot of set with lights, etc.	
3/15:07	Hard cut	Interior, day, funeral, quiet presence, then Liam speaks	
3/16:07	Bay City Rollers: *Bye Bye Baby* as source music		He cues it in over his tears
3/16:48	Music continues across cut as source music in a new location	Interior, wedding reception, continuous time	Timbre change at cut indicates scene change in source music— both scenes are playing the same song!

Continues

Table 8-2 *Continued*

Scene Change or Event Chapter/Time	Sound Transition/ Technique Used	What Happens	Notes
3/18:02	Source music continues across cut, becoming score	Exterior establishing shot, footbridge over river	
3/18:05	Music continues across cut, then fades out	Interior, office, day	
3/18:48–19:22 19:24–19:36	Music cue: score		Emphasizes the point: she's in love with Carl and everybody knows it; broken into two pieces, it is probably more effective than one
3/19:48	Tune is on the radio		We've heard this one before
3/19:51		Her obnoxious phone rings	
3/20:04		"What is that?"	
3/20:07	Music continuous across cut, but with different timbre; it is source music in both cases, but now we're in the originating studio	"That was..." a very funny way to answer the question posed before the cut	

Continues

Table 8-2 *Continued*

Scene Change or Event Chapter/Time	Sound Transition/ Technique Used	What Happens	Notes
3/20:22	Hard cut: we hear the voice of the announcer continue, but worldized	Interior, day, continuous time; faded pop star and manager in radio studio waiting room	
3/20:25	Hard cut	Back to studio announcer on the air	
3/20:28	Prelap edit "so"	Interior, day, new studio, interview	Time is compressed: it passed in the cut
4/22:40	Source music plays across picture cut, but fades out rather quickly	Interior, day, the cabinet room	Music not desirable under tense cabinet meeting, set up by announcer, "Is the new Prime Minister already in trouble?"
4/23:24	Music cue score under		The PM's love is obvious—she has entered
4/23:32	Score continues under scene change	Interior, PM's office, day, later	Time compressed
4/24:10	Hard cut	Interior, day, studio	

Continues

Table 8-2 *Continued*

Scene Change or Event Chapter/Time	Sound Transition/ Technique Used	What Happens	Notes
4/24:40	Music cue score under		Even in the most outrageous of circumstances, people can relate
4/24:49	Bang hard cut	Car, exterior, day	We hear car radio more than the street
4/24:52	Hard cut, continuous	Car, interior, day	Car radio continues over dialogue but it's lower level in the interior than the exterior
4/25:42	Hard cut	Office, interior, day	
4/26:20	Music cue score under		"Hoping to Be Kissed"
4/26:32	Score continues under scene change, then fades out	Interior, Liam's house, day	
4/26:49–27:32	Music cue score under	Camera cranes us to boy's room, then cuts back to live action	Mysterioso music: "What's he up to?"
4/28:08	Music cue score under, same theme as last one	Continuous	The scene ends with them going for the comfort food

Table 8-2 *Continued*

Scene Change or Event Chapter/Time	Sound Transition/ Technique Used	What Happens	Notes
4/28:15–28:55	Score continues under scene change	Exterior, day, park bench overlooking Thames	Liam and stepson have the big talk
4/29:04–29:37	New music cue	Continuous	"Truth is, I'm in love" to "worse than the total agony of being in love"
5/29:44	New music cue	Continuous, but we are back on the wide shot	Helps get out of the scene
5/29:46	Score continues under scene change	Interior, night, office	Laura Linney at work—she's working up her courage to ask Carl out
5/30:27	Her cell phone goes off	Continuous	She's always being interrupted (as it turns out, by her incapacitated brother)—the music is bittersweet
5/30:38	Score continues under scene change		

- *The hard or bang cut*. This breaks the ongoing scene and slaps you in the face that a change has been made. Illustrated by the scene change to the blond and black guys in a car, first exterior with their radio playing, then quickly to the interior. Chapter 4, 24:49. Also used at the end of the scene.

- *A music cue bridging across a scene change*. This helps indicate that time has elapsed and softens the change compared to the hard cut. Chapter 4, 23:30; also 26:33.

- *Fade-out/fade-in*. Marking a more significant change than a simple scene cut, this implies a major marker, such as the passage of time or an act change. In *Love Actually,* it marks the change from the opening montage of people loving at Heathrow, with music and a voice-over, to the start of the more narrative part of the film, the recording studio sequence. This transition is actually made rather quickly, because there's no point in stopping the flow so early in the film, and might even be called a cross-fade, but fade-out/fade-in better characterizes it. Chapter 1, 2:02.

- *The prelap sound edit*, also called a J-cut (because of the shape of the letter "J" indicating something happens in the audio track before the video) in some circles. Sound is heard before the picture change of the incoming scene. This helps propel the story and gives it a little more energy than a straight cut. It causes anticipation for the picture to change. Chapter 2, 9:45. The start of the marriage vows are heard before they are seen, and also the word "so" in the scene change at Chapter 3, 20:28.

- *Post-lap or L-cut*. Sound established in one scene overlaps into the next. Music of the wedding carries over a character arriving home unexpectedly, both over the exterior establishing shot and into the interior, where it comes out. Chapter 2, 11:22.

- *Source music becomes score*. By changes in orchestration or worldizing, the two can be transformed. In *Love Actually*, the recording studio live-sound source music changes into score in several ways: the scene changes to an exterior, the vocals drop out, and the strings swell. Chapter 1, 4:00.

- *Same source music across a cut, but with different perspectives*. In the funeral scene, Liam Neeson fulfills his deceased wife's request to play the Bay City Rollers' tune *Bye Bye Baby* at her funeral, and in the middle of it we cut to the wedding with the same tune playing in continuous time. The change is marked by a difference in how the sound was worldized to sound different. Also, listening to a radio station in an office, the tail line in the scene is "what is that?" and the picture cuts to the radio studio originating the broadcast, with continuous sound but in the new perspective of the station and the announcer says "That was . . . ." at Chapter 3, 20:07.

The Director's Cut

- Computer-based digital audio workstation (DAW) editing employs a non-linear, random-access, nondestructive, visual waveform–based editing model. These developments together have greatly increased editorial productivity. Cutting sound on film averaged about 4 sounds cut per editorial working hour; with DAWs, the rate is much faster.
- There are two or three basic file types: the audio files themselves, called audio files or clips, possible fade files constructed from the audio files for use in making smooth transitions, and project/session files. Project files control when the audio and possibly fade files are played out. Both or all three file types need to be available to play back.
- Audio plug-ins are of two types: one processes entire clips and substitutes new copies with the effect desired, and the other works in real time upon playback. The first is less computer intensive because it can occur outside of real time, whereas the second can have automation functions.
- Many plug-ins represent processes that traditionally were the province of mixing, and still sometimes that is the best place to apply particular processes. On the other hand, fine surgery of sound may be done with plug-ins during editing for which there may not be the time to deal with during mixing.
- Individual editing systems will have slightly different methods of routing signals, grouping tracks, soloing or muting channels, and the like, so these skills must be learned for the particular system.
- Sound editing of production sound occurs along with picture editing, but tracks are usually limited in number, and picture editors do not concentrate on the issues that affect fine sound editing. Thus, editing may occur in two phases, first with just production sound and perhaps a few added effects, and then after export to a sound editing system, in fine detail.
- Track splitting of a continuous track is done when a mixer has to make a change at an edit, for example.

The Director's Cut (*Continued*)

- Dialog smoothing uses multiple sources: production sound, wild lines, and ADR, and is interspersed with presence, also called room tone.
- Sound effects libraries on CD or the Internet are often used for effects, except for specialized ones for each program.
- Sound edits across scene changes can be of various types, which have different feels. Among them are the straight cut, the dissolve, the prelap edit, the postlap edit, score carrying one across the edit, and source music carrying one across the edit with appropriate change.

CHAPTER 9

Mixing

There are two primary ingredients to mixing: performing a variety of audio processes on the tracks and configuring those processes together, within and among the tracks. With the advent of the digital audio work-station (DAW), plug-ins representing many different audio processes that traditionally had been the province of mixers became available to editors. So the question becomes the division of labor: how much equalization to do during editing versus how much to leave to the mix, for instance. There are several primary differences between editing and mixing:

- *The training and experience of editors and mixers is different, although the disciplines are converging.* Nonetheless, on the highest levels of the Hollywood feature film, for instance, the roles are separate. Editors tend to concentrate on the trees (e.g., work within a track especially at the edits and getting blend within a track so that it plays across edits without bumps, and how the tracks are laid out), whereas mixers concentrate on the forest (e.g., how the overall equalization of a track is working and how tracks are blending).

- *The environment of mixing is one with appropriately scaled presentation of picture and sound.* It also incorporates explicitly standardized calibra-tion of the level and spectrum (frequency range and octave-to-octave balance over the range) and de facto standards on the direct-to-rever-berant ratio of monitoring, picture-loudspeaker arrangement, sur-round layout, and others. Mixing in a calibrated environment has a much better chance of making recordings interchangeable with others with respect to dialogue level, timbre, and so forth.

- *Editing is almost always a solitary activity, preparing for the mix.* In a professional environment, the mix may occur with the producer, director, picture editor, or others in the room.

Even with just one person performing editing and mixing, there is some difference between what is best done editorially and what is left to the mix, for the best efficiency. Generally speaking, even though they use plug-ins, editors concern themselves with using them for matching within a track. Thus, a gain plug-in may be used to match levels of a region inserted within a track and time-compression to fit sound to a specific clip length. On the other hand, extensive volume graphing to achieve balance among tracks at the editing stage may just hamper the mixing. So while an editor might use volume graphing for balance among tracks, these automation instructions might be erased for the mix. A better way to balance tracks during editing if you have the hardware is to run the various channel outputs to an external mixer, to set the relative balance among the tracks for the monitor, without affecting the level that occurs in the track.

Some clean-up activities are easiest for the editor to volume graph. Getting a cough or a sneeze into the right level range by tightly volume graphing around it is very valuable. That's because asking a mixer to catch a sneeze is problematic (and all that could be done some years ago), whereas today it is far easier for the editor to volume graph such an event. The normalize and the gain plug-in functions aren't as good for this because normalize only fixes the insertion at the maximum permissible level, which is certainly not likely to be right, and the gain plug-in fixes the gain throughout the separated region at a fixed value. To use the gain function, one would have to (1) separate the cough from the original region into a new clip, (2) duck the level of the clip with the gain function, and (3) then likely have to do cross-fades both at the head and the tails of the insertion, a total of about five functions. Volume graphing is simpler but has a problem too: you might easily overwrite the volume graphing while you are mixing. For instance, some systems have touch-sensitive faders where if you are touching the fader, you have the volume graph function under your control. If you are touching it during the cough, then the duck provided during editing by means of a volume graph gets overwritten. Avoiding this mistake is an example of the understanding of the grammar that it takes to operate these workstations effectively in editing and mixing modes. Each system is different, as is sometimes each revision of software, so the best advice is to do some testing of issues such as these with your system before committing a major mix to it.

If volume graphing is used editorially for items such as the cough duck, then the question becomes: What is the standardized gain setting of the volume graph, the gain to which we return during editing for all but short, sharp items like coughs? It seems best to leave tracks at 0 dB and to adjust them for relative level in an external mixer for monitoring until the mix occurs.

Likewise, using equalization plug-ins may be useful for matching insert edits to surrounding regions, but determining overall equalization is best left to the mix, where especially the calibrated monitor system affects what is heard so that equalization judgments are best left to the mix room. This is because the frequency range and response of the monitors typically used in editing are poor compared to the mix room.

The Mixing Hourglass

Your sound may be fairly simple, represented by just a few tracks. In this case, it may be possible to mix the tracks together directly to an Edit Master (see the next chapter) in just one step. However, for many mixes, things get more complicated because of the number and variety of tracks involved. In such cases, it is customary to first make a mix of like sounds together into what is called a Premix or Predub for each of the major ingredients: dialog, ambience, Foley, hard effects, music, and so forth. Once these are done, they can be played together to make a Final Mix. A block diagram of the process is shown in Figure 9-1.

Each of the premixes should contain all of the level balancing, such as fade-unders for dialog, that is needed for the Final Mix. This is accomplished by a technique called Mix in Context (Figure 9-2). In this system of working, the dialogue premix is made first, if at all possible, and then is played back while another premix is being made, such as ambience. Then the ambience premix has already been balanced with respect to the dialog. Doing this process for each premix in turn and playing back all of the available ones at that point allows for each of the premixes to be correct in the context of playing against the others. Final mixing becomes rather straightforward, and if everything has gone well, no adjustments may be needed at all.

Audio Processes

Audio processes may be broken down into the following domains over which they have the most effect: level, frequency, and time.

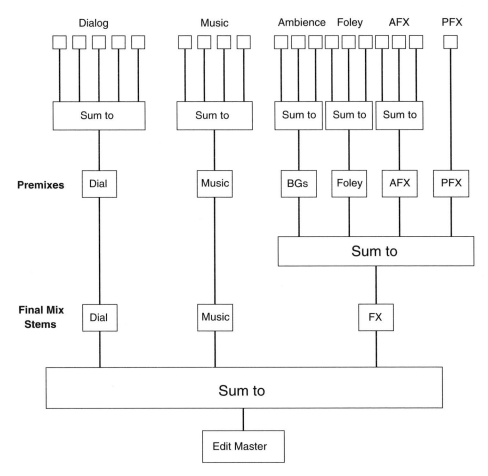

Figure 9-1 Block diagram of the workflow for mixing.

Processes Related Mainly to Level

Level Controls

Among all processes, this is listed first because doubtlessly the mixer's first job is to set both the absolute level and the balance of level among the tracks. In speaking of absolute level, it is remarkable how much agreement there is on the right dialogue level when even neophytes are confronted with the task of setting it, so long as the monitor environment is calibrated. Groups of students given the task of setting the right dialogue level routinely are able to do this within $\pm 2\,dB$ from person to person, so we

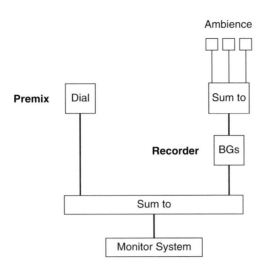

Figure 9-2 Block diagram of the signal flow for Mix in Context mixing.

know that there is a right level for dialog, and it's not all just to be left to taste. However, this experiment only works in an environment where the monitor level is calibrated and all meters are covered up. Mixing for the meter is one way to do it, but not a very good way, because peak meters especially don't tell you much about loudness.

Relative level among the tracks has a lot to do with the style of the program. An action-adventure movie might have peaks to full scale and passages that don't exceed −50 dBFS, whereas a dialog-driven comedy might not use the top 6 to 10 dB of the dynamic range at all and rarely go below −40 dBFS. In the music industry, it would be considered bad practice to not use up all the bits (i.e., peak at full scale) for each piece of program material (all of the time in some instances!), but the major problem with this approach is that it leads to program material that is not interchangeable: the loudness will vary dramatically from program to program as the peak-to-average ratio dictates. This means that with the highest peak of the program just touching 0 dBFS, but with different peak-to-loudness ratios of the program, the playback loudness will vary, potentially dramatically. A close-miked hammer transient at the start of a xylophone note exceeds the running, ongoing level by some 40 dB. If we capture the hammer transient cleanly on a digital recording, then put its peak level at 0 dBFS, its average level will be around −40 dB, and it will play rather softly. This leads to a preference for recording xylophones, for instance, on analog tape machines, where the relatively benign saturation of the analog medium compresses the hammer transients and allows the average level to be raised without noticeable distortion.

Today it is all right not to use full-scale recording level anywhere within a program. In fact, some customers like television networks may not even allow recording to full scale because the nearly universally accepted reference level standard (SMPTE) is −20 dBFS, and the network may have only 10 dB headroom in some distribution channels. So some programs may contain no recorded level above −10 dBFS and still be considered good. In the early days of digital audio, this may have been a problem because keeping the recorded level up helped conceal low-level problems in converters, but 20 years into the digital revolution we can afford not to use the top of the range for some programs in order to achieve greater interchangeability of program material, without excessively exposing noise or low-level converter problems.

Take two movies: *Driving Miss Daisy* and *Terminator 2*. What they have in common is that the loudness of ordinary face-to-face dialogue is the same, but *Terminator 2* uses a lot more of the available headroom than does *Driving Miss Daisy* in its big action scenes. If we were to follow music industry practice and record the greatest peak of *Driving Miss Daisy* to full scale, then its dialogue would play back much louder than that of *Terminator 2*, a kind of absurdity. So we leave some unused headroom in *Driving Miss Daisy,* and then it is much more likely to get played back correctly in theaters and even homes, because both can be played at the same volume control setting. How to handle the wide dynamic range of *T2* for home playback is described as a part of mastering dynamic range control in the next chapter.

Gain Staging

A concern in any complex system that includes multiple level controls is how the relative levels among them are worked out. If a gain control early in the chain is turned down for some reason, and the gain is restored later in the chain, the result is that noise between the two points is exaggerated. The converse is even worse. If a gain control early in the chain is set so high as to produce clipping, then no amount of subsequent level reduction will fix the clipping. This is more of a concern in production, where things are uncontrolled and unrepeatable without at least added expense, than in postproduction, where there is an opportunity to optimize things. The process of gain staging a DAW and an external mixer to monitor its output is described in the last chapter.

Hand Compression

Observing some of the best mixers in Hollywood shows their hands to be always at work, smoothing out dialog, fitting sound effects to it, and so forth. While compressors, limiters, and other dynamics processes are useful, there is nothing so good as a well-trained mixer with a fader in hand. While this seems not to be a purist approach (shouldn't we leave things alone?), in fact it might be more purist than not riding gain.[1]

Good postproduction mixers ride gain, and they do a better job of smoothing out level variations than any device because they can anticipate action and follow the intensity of the script in a way that no equipment can. That is not to say that these adjustments are large or noticeable: in fact, they are typically small (such as $\pm 3\,dB$) and not noticeable. That's the whole point. This does not take away from the dynamic range portrayed by the actor because his or her performance is affected by many factors, not the least of which is timbre. Timbre relates only indirectly to level. It is why we can't turn up a whisper and turn it into a fully voiced speech. So the range from whispering to shouting may be actually rather less in level variation than it would appear to be at first glance, because the timbre of the performance says "whisper" to a listener as much as anything. This is well known in theatrical circles, where a whisper that is audible in the third balcony without benefit of amplification was possible for classical actors: it is more a matter of timbre than level.

---

[1] Here's why. Voice recordings are made at a single point in space, with a boom or lavaliere microphone. Speech has a rapidly changing spectrum, with changing frequency elements from moment to moment. The recorded level picked up at a single point varies with the various frequency elements in the source, as a result of interacting with the standing waves in a room. In fact, frequency-by-frequency from one point to another in a room, the level varies by $\pm 15\,dB$. When we are present in such a room, we hear nothing like this level variation because voice is a broadband source and so strikes many frequencies simultaneously, which tends to average things out, and, principally, because we don't listen at one point in space but at two, with a thing between the points called a head. The statistical level variation is rather less for two-eared listening than for one-microphone listening. Thus, the microphone hears the timbre variations caused by standing waves rather more strongly than natural listening, and the level variations are greater. At least this is my explanation why it is observed that a little compression actually sounds more like a talker than having none at all.

Compression

Audio compression may prove useful too, especially in particular situations. Compression is use of an automatic gain control. Such plug-ins or hardware boxes have a variety of controls that affect the range of level over which they are working, the amount of compression, the time effects of compression, and so forth. Here are some controls that may occur on specific models:

- *A threshold control*. This determines the beginning (i.e., lowest) level at which the system starts compressing.

- *A ratio control*. Above threshold a ratio control determines the amount of compression. A 2:1 (mild) compression ratio makes a 40 dB range into 20 dB. High ratios, such as 100:1, act as a limiter, described as follows.

- *Input level, output level, and gain makeup controls*. Changing the input and output gains affects how much of the signal is above or below threshold, similar to the threshold control in function. Gain makeup controls are used because the natural course of compression has the overall effect of lowering the level, so they then turn the level back up after the compression.

- *Attack and release time controls*. These are used to set the dynamic properties of how fast things work. With very fast times, short sounds that don't sound very loud control the level, but such times prevent any possible overmodulation of a following medium. Short release times demonstrate fewer effects that might become audible, such as a changing gain on a background after a main event has passed. However, short release times also have the potential for distorting the signal because any quick gain change actually changes the waveform. These controls are often variable, as they are widely used on things like drum kits to achieve a particular tight sound. On voice, the best attack and release times are likely to be in the tens of milliseconds for attack and the hundreds for release time, to be most effective. On background music, these times might be even longer in the case of keeping, say, classical music to a steady level. Short attack and release times may be most useful on Foley footsteps, for example, since we are trying to tame a short, sharp sound.

Compression is used especially during mixing in instances where there is no time to rehearse, particularly on dialogue tracks. It is also useful on tracks whose dynamic range must be tamed. Let us say we have an orchestral score that must play under a scene, but that has been recorded with a wide volume range. If played under, there will be times when the orchestra is too loud and interferes with the dialog, and other times when it seems to drop out. Using compression helps to keep it smoothly under the dialogue as accompanying music.

Compression used on specific tracks before they are combined into the mix is much more effective, and more easily hidden, than compressing tracks after mixing. That's because of artifacts that occur when multiple elements are present at the compression controller simultaneously. We hear dialogue pumping the level of background music, for instance, if both are present and the dialogue level range is controlling the compressor.

The amount of compression may be indicated by a display that shows the amount of gain reduction. Typical amounts are in the 6 to 10 dB range of maximum gain reduction, for good audible performance. Going beyond 10 dB usually leads to audible consequences, heard as gain pumping, a kind of breathing of the level that can be heard most readily on vowels in speech.

Limiting

Limiters have the same basic configuration as compressors, but their ratio control is set very high, such as 100:1 or infinity:1. Thus, no audio is permitted through that exceeds the threshold level cause for every decibel of input change, the gain is turned down by the same amount. Thus, limiters cause an upper limit to recorded level for that track. They have three principal uses:

1. *To contain the maximum level, for use on a medium that may not be able to handle 20 dB of headroom.*
2. *To control the level of certain sounds that might otherwise interfere excessively with foreground action.* Such is the case with the Foley footsteps, where one or two stick out of the mix. They could be volume-graphed down to the proper balance, but it may be easier to limit them. This could also be true of certain other kinds of sound effects.
3. *To put a lid on the maximum dialogue level.* Let's say we have two characters interacting, one at a normal level and one with a raised voice.

A compressor might do to even out the performance (with the raised voice still sounding raised because of the timbre difference that raising the voice causes), but a limiter may be effective too. In fact, both might be useful simultaneously, as first the compressor works over a particular range of levels and then a limiter puts a maximum lid on the level.

De-esser

A special form of limiter is a de-esser. The "s's" in speech cause problems for various media, usually downstream of the DAW. For instance, television broadcasting uses strong pre-emphasis and de-emphasis in the transmitter and receiver, respectively. This means that the high frequencies are turned up a lot in transmission and cut back in reception by an equal amount. The result is flat frequency response, but hiding a lot of noise that would otherwise be audible. The consequence of pre- and de-emphasis is that the headroom of the broadcast channel is much worse at high frequencies than in the midrange. Strong "s's" will splatter and distort. Thus, it is standard good practice to de-ess the dialog. This is a limiter process that responds only to high frequencies in the content, so it does not affect most of the dialogue but just turns the "s's" down. Actually, a good process will do this transparently, and you won't notice a lack of highs in the dialog. Controls are similar to a limiter. The amount of de-essing in the range of 6 to 10 dB is usually audibly transparent.

Noise Gate

A noise gate is a device that only turns on the signal when it exceeds an adjustable threshold in level. Noise gating may be useful to conceal changes in background level from clip to clip in a dialogue channel, although using it alone to process sound, with nothing else to cover the resulting holes, would cause problems. Using noise gating to conceal the background changes, and then adding ambience to make a smooth background, may well work to ensure good continuity. Noise gates may have controls similar to compressors, such as principally a threshold control, among others. The object is to set the threshold control so it has minimal effect on dialogue but conceals the background noise. Attack and release times may be adjustable too, with the object being to conceal the noise but allow through the voice, without hearing noise tails at each pause in the speech. The attack time has to be fairly fast, too, to not affect the timbre of the speech through altering its attack characteristics.

Downward Expander

Less abrupt than the noise gate are a variety of downward expanders, of varying complexity, all meant to reduce the effects of background noise. The simplest of these are like a noise gate, but instead of turning the signal fully off, they simply reduce the lower level signals. The advantage is that while the noise is reduced, no separate ambience need necessarily be cut to cover the holes in the sound. There are also devices that work in both the level dimension and the frequency one, described later.

Processes Related Mainly to Frequency

Equalization

Second only to gain controls are equalizers in their relative importance to most mixes. These are more sophisticated types of tone controls, the basic idea of which is familiar from home and car sound systems. Equalizers are first characterized by the number of bands they control. Whereas typical home stereo tone controls are just bass and treble, professional equalizers are usually of four or more bands, such as bass, midbass, midrange, and treble. Thus, equalizers are used to affect principally the timbre of sources, by making separate adjustments to level in a particular frequency range. More sophisticated equalizers may have more frequency bands, adjustable frequency for each band, and adjustable sharpness for each band, called Q. All of these are meant to increase the precision over which control can be exercised over timbre.

Learning how to adjust equalization is a great deal of learning what mixing is about. One way to study it is to adjust a pink noise source (available from the Generator function of most DAWs). You can arrange two different channels to have two different equalizers. Then have someone set one of them to serve as an unknown and conceal its controls. Now switch freely back and forth between the unknown channel and the second over which you have control. Equalize the known channel to match the unknown, by ear. This exercise is valuable in characterizing the voice with which each frequency range is identified. Using pink noise makes the job easier and harder: easier because it is a steady sound unlike the changing timbre of real sources, and harder because by containing every frequency and being continuously present, it is revealing of differences in timbre. Useful hours may be spent with this exercise.

Table 9-1 Effect of Various Frequency Ranges.

	Frequency Region			
	Low Bass	**Midbass**	**Midtreble**	**High Treble**
Increases in this range	Powerful, boomy, woofy	Emphasis on uhh uhh utterance; rooms often emphasize	Greater presence, honky	Bright, sizzly
Decreases in this range	Thin, weak	Thin on male voices; cut frequently needed due to room acoustics	Greater distance, lacks intelligibility	Dull

Another way of looking at equalization is by its effect in subjective terms. A way to characterize the effect of various frequency ranges is given in Table 9-1.

Common equalization for well-recorded boom microphone work is perhaps to pull out some midbass. That's because rooms emphasize this region through standing waves. This effect is most obvious in small rooms, like bathrooms, which is why people like to sing in the shower: the bass frequencies are emphasized. So cutting them back in postproduction by dipping this region can be effective.

If a great deal of windscreening has been used on a boom mic, like the combination of a silk windscreen and a Windjammer, highs may have been lost, calling for some high-frequency boost.

Equalizing lavalieres is probably the trickiest problem, especially if they have to be made to match a boom. It can be done, but it is a difficult task because several effects are simultaneously in play:

- The position of the microphone tends to lose high frequencies, as if the lips are shadowed by the chin. Most lavalieres have built-in high-frequency boost to overcome this loss, but the shape of this equalization may not be a particularly good match for any individual mic location chosen. Thus, the high-frequency sound may be anything from dull to bright, depending on the interaction of the particular lavaliere's frequency response and placement.

- For fiction filmmaking, the lavaliere is often buried under clothing, resulting in a loss of highs.

- There is a resonance recorded by placement on the chest, emphasizing the region around 630 Hz. So a 630-Hz equalization dip is usually useful.

- The 2-kHz region is most responsible for the sensation of presence, yet this region can be lacking because of the lavaliere placement, and thus may need emphasis.

- Lavaliere design sometimes de-emphasizes midbass frequencies, in a search for clarity. Thus, male voices can sound a bit thin. It is uncommon to boost bass because it often gets one into trouble with noise, but a little bass boost around 200 Hz can be useful to make males sound more like themselves.

There is an analytical way to equalize lavalieres, and its use is illustrated on the accompanying CD. However, this method is not yet practical for day-to-day operations. It involves measuring the spectrum from a boom mic and a lavaliere and comparing them, and then equalizing the lav to match the boom. An example of curves found this way is given in the figures, which, for several conditions, is an exact solution, with the timbre of the lav and boom matching after this equalization is performed. Note that the response shown is largely a function of placement on the chest and is not a reflection on the free-field response of the microphone. For raw microphone response curves for a variety of lavaliere microphones including the one used here, consult www.microphone-data.com.

The curve in Figure 9-3 is the response of the microphone, so each dip has to be equalized with a corresponding peak, and each peak in the response has to be equalized with an equalizer dip to achieve the response shown in Figure 9-4. Even though this is just one microphone model on one person in one acoustic environment, nonetheless it offers guidance for where equalization will be the most useful. Other researchers have found the 630-Hz centered peak, for instance, which tends to make the sound chesty, and a corresponding dip in that range is quite helpful. Likewise, to a slightly less degree, the 3-kHz dip can be equalized with a peak. (The 3-kHz dip is not quite as audible as the 630-Hz peak because of the differing nature of peaks

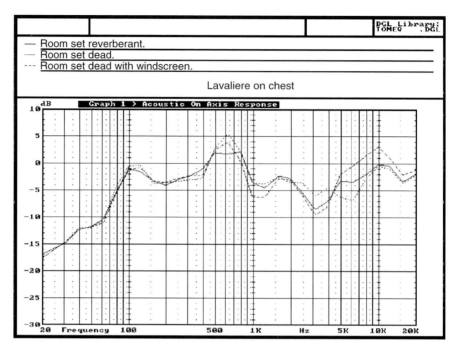

Figure 9-3 Unequalized response of a professional lavaliere microphone on the chest. Curve made by comparing long-term spectral average response of this mic versus a reference measurement mic at 1 meter on axis.[2] Microphone: Tram TR-50.

versus dips: for the same dB amount and frequency range, a peak is more audible than a dip.)

Filters

The effect of equalizers is generally broad across frequency, most useful for adjusting overall timbre of an element. However, there are also sounds we want to exclude, such as low-frequency rumbles that change at cuts. For such clean-up work, filters are more appropriate because their change

---

[2] The variation in responses is caused by differing conditions in the room and wind-screening. This experiment was conducted with several microphone types and positions, and the room variations are far more important in more distant mic positions than for the lavaliere. In this case, the variation seems mostly to be caused by small differences in mounting the lavaliere from one section of the experiment to another, and possibly the angle of the head of the talker. The variation shows how difficult it is to get a match for lavalieres, but also shows that a certain fixed equalization seems useful, with some variability for specific conditions. This work was published as "Improving Microphone Equalization for Dialogue," *SMPTE Journal,* Vol. 108, No. 8, August, 1999, pg. 563–567.

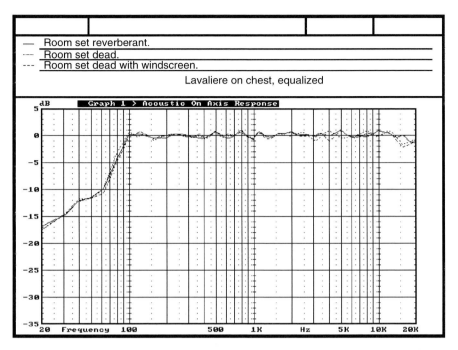

Figure 9-4 Equalized response of the same microphone. The peaks and dips over the range from 100 Hz to 15 kHz of the microphone condition shown in Figure 9-3 have been equalized out with a 10-band parametric equalizer plug-in (Waves Q10).

across frequency is usually more abrupt than that of equalizers, so they do a better job of separating close-by frequencies. The various filters are as follows:

- *The high-pass filter, also known as low-cut filter.* This type passes all frequencies above its cutoff. A common frequency is 80 Hz for dialogue channels, in use virtually all of the time because it won't damage any but James Earl Jones type of male voices, while it eliminates noise. If only female voices are heard in the channel, the frequency can be increased to perhaps 160 Hz. Besides frequency, the only other parameter might be slope, the amount of attenuation per octave. If this is available, the steepest slope is usually best for dealing with the issues of film sound tracks

- *The low-pass filter, also known as a high filter.* This cuts all frequencies above the stated one. A common frequency for dialog channels is in the range of 8 to 10 kHz. It is useful because matches at edits at very high frequencies are problematic, and almost all of the voice energy lies below this frequency. It also helps when an eventual optical track or television broadcast is going to be made to limit the amount of very high frequencies in the material. It would be unusual, on the other hand, to use a low-pass filter on music. It may be useful on sound effects to strip off undesired parts of the sound, where it may be used down to a fairly low frequency

- *The bandpass filter*. A combination of high- and low-pass filters commonly used to simulate a telephone. The frequency range limited from 250 Hz to 2 kHz sounds reasonably like a telephone, especially when compared to full-range voice.

- *The notch filter*. This cuts out one narrow part of the frequency spectrum and is useful to attenuate a tonal sound that could be annoying. Some equalizers have such a range of adjustment that they can be considered to be notch filters when turned fully to their sharpest setting (highest Q).

- *Hum and buzz reduction*. In the United States, 60-Hz hum and its harmonics at 120 Hz, 180 Hz, and so on are bothersome because they make stray electrical fields that may have been induced into the signal along its way. Also, devices that run from the power line, like fluorescent lights, can make mechanical noise at these frequencies. A single-notch filter will only attenuate one frequency component, which is only occasionally what is needed for such problems. A multidip filter at the fundamental and its harmonics is better.

Processes Involving Combinations of Level and Frequency

Some plug-ins combine features working on both level and frequency domains simultaneously. Many are aimed at specific problem areas, particularly in production sound recordings. Among them are the following:

- *Broadband noise reduction systems*. Utilizing multiple frequency bands, these systems rely on the fact that the desired signal is above the noise level, and discriminate between the two, applying downward expansion to reduce the noise. Some of them can be fed a background noise passage for analysis and then automatically set the threshold level in multiple bands

- *Click and crackle removal.* Phonograph records exhibit ticks from dust. Bad mic cables may crackle and leave gaps in the audio. These software plug-ins attempt to smooth over such abrupt transients and substitute best guesses, perhaps human aided, at the underlying desired signal.

These kinds of devices range from relatively simple plug-ins, through ones that cost many thousands of dollars, to outboard pieces of equipment such as the widely used Dolby CN 430 and the Cedar DNS-2000. The effectiveness of each of the methods varies depending on the type of background noise to be reduced. Use of such devices is widespread in high-end postproduction. In fact, over the years there has been a steady increase in using tracks that would previously have been considered too noisy.

Time-Based Devices

Reverberation

Reverberation plug-ins and outboard equipment to do it are used to add to original recordings to set the space for the sound to exist in. Various plug-ins and devices offer several different adjustments, such as the following:

- *Reverberation time.* Classically defined as the time it takes for an abruptly stopped signal to decay by 60 dB or, for practical purposes, to inaudibility. This is the basic adjustment that we associate with size of a space being portrayed. Ordinary small rooms might have 0.5 s RT60, whereas a concert hall could have 2.0 s and a cathedral 5.0 s or more.

- *Initial onset time.* This is a delay between the incoming sound and the start of reverberation, and it also tells the ear something about the size of the space, longer times indicating a larger space.

- *Adjustments across frequency.* Most rooms have longer reverberation time in the bass than the treble, and this factor becomes larger in bigger rooms. Most reverberators thus provide means to adjust a difference in RT60 across frequency.

Reverberators are potentially used on each element of a sound track, although all reverberators are not set to the same parameters. From the driest type of recording with no reverberation to the wettest, the most reverberation, here are some items that use varying amounts and reverb times:

- *Dry sound*. Utterly without reverberation, whispered narration (*sotto voce*: the whisper that reaches the back of the house in theater). Example: voice-over in *Apocalypse Now*.

- *Room sound*. Production recordings contain some room sound according to the location. A task in postproduction is coming up with a reverberator that matches that reverberation, for use in matching lavaliere to boom recordings and ADR to reference boom miked recordings, depending on the coverage of the scene. Foley recordings and other on-screen effects may also use a reverberator to make it seem more like the sound is associated with the right setting of the picture.

- *Off-screen effects*. Occasionally, off-screen effects are more reverberant than on-screen, as though heard from a distance. Example: Indy meets the girl in a portico above a stadium in which a book burning is being performed by the Nazis in *Indiana Jones and the Last Crusade*.

- *Music*. Traditional large-scale orchestral score is often the most reverberant element of a sound track because classical music is traditionally heard in concert halls with fairly long reverberation times.

By automating the plug-in's reverberation time and/or the faders controlling the amount of reverberation reproduced along with the dry, nonreverberated signal, an acoustic zoom can be performed. Note that the use of reverberation is a way to introduce a sense of space even for monaural productions. On the other hand, for multichannel productions, each reverberated signal has potential reverb returns to all the channels, so the question becomes the balance among them. There are two classical ways to do this: return the reverberation device's outputs just to the screen channels, or to both the screen and the surround channels. The former gives us a view of listening into a space portrayed in front of us, and the latter envelopes us and places us in a shared space with the screen. There is no one right answer, and the answer may well vary from time to time within a show, but it is always a consideration.

An unusual example of the use of reverberation in storytelling is the opening of *Midnight Cowboy*. It starts with a reverie by Joe Buck of being in an open-air drive-in and singing. Although it is open air, the sound is reverberant—this is a dream, how he remembers it. When the picture cuts to him in the shower signing the same song in continuous time, the reverberation is cut out. This reversal of the normal order of things— outside reverberant, singing in the shower less reverberant—helps establish this sequence as montage, before the title. Interestingly, the idea is carried through with panning a moment later, when a chorus of voices asks "Where is that Joe Buck?" from one direction and another, an unusual thing for dialogue to do. When the real dialogue starts a minute later (after the song), it is normal, centered.

Other Time-Based Effects

A wide variety of effects are possible once a signal has been digitized. A simple, single delay may cause an added thickness through comb filtering up through a discrete echo, depending on the time of the delay. Multiple delays lead to curious effects, potentially useful to modify voices or effects. Some outboard devices, operating mainly in the time domain, offer many dozens of effects that are useful in modifying voices, sound effects, and music. Plug-ins are available in the hundreds, with active online communities built up around them. The areas covered include synthesizers (making sound from scratch), samplers (capturing, storing, and manipulating sound), and DAW processing plug-ins. The issue to be concerned with in order to use these is the environment for which the plug-in was designed, such as AU, AudioSuite, DirectX, HTDM, MAS, Premiere, RTAS, TDM, or VST. See the Table 8-1 for more information.

Other Plug-Ins

A wide range of other plug-ins is available, many of which may see only occasional use in editing/mixing for picture. The following are ones that are highly valuable when their specialized functions are needed:

- *Dither.* Low levels of signal in digital audio may suffer from hearing the steps of which it is composed—a particular kind of distortion that increases with decreasing level. Overcoming this problem completely is dither, a small amount of deliberately added noise. With the right type and frequency spectrum of noise (equalization applied to it), its addition is benign insofar as audible noise is concerned, and low-level sounds remain undistorted. Although it is a complex topic, most sources that are used in sound for picture have enough associated noise to dither the output conversion. For wide dynamic range sources, it is a good idea to use a dither plug-in as the very last thing in the chain (such as a plug-in for the output channel master) with exactly correct gain (fader set to 0 dB [unity gain]) following the plug-in. The dither amount should be set to the number of bits expected in the least resolution system. For instance, if the output recording is to be to DAT, then dither should be set to 16 bit.

- *Generator*. Useful in calibrating systems, they usually offer a variety of test signals, such as sine waves for head line-up tones of Edit Masters and level setting throughout a system as described, and pink noise, for aligning sound systems acoustically. Defining the level of pink noise is a bit tricky. You want noise that's at exactly the same long-term level as a sine wave, say, of −20 dBFS. However, such pink noise will read about 10 dB higher on a peak meter than the sine wave or the same long-term or rms level. The Pro Tools generator function does this correctly, setting the level for long-term value rather than short term. Thus, the peak level seen on its meters goes up when switching from sine to pink, but this is correct; the pink noise is at the right level. Also interesting is that the pink noise will sound louder, which seems to correspond to the meter reading, but this is actually true for a more obscure reason. By reproducing a wider frequency range, pink noise stimulates hearing more, and thus sounds louder than a sine wave of the same level.

- *Pitch correction*. By feeding in a MIDI file typically used by synthesizers for control, a performance on one track can be compared to the correct pitch and pitch shifted moment-by-moment to get it in tune.

Other plug-ins are described in Chapter 8, those that are perhaps more frequently used by editors, although they may be necessary for mixing too.

Panning

Panning bridges the domains processing and routing, which is described next. Panners take in typically one channel and redistribute its signal among multiple output channels, such as the five: left, center, right, left surround, and right surround. The panning law or rule by which the energy is redistributed is that exactly half way between any adjacent pair, each will be fed the same signal attenuated by 3 dB (equal power panning), in normal operation. An additional control called *divergence* tends to spread the content out among all of the channels, not just the adjacent pair where the sound is panned, with it ultimately leading when fully turned up to the same signal in all five channels. The idea behind divergence is to thicken up or broaden a source, but in fact it doesn't work very well to do that, creating comb filters and often a sense that it's coming at you from multiple directions, not a fuzzy cloud that's expected when divergence is fully up. Some chorus and other programs of reverberation devices or plug-ins do a better job at thickening up sound, and a surround decoder may be useful in decoding two-channel stereo into more channels. For some kinds of nontonal sounds, slight pitch shifting inserted into multiple channels will make the source seem bigger.

Routing and Limitations Caused by It

Busses, Channels

The basic idea of busses is described in Chapter 7, in the section on how to use the two channels. Hardware inputs are connected to edit workstation tracks through input routing by means of input busses (Figure 9-5). Tracks are connected to the outputs by way of output busses, or they may be routed through an intermediate path to do more processing by way of an auxiliary bus. An aux bus has its input from one or more tracks, and outputs to an output bus, providing by way of plug-ins in the aux track common signal processing for several channels, for instance.

An aux bus may also be routed to external equipment, such as more complex reverberation devices than can run as plug-ins on conventional workstations. In this case, it has an input from the tracks, a send (by way of an output channel, either analog or digital) to the outboard equipment, a return from the outboard equipment (by way of an input channel, either analog or digital), and an output assignment to a track.

Delay Compensation

A consequence of digital audio processing is associated delay. Audio conversion and signal processing both cause delay. If a signal is routed by two

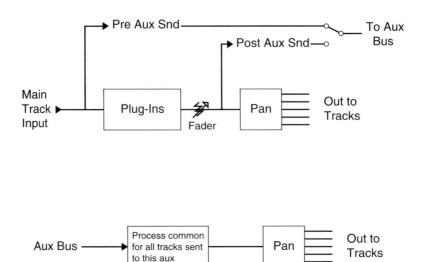

Figure 9-5 A block diagram including inputs, outputs, and main and auxiliary busses.

routes, one for extra processing such as in an aux-send/aux-return situation and one more directly, the signal encountering the added path will be delayed relative to the shorter path. The consequence of adding two signals together with one delayed relative to the other varies depending on the delay time. For short delays, a notch filter will be caused at high frequencies. For longer times, comb filtering occurs, which once heard is an obvious coloration. System designers know about such delay and take various measures to overcome it. One is to put in all the delay one would ever think necessary in every path and then remove the delay as plug-ins, buss routes, and so on are patched in according to the length of delay that the item being installed represents. This system works all right, but it consumes system resources, at the least.

Voice Limitation

Only a limited number of tracks, busses, and input/output channels are available for use at one time. Another limitation is caused internally by the number of sounds that can be reproduced simultaneously. In a system where almost everything is virtual, this limitation is a little more obscure than the others. Called the number of *voices* available, a term borrowed from synthesizer design, this number represents the number of sounds that can be played simultaneously. This number may be fewer than the number of tracks cut or the number of input/output busses available. It depends generally on the amount of computer horsepower available in a given configuration of machine.

How to Mix

While there are many ways to mix, one way to approach the problem of conventional dialog, music, and effects mixing is as follows. Clearly this is an area where the particular type of program can change the order of doing things, the time available to do them, and the specificity with which they can be done for a given budget. It is assumed that you have calibrated your monitor system according to the instructions in Chapter 10. A valuable exercise is then listening to good feature-film mixes of the style you are working in over the system, to begin to understand the desired timbre for speech, its balance with other elements, and so forth.

That having been said, here is guidance on a way to proceed, perhaps most of the time:

1. *Mix the dialogue first.* It usually tells the story and is essential for the understanding of the audience. Remember that your audience usually hears the program only once, whereas you may have heard it hundreds of times. Something that happens in feature-film mixes is that the directors have heard the dialogue so many thousands of times during editing that they can recite it in their sleep, and what they are looking for in the mix is a new, heightened experience, so left to their own devices, sound effects and music will be slathered liberally over all of the dialog. The competent lead mixer will resist this trend, making sure that he or she sits in the shoes of the audience, which is trying to understand the words on the first pass.

   Mixing dialogue means mixing the dialogue stem. That includes intercut presence, wild lines, ADR, and so on. The editing should already have provided a complete track, with no holes, or at least without holes that won't be covered up by other sound effects. There should also be no bumps, undesired discontinuities in the tracks. Editorial principles such as filling out split track with presence should have been followed.

It does not necessarily mean mixing production effects, called PFX, which although recorded along with the dialogue during production, may have been pulled out to sound effects tracks in order to exercise more control in the final mix over the parts.

With SMPTE reference level of −20 dBFS, and video level calibration, you are likely to see dialogue read peaks of about −15 to −10 dBFS on peak meters.

The order of signal processes matters. While conventional processes like equalization and filtering can be exchanged in order without consequence, dynamic processes perform differently depending on their order. Here is an order that will normally work:

a. Clean up first. Apply high- and low-pass filters to avoid undesired noise and changes at edits in production sound tracks. A normal high-pass filter that won't damage most male voices is 80 Hz. A low-pass filter is a little less necessary, but can be valuable, say, set to 8 to 10 kHz. Apply a notch filter for a discrete tonal noise (fairly rare), or a hum/buzz plug-in if that is a problem.

b. Next perform broadband noise reduction with a plug-in or by routing to an outboard signal processor and back into the signal flow. Occasionally you might want to follow this with a noise gate. These devices will help reduce noise from traffic, airplane flyovers, camera noise, and other sources of broadband (nondiscrete tonal) noise.

c. Equalize for good timbre on voices. Lavaliere tracks will typically require more equalization than boom mic ones. If the editor has separately equalized clips or regions so that they work more smoothly, be certain that the automation of the plug-in you are using does not interfere with this equalization. For instance, in Pro Tools, AudioSuite plug-ins applied to whole regions create new audio regions that are inserted instead of the original during editing, and then during mixing, an automated TDM plug-in can be used to set the overall equalization, and even dynamic equalization as required.

d. The level control is here in the chain typically, but is the last used after all of the others have been adjusted correctly. Perform the mix function here. Usually the adjustments will be fairly small, say ± 3 dB if the editing job has the matching right from clip to clip.

e. Compress lightly for better intelligibility in view of other sound sources that will interfere with intelligibility, poorer listening conditions, and the like. This is easy to overdo. Peak gain reduction value typically should not exceed 10 dB. The attack time can be 10 to 50 ms, and the release time 100 to 500 ms. Input level, output level, threshold, and gain makeup controls are adjusted to get a peak gain reduction of 10 dB and a peak recorded level of -15 to -10 dBFS maximum.

f. De-ess lightly for best compatibility with all downstream recording processes. This is audibly benign but will prevent splattering "s's" later on in the program's life. Adjust the de-esser for the correct frequency range of a particular talker's "s's," and adjust the levels, threshold, or other such controls to produce a maximum amount of reduction of about 10 dB. Some plug-ins provide a way to listen to the sound that is controlling the de-esser (that is, the bandpass filtered "s" sound) so that you can tune it to the particular "s" range for a given talker.

g. Apply peak limiting adjusted to create a maximum level of -10 dBFS, with no more than 10 dB of gain reduction. Excessive peak limiting will probably bring up the effect of background noise, as the louder sounds are constrained in level, meaning the softer ones are actually being exaggerated and will cause funny, hard-sounding dialog.

Some of these processes are likely to need dynamic adjustment, particularly level, equalization, and broadband noise reduction. Thus, they need to be dynamic plug-ins (RTAS, TDM, H-TDM) in Pro Tools, not the region-oriented AudioSuite ones. Often the compression and de-essing can be set once and not need to be dynamically varied throughout the mix.

In addition, occasionally reverberators will need to be applied, either plug-ins or outboard, particularly to ADR tracks to get them to match production sound tracks.

2. *Set up the bussing and routing for Mix in Context so that you can hear the dialogue premix you've made while working on the next ones.*
3. *Make an ambience premix from the ambience elements.* Ambience may use equalization (with more extreme values than dialogue often useful), level, and so on but would rarely have so complex a patch as a dialogue mix.
4. *Make a Foley premix from the Foley elements.* Here again, stronger equalization may be useful because of the skin, grass, and sky ana-

logy (we only know what color those are for sure, not other objects; we only know what dialogue and some musical instruments sound like, on the whole). Peak limiting can be helpful so that particular Foley events don't stick out too much when the average level of Foley is right.

5. *Make one or more hard effects mixes.* If you make more than one, the principle to apply is to checkerboard the several mixes (i.e., with sound first in one, then another, along the time line). This helps in going back and making corrections later. PFX is one of the multiple hard effects premixes. In simpler productions, all of the hard effects can be mixed together.

6. *In performing the foregoing, add each of the finished mixes to the Mix in Context monitor busses as they are completed.* At the end, you have a master mix, with each of the premixes having the right level relationship to the dialogue premix.

Mixing is affected in the number of tracks, routing, and panning by the required format of the final master, two-channel or 5.1, as described in the next chapter. Also the next chapter has a great deal of information on mastering for overall level, which is a part of mixing. It is covered under mastering because final work undertaken is the overall recorded level for the target delivery medium.

Several operational matters principally affect mixing. For many years, sound systems for mixing have been slaved to picture sources, such as tape machines. The whole speed of operations was controlled by the dynamics of the deck transport, how fast it could rewind, and so forth. Once rewound and playing, time code from the source machine was used as control to lock up the audio system and slave to the picture. This process was fairly slow. In recent years, the use of digital picture for mixing has become prominent, so there is essentially no waiting time, and the DAW can contain a picture representation good enough to mix to as a track, so there is virtually no time waiting for sync.

A feature derived from film mixing is not widely available yet on workstations but would be a valuable addition to the working environment, and that is the ability to mix in reverse. Winding over and over a particular passage permits comparisons at its in- and outpoints with what preceded and follows it, which is particularly useful for equalizing. Although today's systems can loop quickly over a passage, they do not typically run in reverse, which old film dubbers could do. Listening to a voice in reverse, for example, allows one to concentrate on the timbre rather than the content, and this may be a valuable addition in the future to DAWs.

The Director's Cut

- The most important part of mixing is getting the various tracks into the right balance of loudness. It is usually useful to start with the dialog, and then add to it.
- Stem mixing is valuable because it allows balances to be changed until the end of the process. Stem mixing is keeping dialog, effects, and music tracks separate until print mastering.
- Mixers employ a wide variety of sound processes: equalization, compression and limiting, noise clean-up devices, and so forth. In some cases, the order that the processes are applied matters.
- Today's debate is over how much processing to do editorially and what to leave to the mix. Generally, overall equalization and balances should be left to the mix because that is where the best monitor environment exists and the training and experience of a mixer is different from that of an editor. What is most useful editorially is to be able to operate on, say, a cough, which will be harder for the mixer to jerk down in level and sound smooth than it is to do editorially.
- It is useful to develop your ear for timbre, particularly for dialog, because that is so important.
- There are issues regarding sound localization within a surround-sound field. Normally, dialogue will be centered unless it is supposed to be off-screen or at the extremes of a frame. This is because dialogue edits jumping around are distracting from the story.

CHAPTER 10

Masters and Monitoring

The final output of the postproduction process is a Delivery Master. While there is a desire among program producers to make a "one size fits all" master, in fact if the program is intended for both theatrical distribution and video distribution to homes, the differences between the sound systems and environments is large enough that different masters are required for optimal sound. Using a cinema master on a home system requires special playback techniques to be optimal,[1] and while these are available, they aren't accessible to everyone. Using a home master on a theatrical sound system also requires special playback, which is virtually never available. Thus, masters and monitoring are covered here in one chapter because they are interwoven.

Master is a slippery word in film and video production because just what does it mean? Basically, standing alone it means just about any postproduction recording, anything other than an item of finished goods. In postproduction, the word *master* has lost its meaning through overuse—almost everything in sight is a master of one kind or another. To differentiate among the various items used by program makers, we can better use the following terms:

- *Camera original.* This more clearly states than using the word *master* that this piece of tape or hard disc file is one onto which the original capture from the camera to the medium was made.

- *Camera original clone.* A digital copy at the full resolution of the original recording, such as 25 Mbps for DV. That is as opposed to *camera*

---

[1] Home THX® uses re-equalization and timbre matching to equalize the octave-to-octave balance of a home system to make it better match the cinema experience when playing movies that have been mastered directly from the theatrical masters with alteration.

original copy, which could be an analog copy of a digital original; the use of the word *clone* is specific in meaning a bit-for-bit copy.

- *Intermediate master.* This could be a tape or disc file containing typically all of the content at just about any stage of postproduction that is not a camera original or a delivery master. For instance, it could be a work copy of a cut used to export picture from a picture-oriented editing system to a sound-oriented one.

- *Edit Master.* The finished program on tape or disc. An Edit Master typically contains a header consisting of identifying information, color bars and tone, a countdown leader with a 2 pop, followed by the program with accompanying master audio. In the case of 2.0-channel masters, the audio is on the medium. In the case of 5.1-channel masters, only some of the highest-end media have space for the audio, and if there is not enough space, two methods may be used for it. One is called double-system, where the audio is on an accompanying medium, such as DTRS[2] tape, with time code matching that of the picture so that the two can be locked up by a synchronizer and played simultaneously. The other is to use a special bit-rate-reduction scheme for such masters, Dolby E (E for Editable), to fit 5.1 channels into the space normally used by two channels of conventional digital audio, and record it on the medium.

- *Delivery master,* also called *studio master.* This is a master tape or disc file that contains the program in its finished form, plus potentially added content intended for distribution through one channel. Compared to the Edit Master, it may contain studio trailers, identifying logos, MPAA rating card, FBI warning, and other such types of content at the heads and/or tails of the principal program. The term *channel* in this case means a marketing channel, not a television one, with particular response and level characteristics intended for a specific market, as described later in this chapter.

- *Protection dub.* Any one-to-one copy of any of the above. *Protection clone* is a more descriptive term for a bit-for-bit verified digital copy.

---

[2] Special digital audio tape housed in the same type of cassette as Hi-8 tape. Such tapes are often called DA-88, for the model number of the machine that popularized the format, but the more general formal name is DTRS.

Choice of Sound Format on Edit and Delivery Masters

One big question facing DV producers is what form of spatial sound to choose: mono, stereo, matrix encoded surround, or discrete surround. Mono is used today generally for informational programs aimed at cable and network television and what used to be called the industrials market. Because virtually all media are at least two-channel today, for mono programs the content should be recorded identically in the two channels. This will permit stereo systems to reproduce them from both loudspeakers, and will thus render the content acoustically as a phantom image. For a listener who is precisely on the centerline of the two speakers, the phantom is heard between the speakers, but it is fragile. Moving just a few inches closer to one than the other loudspeaker will shift the image dramatically toward the closer loudspeaker, and the timbre is affected by the crosstalk, which is left loudspeaker sound reaching the right ear just 200 µs after the right channel loudspeaker sound has reached the right ear. The delayed sound creates a dip in the response in the 2-kHz region and ripples above that frequency, which damages timbre. The dip can also make centered sounds more distant appearing because this frequency range is called the presence range; increasing amount of level in this range tends to make sound seem closer, while decreasing level such as the dip encountered with phantom-image centered stereo makes it seem further away. You can hear this by panning a sound source across a front two-channel stereo sound field. The timbre and distance should sound the same at left and right but will sound darker and farther away as a centered phantom.

Recording mono programs to both channels is good practice despite these problems because a phantom sound image can be arranged to appear centered on the picture, if left and right loudspeakers have been placed to the two sides of it. It sounds strange when, for instance, the output of an Avid set to Channel 1 is recorded on a DVD in two channels. The resulting left-only speaker signal doesn't permit matching the position of the picture—the sound image is always off center to the left. For instance, listen to the alternative ending in the supplementary materials of *Ronin*. Here is a glimpse at the postproduction output from a picture editing system raw, before any sound postproduction has been done, and one of the problems is the left-only recording.

Two-channel stereo can now be seen as a detour in the history of sound recording and reproduction. It arose in the late 1950s because of the two groove walls of the phonograph record, the first way to distribute stereo widely, and thus was cast as the home system, with other media (e.g., FM, cassette, CD, television broadcast, VHS tape) just meeting the requirement to match what was already available. Two loudspeakers became the norm at home, and the chicken-and-egg problem applied to all subsequent media for many years. Actually, the beginnings of stereo were multichannel, with three front channels in 1933, to which surround was added about six years later. While early multichannel systems could be chalked up to experimentation, it became widespread for movies in the early 1950s. When the stereo LP was introduced in 1957, practicality called for just two channels to get stereo launched into the home. Today it is hard to buy a stereo receiver—they're virtually all multichannel. So the main reason two-channel stereo survives is as a legacy format for the many existing programs recorded that way. The problems with it include the phantom imaging problems discussed previously (i.e., image pulling for off-center listening and timbre of centered sound for every listening location) and the fact that it lacks the capability for the enveloping sensation that is a major ingredient of surround sound. Today, to distinguish two-channel stereo from two-channels used to convey surround-sound information, the left/right or stereo designation has been renamed LoRo for left only, right only. So a proper labeling for a two-channel stereo master is Program Name—Edit Master—2.0 LoRo. The 2.0 designates there are two front channels and no low-frequency enhancement channel.

Arising from the need to deliver a surround-sound experience over just two channels, amplitude-phase matrix technology first became employed in the ill-fated quad era. It was reworked for film sound by Dolby Labs in the middle 1970s and remains to this day a widely distributed format for film sound. Such tracks are called LtRt, which stands for left total, right total and indicates the fact that this two-channel delivery is intended for decoding into left, center, right, and surround channels. The advantage of this format is that distribution can be by way of the stereo infrastructure built up since the 1950s, both for broadcast and packaged media. The disadvantage is that the channels are not in fact perceptually discrete; if they have complex content, your results may vary. For instance, trying to record four voices in four channels and have them continuously come out in the right places just isn't possible with a matrix. On the other hand, for most sounds most of the time, the matrix technology, which has seen further development in recent years, is adequate to convey the surround impression, and mixes made to it fit in a lot more channels to market than 5.1. Table 10-1 compares the two systems.

Discrete multichannel sound in the 5.1-channel format has to be said to be the ultimate widely observed standard today. While available on fewer media, its use has come to dominate thinking about film programs, and by extension in some cases, DV. The advantages of discrete sound are that much more complex mixes can be heard more clearly because there is less spatial interaction of the component parts of the mix, no sound ever winds up in a position where it wasn't put by the mixer, there is a left-right sensation in the surround field that is at least difficult to achieve with matrix techniques, and there is the 0.1 LFE channel to handle higher levels of bass.

The trade-off for most video producers among mono, stereo, matrix surround, and discrete surround probably falls on matrix surround a good deal of the time. The simpler distribution to most listeners, many of whom are listening to decoded surround sound, wins the day, and for those who are listening in stereo, there is backwards compatibility. This means that a stereo listener hears all of the sound, and most of it in the right place. Left and right alone are easy: they come out of the respective loudspeakers. Center is rendered as a phantom image. Surround is rendered as an out-of-phase signal from both the left and right loudspeaker, which tends to make it at least a little more spatial and harder to localize. For backwards compatibility all the way to mono, a problem is that the mono listener does not hear the surround component of the sound field because it is transmitted as a Left minus Right signal, which results in zero output when summed into mono. So it is important not to transmit essential storytelling content by way of the surround channel in a matrixed system.

In most studio environments, a hardware encoder/decoder pair is used for matrixed stereo (Figure 10-1). These are placed in the signal path for making the Edit Master in the Lt Rt format. There is also a plug-in available for Pro Tools called Dolby Surround Tools, which may be rented or purchased from Digidesign's web site (www.digidesign.com). In addition, if you own the hardware, it is possible to listen to the effect of the encoder and decoder continuously while editing and mixing, by putting the encoder and decoder in the monitor path, and thus understand better the effects that the process has on the surround-sound field, and prevent errors. For instance, a common audio problem is called a *phase flip*. Using balanced lines, this is easy to occur because one pair somewhere just has to

Table 10-1 Comparison of surround produced by way of LtRt matrix with 5.1 discrete technologies.

Surround Format	Two-Channel Matrix-Encoded Surround	5.1-Channel Discrete Surround
Tradenames of encoding processes	Dolby Surround Dolby Pro Logic II SRS Circle Surround	Dolby Digital, AC-3 dts SDDS (cinema only)
Tradenames of decoding processes	Dolby Surround Dolby Pro Logic Dolby Pro Logic II Dolby Pro Logic IIx dts Neo:6 Logic 7 Circle Surround	Dolby Digital dts
Application area	To deliver surround sound to the widest possible audience. This means delivery over media limited to two channels, which includes a broader range of possibilities than the more limited distribution formats for 5.1-channel sound, with some compromises	To deliver a more complex surround sound field over more specialized media than two-channel delivery permits

Continues

Table 10-1 *Continued*

Surround Format	Two-Channel Matrix-Encoded Surround	5.1-Channel Discrete Surround
Primary enabling technologies	Amplitude-phase matrix encoder and decoder; encoder and decoder use sum-difference matrixes with phase-shift networks to produce a 4:2:4 basic matrix (four input channels to two recorded channels, decoded by the end user's equipment back to four channels), and the decoder typically includes playback delay of the surrounds by 20 ms to help prevent crosstalk; systems introduced more recently such as Pro Logic IIx derive up to 7.1 channels from the LtRt	Bit-rate-reduction of original linear PCM audio to fit into the digital space available on restrictive delivery media, typically by a factor in the range of 8.6:1 to 12:1; this is accomplished by using frequency- and time-masking perceptual algorithms to discard signals that are said to be inaudible to human listeners; extensions include using matrix techniques on the LS and RS channels to derive separate back surround, for instance
Delivery media	Theatrical film analog, DV and other digital tape formats,* DVD, NTSC TV broadcast, most satellite cable broadcast, VHS tape	Theatrical film digital (SR-D, dts, SDDS),** DVD, professional digital tape formats utilizing Dolby E compression used largely for digital satellite and television
Encoding requires	Hardware from manufacturer or software such as DVD Studio Pro or others	Hardware from manufacturer or software such as Digidesign Dolby Surround Tools
Minimum monitor requirements	Decoder such as a Pro Logic II one in a consumer receiver, calibrated level monitor	Proper hardware decoder corresponding to encoder, bass management, calibrated monitor level

* Many professional tape formats have four channels, which is not enough to do a 5.1 mix directly. Thus, they are used for two sets of matrix-encoded surround mixes with differing headroom depending on their usage, or they are used with Dolby E bit-rate-reduction to fit 5.1 channels into a two-channel space.

** There is an analog backup of two-channel matrix-encoded surround on digital prints.

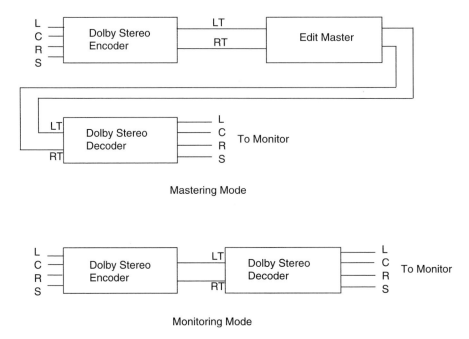

Figure 10-1 Mastering versus monitoring with a matrix encoder/decoder.

be reversed from others, and you will have a phase flip. A phase flip in a matrixed surround system will cause center and surround to be reversed, so things panned center front will come out of the surrounds, and vice versa. In a multichannel environment, it is easier to hear this effect (with an encoder/decoder in the monitor path) than it is to diagnose the problem just about any other way. So the encoder/decoder has two jobs: actually encoding the master from L, C, R, S channels into LtRt and corresponding decoding at a mastering stage, and being placed in the monitor path to hear its effects at earlier stages.

Possible negative effects of the amplitude-phase matrix include the following:

- *Static narrowing of stereo sound fields.* If there is a strong center component to the sound field (i.e., if left and right have a lot in common), the matrix systems will tend to emphasize this and reproduce the content with a dominant center channel. This can reduce the apparent width of the sound field.

- *Dynamic narrowing of stereo sound fields.* In an early scene in *Young Sherlock Holmes,* the teenage Holmes and Watson cross a courtyard on their way to class, and there is a music cue underneath their dialog. A poor surround decoder will modulate the width of the music with their dialog, making the orchestra sound narrower when they talk and wider when they don't.

- *Magic surrounds.* If two-channel stereo sources have a strong difference between the two signals, expect a high level of surround output. Because this is often unexpected, the result is, well, magic.

- *Image pulling.* Strong content in one channel may pull content following it in time to its location. If a sound effect in, say, the left channel comes just before a line of dialog, then the first syllable may be pulled left and then the subsequent dialogue may center. This is generally most audible for misplaced dialog, but it also occurs with sound effects and music.

- *Uneven pans.* Some systems can reproduce sound panning smoothly, and some may appear to stick for a long time at a particular location as sound is panned and then jump all at once to the position planned.

- *Dialog leak into surrounds.* Because dialogue is almost always anchored with a screen image, to hear it from the surrounds breaks the sound image.

The extent to which these problems are manifest depends on the particular encoder/decoder system chosen. Because what is being done cannot be strictly done scientifically (you can't really get four discrete channels from two recorded ones, as that violates information theory), there will always be subjective judgments involved in the design and use of these systems, and it takes lots of program material, not test signals, to understand what they are doing. The market is in the many tens of millions of decoders, so it is a hot area for competition. About the best a user can do to make a decision is to compare the encoder/decoder systems in a fair evaluation, with matched levels, over the same sound system, with content with which you are familiar.

The 5.1-channel system is the current leading one in providing discrete, multichannel sound. By discrete we mean that the channels are separate for all practical purposes.[3] They are Left, Center, Right, Left Surround, Right Surround, and Low Frequency Effects (LFE), which is also known as the 0.1 channel. It is a low-frequency-only channel with a frequency range up to 120 Hz, and it has 10 dB greater headroom than any one of the main channels. The reasons for the channel are psychoacoustic: greater sound pressure level is needed at low frequencies to sound equally as loud as in the midrange, and only a single channel is necessary because localization of sound is increasingly poor as frequency goes down.

With multichannel sound there are two principal ingredients of surround sound to consider: imaging and envelopment. Imaging has to do with hearing the direction and size of a sound source. A more limited case of imaging is localization, just where a pinpoint sound source is located in space. The three front channels of 5.1 provide a means to locate sounds well across the front sound field. The center channel provides an "anchor" so that centered sound is always reproduced from the center of the sound field no matter where you are sitting (unlike stereo), and with sounds anchored at left, center, and right positions, frontal imaging is very solid. To a lesser extent, imaging works across the space between left and right surrounds. That's because phantom imaging more or less works across the listening area (in a cinema with an array of surround speakers) or behind a listener (in a home setup with the speakers somewhat behind the listening location) as well as in front. However, because of the lack of a center back channel, off-center listening will favor the closer side when sound is panned precisely between the two, just as in front. Panning between the front and surround channels on the same side, on the other hand, creates poor phantom imaging because with two ears at the two sides of our heads, humans aren't built for such phantom imaging. This disposition of the channels, with more in front than behind, is thus tuned to perception and to the fact that sound is meant to have better precision of imaging where there is a corresponding picture than where there is no picture.

Uses of Surround Sound

With the foregoing perceptual discussion, it can be seen that various parts of the sound field are reproduced differently by the 5.1-channel system. This corresponds to the aesthetics of surround sound making

---

[3] Although joint low-bit-rate coding of the channels is done, thus the five channels cannot be used for five separate mono programs, for instance.

too. Generally speaking, sound objects with hard sound images, such as dialogue and hard effects, usually appear on the picture, which means in the LCR channels. Sound without such a hard image may appear in the front as well or include the surrounds. Such sound includes ambience and reverberation as prime elements. One problem is that most sound effects libraries are two-channel stereo, and yet we'd like to have sound light up the surround channels. One way to do that is to use a two-channel amplitude-phase matrix decoder to produce an LCRS output from a two-channel library source, and then decorrelate the surround output into left and right channels. Decorrelation can be done by adding reverberation, by slight pitch shifting between the two channels, or by other custom means.

A special case that violates the norm of having only reverb and ambience in the surrounds is the transient fly-by. A famous one is a bird that flies from screen left to surround right in the jungle scene in *Apocalypse Now*. This effect alone sold the idea of two surround channels over one to international standards bodies. Fly-bys may be enhanced with added Doppler shift and perhaps varying reverberation, along with panning.

The ultimate usage of surround sound is to engage the audience. This is often found in some of the best movie sound tracks by not sticking to just one recipe throughout, but by aesthetically determined variation throughout the piece. That is to say that there are times when a fully rendered sound field all around one is appropriate, and times when it is not, and variation between these is engaging.

Mastering for Level

As anyone who has tried to run a DV film festival can tell you audio level is the single most annoying part of running things. That's because the levels are so inconsistent among the sources from various producers: one will blast while the next one will be too soft. One producer will have the monitor system they are using turned way up, and so they make the recording level low, while another will run the monitor system with the volume down, causing them to master hot. The problem is complicated by the fact that there are so many level controls in the system. Even within a computer, there may be playback level controls for the application software, for the operating system software, and even possibly for the digital-to-analog output board in software and/or hardware. To this must be added any external mixer used for monitoring with perhaps three level controls in the signal path and those on any external-powered loudspeaker. With so many level controls—each of which affects what you hear and some of which affect what gets recorded—confusion reigns. Each developer of a product in the chain thinks it has to provide flexibility for customers, so provides such controls, yet the sum of them all in series actually greatly complicates matters for getting things right on the master. What is needed is an orderly approach to setting each of the controls so what you record and what you hear are related correctly, and such an approach will be explained later. This is reminiscent of the production sound problem with multiple pieces of equipment in the signal path described in Chapter 5.

At the very least, people use both −12 dBFS and −20 dBFS as a reference level, which is a long ways apart psychoacoustically, being nearly 2:1 in loudness. Plus they then place program material at various peak levels with respect to the reference level. And even if peak levels were standardized, they don't correlate very well with loudness because peak level is measured in the very short term, by definition. It takes some 80 ms or roughly 2.5 frames to reach more or less full loudness, yet a digital peak meter will read a 1-ms glitch at the same level as a full 2.5-frame sound that sounds much louder. So a program filled with 1-ms events like clicks will sound softer than one filled with longer events, even though they have the same peak level. (It is argued that the meter is this way in order to capture the peaks that will cause audible distortion rather than indicating loudness. This is a fair way to look at it; just realize the peak meter is all about preventing distortion rather than reading loudness.) Thus, the first thing that needs to be done is to standardize the settings of all the level controls in the signal path. With such standardized settings, much greater consistency can be achieved among programs.

By the way, the best contemporary answer to the DV film festival problem, before monitor calibration is widely accepted and done the same way by many producers, is for the festival operator to screen everything in advance and set a level for each program, with a chart for the operator/projectionist to use to set the volume in playback in front of an audience.

Background on −20 Versus −12 dBFS Reference Level

The motivation behind the −20 dBFS reference level was for digital to more or less match the headroom of 35-mm analog film masters so that movies could be transferred to digital with little hassle, especially given that Hollywood postproduction studios were among the first to use digital video, and thus their viewpoint set the early standards. Unfortunately, a lot of conventional systems located downstream from the digital master could not handle 20 dB of headroom, which gave rise to −14 and −12 dB as reference levels. Digital masters made with a −12 dB reference and thus only a maximum of 12 dB of undistorted headroom provided a better fit into the capacity of such media as broadcast television, interstation microwave relay links, analog satellite distribution, VHS tape, and so forth. Interestingly, more recent media developments like DVD have no problem with using −20 dBFS as a reference with 20 dB of potential headroom; only legacy systems have to be protected. Thus, the two sets of reference levels are at cross purposes, and in some sense never the twain shall meet. However, there is a way to solve this seeming conundrum by untying the Gordian knot, to be described later.

A field that exhibits much better level consistency than general DV is movies. That's because a standard is in place in postproduction for the reference level, both on the medium and acoustically in the room (Table 10-2). Thus, the volume control of the dubbing stages that make movies is controlled by technical means, and that makes for better consistency.

Level Calibration

What is required to do the best level calibration of your monitor system is the CD in the back of this book and a simple sound level meter such as a Radio Shack 33–4050 ($39.99). (Do not fall into the trap of thinking the digital meter for $10 more is better: it can only be read to the nearest dB, whereas the analog meter can be read to 0.5 dB.) To calibrate, do the following:

- Import the CD digitally into your editing system, either by transferring the file (commonly called *ripping*—you can have it: the copyright per-

Table 10-2 Monitoring reference levels for various playback environments.

Field of Application	Room Size	Digital Sine Wave Reference Level	Acoustical Reference Level	Monitor System Frequency Response
Cinema	Large	−20 dBFS	85 dB SPL	X curve
Cinema	Small	−20 dBFS	82 dB SPL	X curve with small room adaptation
Video with high headroom	Small	−20 dBFS	78 dB SPL	Flat to 10 kHz, then natural roll-off
Video with low headroom	Small	−12 dBFS	70 dB SPL	Flat to 10 kHz, then natural roll-off
How measured		Console VU meter set for 0 VU on −20 dBFSrms pink noise (Ignore peak meters as they will read higher on the same signal!)	Sound level meter at primary listening location set to C weighting and slow reading	Real-time spectrum analyzer

mits this) or by a digital streaming transfer. Note that because of the standard sample rate of CDs at 44.1 kHz, you should make a 44.1-kHz session file for this calibration. It need not be intermixed with 48-kHz DV sessions.

- Be sure that all of the editing system's playback level controls in the chain, such as volume graphing, are set to unity or 0 dB gain, and that channel 1 is panned left and channel 2 right. In the case of 5.1-channel monitoring, such as with an external Pro Tools system, copy each of the sections to each of six channels and perform routing to six outputs. Mute/solo controls should both be off. Equalization should be set flat or switched out.

- Note when playing the sine-wave tone that it reads exactly –20 dBFS on the editing system's software and, if present, hardware meters.[4] Some digital meters have such coarse resolution that you cannot read –20 dBFS accurately, so for these systems just be certain that the volume graphing is reproducing the tone at unity gain.

- Set the output controls in your computer's system software to a standard position that's repeatable, such as at the 80 percent point for the slider, which is the fourth of the five fixed markers on Mac OS X, Apple Menu, System Preferences, Sound, Line Out: Built-in Audio, Output volume. If you have control over the level of the hardware, such as with a Pro Tools system, it is also desirable to standardize the electrical voltage level by measurement with a voltmeter at each output channel, setting the output potentiometers for a nominal value such as 775 mV when playing the –20 dBFS sine wave.

- If you are using an external mixer as a control device, set its relevant channel level controls for unity gain ("U" on a Mackie, 0 dB if the scale goes above and below 0), and its master level control for unity or 0 dB. Set the mute/solo controls to be not engaged, and set the equalization flat or out on the external mixer.

- Play the sine-wave tone into the external mixer. Set the input trim controls so that the –20 dBFS tone reads 0 VU on VU meters (usually those that have 0 somewhere near the top, but with numbers above 0 VU) or –20 dBFS on digital peak meters (those that have 0 dB right at the top and a descending scale of numbers below it). Note that some digital peak meters neglect to use the minus sign (–) for dB below 0 because of space limitations.

- Roughly set the monitor volume control level on the external mixer and any input level controls on the loudspeakers for a comfortable level playing the tone (for now). These should be at nominal, repeatable settings.

---

[4] If other level systems are in use than referencing directly to full scale, you may have to make an adjustment for where –20 dBFS lies. For instance, on the individual channel track meters in Final Cut Pro, reference level is –12 dBFS, and db numbers are scaled from there. Thus, –20 dBFS is –8 dB on this scale.

- Play the band-limited pink noise. This sounds like a kind of filtered waterfall. Ignore all of the meters. Peak meters will read something around 10 dB greater than they did on the sine-wave tone, but ignore this. The higher reading is caused by the time properties of the noise and does not reflect its long-term value. A VU meter will read it much more closely to its long-term value, but because it bounces, the exact level will be difficult to tell. Trust that the disc has been made correctly and that the level is in fact precisely –20 dBFS measured on an rms basis, which is how engineers measure the long-term value.

- Use the mute function of the editing system on all unused channels to play the noise from each channel in turn.[5] Place the sound level meter in the center of where your head would be while listening and stand off to one side while holding it, not behind it. Set the meter to C weighting and slow reading. Adjust the level control of each powered speaker or power amp level control in turn so that the noise reads the value in Table 10-3.

- If you are using a power amp and set of loudspeakers with no gain control and your console only has a common, ganged monitor volume control, you'll have to check that each of the channels produces the same sound pressure level for one level control setting. The alignment should be within 0.5 dB. If you can't achieve this degree of balance, a trim should be made to each channel's level to reach the correct SPL.

In film dubbing operations, these settings are rarely changed. While editing, you may find a need to increase the level to hear a background, and possibly while mixing occasionally to listen to the backgrounds. In that case, doing so on a calibrated control, such as the main channel level faders, allows you to reset it to the calibrated level once your increased gain listening is complete.

When You Can't Calibrate with Test Signals

Although the aforementioned procedure looks rather long, it can actually be performed quickly once you've done it a time or two. But what if you've lost track of the CD and don't have a sound level meter? The first thing to know is that typically dialogue controls the volume level that people set. For pro-

---

[5] Note that while the solo function might work, especially on external consoles, solo may change the level or position; thus, using mutes is more certain.

Table 10-3 Reference sound pressure levels for monitoring.

For	Reading
Monitoring for video release in edit rooms, mix rooms, and control rooms, with all channels set each in turn	79 dB SPL (−1 dB on the 80 dB scale)
Monitoring for theatrical distribution masters in edit rooms and small mix rooms, each channel in turn	
L, C if used, R	81 dB SPL (+1 dB on the 80 dB scale)
LS, RS	78 dB SPL (−2 dB on the 80 dB scale)
Monitoring for theatrical originals being redistributed into the home (DVD) in edit rooms and small mix rooms, each channel in turn	
L, C if used, R, LS, RS	81 dB SPL (+1 dB on the 80 dB scale)

grams like action-adventure movies, extra headroom is needed beyond the level of dialogue for momentary loud sounds, so dialogue cannot be recorded up to full scale. It is typical for normal dialogue to peak around −15 dBFS, again, on a digital peak meter, which is not very reliable for reading loudness. Because of the relative sluggishness of VU meters, the dialogue will normally peak somewhat below 0 VU, perhaps reaching 0 on the maximum dialogue level. This recorded level allows then for 15 dB peaks above the running level of the dialogue for those big scenes.

Set the system up in a similar way as described under calibrating: every control should be run around its nominal level. If one control in the chain is turned down, and a subsequent one turned up to make up the gain, the result is excessive noise that is increased from the stages between the two controls. If one control is turned up relative to normal, and a subsequent one turned down to get the gain right, the potential is for clipping distortion to occur between the two controls, just as bad as digital clipping. What you do in setting all of the controls around their nominal values and then trimming to get the overall system level correct is called *gain staging*.

Then, having set the controls nominally and with dialogue that's recorded well as a source, set the monitor volume control to the right level. The surprising thing about this is how close even untrained people come if you just let yourself go, don't look at the meters, and set the level. I ask beginning mixing students to take a blind vote on the level of dialog, and the agreement among them is remarkably good, certainly in the range of ±2 dB—this seems to be one experience that's universal.

Best One-Size-Fits-All Approach

Once the monitor system has been calibrated, we can get on with recording. Interestingly perhaps, this is the point at which I cover up all of the meters and make mixers respond to what they hear rather than what they see. After all, mixing is experiential in the end. However, we still have to peek at the meters because there are still delivery requirements to deal with set by the company to which you are to deliver.

For a program that is completely dialogue driven, the temptation is to master the program so that the highest peak in the entire program just reaches 0 dBFS; you might say that the program has been normalized, in the plug-in sense of the term. However, this leads to an absurdity when then intermixed in an overall film festival or broadcast day that contains a action-adventure film mastered with dialogue peaks hitting −15 typically—there's a 15 dB difference! The answer is: *do not* do this! Do not master the dialogue-driven program at peaks of 0 dBFS. This is a bad habit that the music industry is in, and it shouldn't be copied into the audio-for-picture industry because it only leads to badly noninterchangeable programs. You might actually get rejected by a network too because some of their distribution paths only have around 10 dB headroom, and their reference is −20 dBFS (as you can see on virtually any digital television tape machine). Instead, peak at a maximum of −10 dBFS with a reference level of −20 dBFS and you will have made one universal product. Losing about a bit and a half of dynamic range is not too much of a price to pay even in a 16-bit environment, and the world is evolving to 24-bit mixes, where it just doesn't matter that you are under-recording by 10 dB.

Considering this argument in terms of the two widely used reference levels produces the following prescription: The reason the −12 dBFS reference level exists is that there are downstream media and equipment from the master that can only handle 12 dB of headroom. Yet intermixing media referenced at −12 and −20 leads to big problems. There is a solution: reference to −20 dBFS and use only about 8 to 10 dB peaks above there, thus keeping to the headroom requirements of those paths having low headroom but producing better interchangeability with sources referenced to −20 dBFS.

This goes against the grain of those who have been trained that to get the best dynamic range in digital audio you ought to put the highest peaks at 0 dBFS because it leaves unused the top 10 dB of the dynamic range. As with all folklore, there is something to be said for mastering to the highest levels: it's supposed to keep you well above the noise floor. And in the early days of digital audio, the low-level region of converters was quite bad, turning low-level smooth sine waves into coarse square waves. These problems are long gone with good equipment today, so the prescription passed down for years does not necessarily apply. Furthermore, we have seen that the actual limitation on dynamic range is typically not the basic medium, but is the actual implementation of the camera electronics, source recordings, and so on, so the idea of recording hot to prevent low-level problems in converters isn't even a problem in practice—the program controls the noise, not the converters.

The bottom line on mastering for level is the same as the mixing prescription: start with the dialogue and then scale the backgrounds, Foley, effects, and music to it. In music mixing, the equivalent is adding a track at a time. Because of the masking effects of one track over another, music mixers will compress and equalize each track in turn so that the mix elements read through one another, which is one reason music mixing takes a long time. Mixing for accompanying a picture, with dialog, music, and effects, has two things going for it that music mixing doesn't have. First there's the relatively strong difference among the types of sources; the elements are less likely to cover one another up when presented together, and good editing involves leaving "little holes" for the dialogue to shine through that music does not do as often, although music composition can leave room for a solo to shine too, for example. Second, there's the fact that much mixing for picture is in surround sound. Spreading sources out around a surround-sound field allows the individual tracks more clarity than having to squish them into two-channel stereo.

You might need to apply some peak limiting to stick to the prescription for a universal master of peaks at −10 dBFS. Let's say you've first prepared a wide dynamic range LtRt mix for DVD release, with 20 dB of headroom and −20 dBFS reference. Now you have to make a new delivery master for, say, VHS tapes. VHS has two different headrooms on the linear versus the HiFi tracks, but few duplicators have separate distribution of signals for the two types of tracks. A one-size-fits-all approach calls for 10 dB of peak headroom above reference level, which will distort the linear tracks (but they are analog and so saturation is not as nasty as digital overload) and leave the HiFi tracks clean. Applying SMPTE reference of −20 dBFS, you should peak at −10 dBFS. So one way to do this would be to set a limiter with an infinite compression ratio to −10 dBFS. However, substantial limiting may be audible as unnatural ducks in the content. So the best way to proceed is probably to turn the level down of the original mix by about 5 dB, and add 5 dB of peak limiting gain reduction, thus limiting the 20 dB headroom master to 10 dB of headroom.

Mastering for DVD, Digital Broadcast, and Digital Satellite Television

When DV tape masters or files are transferred to DVD with a program like DVD Studio Pro 2, another mastering stage occurs, one to translate the linear PCM conventional digital audio used in postproduction to the bit-rate-reduced form necessary to fit on the DVD. In addition to simply compressing the bit rate, Dolby Digital has features called *metadata*, or data about the digital audio. Metadata contains, among other things, two different level-affecting mechanisms: dialogue normalization and dynamic range control. So in mastering for DVD, a measure of standardization can be added to that present on delivery masters.

The program that encodes Dolby Digital is called A.Pack, which is delivered with Studio Pro 2. Some media such as DVD and digital broadcast have space for more than one audio service, with Complete Main being a dialog, music, and effects main mix but also capable of handling special content for the hearing impaired (compressed dialogue only), the visually impaired (description of the picture), and so forth, as separate, parallel bit streams. Each of these different services needs a separate coding pass to produce its own files. The parameters that are to be set for each service before encoding can occur are as follows:

Under the Audio tab of A.Pack:

- *Target system.* Whether DVD Video, DVD Audio, or generic AC-3, depending on where the master is to be used.

- *Audio coding mode.* This specifies the number of channels and their distribution. The possibilities are 1/0, 2/0, 3/0, 2/1, 3/1, 2/2, 3/2. The two numbers are the number of front channels and the number of surround channels, respectively: 3/2 is the five-channel system because it stands for three front and two surround channels. Note that those with one transmitted surround channel would have that channel reproduced by all of the surround speakers in a system: it's mono surround, not single-speaker surround. Also, of these, 1/0, 2/0, and 3/2 are the popular choices.

  Beneath the Audio Coding Mode pulldown menu is a box labeled Enable Low Frequency Effects that should be checked if an LFE channel is available. Note that most, if not all, set-top cable/satellite boxes ignore the LFE channel when mixing down 5.1 content to their two-channel outputs, so no essential storytelling information can be put only in the LFE channel. It is meant to be an enhancement channel, not an essential one, in home distribution. For this reason alone, there may need to be different delivery masters for cinema and home because in the cinema the use of a dedicated subwoofer system is assumed, and so its content will be heard. For corresponding delivery masters aimed at the home, some studios choose to redistribute the LFE content from cinema masters into the main channels and LFE channel to make masters wherein the LFE content will survive mixdown to two channels, but others do not. This is one reason why separate cinema and home masters may be needed—other reasons are described later.

- *Data rate.* A variety of bit rates are selectable for this specified service, and the range of bit rates available depends on the number of audio channels to be coded. Higher rates produce a greater likelihood that no coding artifacts will be heard. The maximum coding rate is 448 kbps, but note that multiple streams are possible simultaneously on DVD for separate languages and that each one uses up some of the bit budget, and the bit rate must be traded off against program length, number of audio services, and picture quality. Typical would be two audio services in one language, an LtRt and a 5.1, perhaps coded at 192 kbps and 448 kbps, respectively, for a total of 640 kbps, a fraction of the average bit rate off the DVD of typically 3.5 Mbps and only about 6 percent of the peak rate of 10 Mbps.

- *Dialogue normalization*. The default value for movies is −27 dBFS, and if you have followed the calibration in this chapter and recorded dialogue at normal levels, this is the setting you should use.

- *Bit stream mode*. A variety of audio services may accompany one video program on broadcast and satellite digital television, and on DVD. Complete Main is the most common setting, but ancillary services such as those for the hearing impaired or visually impaired are also possible audio services. They would be coded in a separate pass of the encoder and combined only on the final medium.

Under the Bitstream tab of A.Pack:

- *Center downmix*. This applies to the backwards compatibility of three front versus two front speakers. In the case where the end user has only two speakers, how much of the center signal should be delivered to each of the channels? The goal is to get a sound source that is panned across the front channels to stay at constant loudness throughout the pan. Classical acoustics says that if you are a healthy distance from sound sources in a room, two equal-level sources will add by 3 dB, so the correct downmix level for this condition is −3 dB, which is the typical setting. However, you might expect the user to sit close and be dominated by the direct sound field, in which case a better downmix may be −6 dB. The value −4.5 dB was meant to be correct in all cases, ±1.5 dB.

- *Surround downmix*. This answers the question "how much left surround should be mixed into left front if there is no surround loudspeaker, and the same for the right channels?" The answer here depends on how prominent the surrounds are. If it is felt that a mixdown would be too great at the normal −3 dB, then −6 dB and off values are possible. These might be necessary for a sports game with loud crowd noises, for instance, where the two-channel and even mono viewer could wind up with too much crowd noise.

- *Dolby surround mode*. This is used to distinguish between LoRo (two-channel stereo) mixes and LtRt ones intended for amplitude-phase matrix reproduction (by way of Dolby Pro Logic 2, Neo:6, Circle Surround, Logic 7, etc.). A third value is Not Indicated, but readers of this book should know enough by now to pick one of the other two indicated alternatives.

- *Copyright exists* checkbox. Check with program producer.

- *Content is original* checkbox. Check with program producer.

- *Audio production information* checkbox. Check the box to indicate that the following information has been provided. Again, readers of this book are in a position to understand and use these features.

- *Peak mixing level*. Dialog normalization is relative. To get the right absolute SPL calibration, future controllers would be able to reproduce the sound at exactly the same level as the producer or at a fixed offset from the producer's level (such as always 6 dB quieter than "Hollywood"). The number indicated is the sum of two factors: (1) the headroom, which is the amount between the reference level and 0 dBFS, such as 20 dB, and (2) the sound pressure level that you have set the front channels to. So if you are using 79 dB SPL and −20 dBFS as a reference, set the number to 99 dB.

- *Room type*. The choices are "Small Room, Flat Monitor," which is what you are likely using, "Large Room, X Curve Monitor," which is used on film dubbing stages, or "Not Indicated." Setting this parameter to "Small Room, Flat Monitor" will likely best duplicate your conditions of monitoring. This is more fully explained later.

- *Compression preset*. Many people observe that films mixed in large dubbing rooms for listening to in cinemas sound like they have too much dynamic range when played at home. They say the dialogue is buried, but in fact this usually means that the entire mix has been turned down compared to the original, and the dialogue is the most affected. To reduce this problem, the listener can add audio compression optionally, and this parameter sets what program type and thus how the parameters of the compressor are set. Note that it is up to the end user's controller whether this is ignored, as in a home theater application, used all the time as in a set-top box, or switchable in and out, sometimes called a "night switch," in a receiver. The settings are program dependent: Film Standard Compression, Film Light Compression, Music Standard Compression, Music Light Compression, and Speech Compression.

- *General.* RF Overmodulation Protection is for when the output of a receiver must be retransmitted as a television channel on an RF (antenna) cable within a home. Many VCRs had this feature, so modern receivers sometimes have it too: you can switch the VCR or set-top box typically to put out a standard NTSC television channel 3 or 4. In this case, the wide dynamic range of modern-day programs can overload the simple mono modulator, and therefore the RF Overmodulation Protection should be checked.

- *Apply digital deemphasis* is used only when the PCM (whatever form, .wav, etc.) has been preemphasized, such as with a very few CDs. It is not widely used.

- *Full-bandwidth channels.* The Low-Pass Filter box should be checked when operating at any lower than the maximum bit rate for the number of audio channels. It prevents probably rare problems with the highest frequency audio signals. The DC filter may be useful when there is no other such filter in line, preventing wasted coding of inaudible signals and eliminating potential thumps upon changing programs, for instance.

- *LFE channel.* Apply Low-Pass Filter restricts the bandwidth of the LFE channel appropriately and would normally be used. This is because editing and mixing software often lack this function, and the LFE bandwidth needs to be limited because if it isn't upon recording/ transmission, it certainly will be in playback/reception. This then can create major surprises as the attack of a kick drum, say, heard over a monitoring system with relatively unrestricted subwoofer bandwidth becomes band limited in transmission. The hard part—the transient— of the attack is gone, and this reveals a mixing problem (the content should have been split between a main channel and the LFE one). Or better yet, the entire bass drum should be in the main mix where the time relationships across the various frequencies will be better preserved. Save LFE for when it is really needed, such as with the canon fire in the "1812 Overture."

- *Surround channels.* Apply 90° Phase Shift would normally be checked so that matrix surround decoders work correctly. Apply 3 dB Attenuation is used only when theatrical cinema masters are being transferred to home video because the calibration levels are different between these two domains by the same 3 dB.

Broadcast terrestrial and satellite digital television also use metadata, and one of the metadata is absolutely standardized as required of all digital television receivers, and that is Dialogue Normalization. For these media, the mastering may be performed by a professional postproduction house, which will supply the metadata typically today in written form, so that the parameters may be set upon ingesting the source program into the broadcast channel. The form that follows on page 282 is to be used to label the source media, such as a DTRS tape. The resulting files, and recordings by way of Dolby E, should additionally be labeled with metadata settings as found previously.

Monitoring

Perhaps the most common cry heard from editors in mixes is "it sounded all right on the Avid." This means that in the editing room, with monitor speakers that don't cover the full frequency range and are lumpy in frequency response across the range, with masking by lots of computer noises, and in a hard, small room with awful acoustics, the sound was acceptable. When heard then in a quiet dubbing stage or control room, with controlled reverberation, and over a system that correctly spatializes the sound for the given recording, it sounds awful. This cry is often given in frustration: "Why do sound people have to be so picky?" but the problem of perception nonetheless exists.

The story is told about why "it sounded all right on the Avid," and when engineers investigated it was found that the tweeters, the high-frequency elements of the monitor loudspeakers, were burned out. So the editor missed all of those subtle background changes that make for bumpy edits because the sound system wasn't putting them out.

Multichannel Audio Postproduction Media Label
Postproduction Studio Info

Studio Name _____

Studio Address _____

Studio Phone Number _____

Contact Person _____

Date Prepared (e.g., 2005-01-12) _____

Program Info

Producing Organization _____

The following items are used by the ATSC Program/Episode/Version identifier.

Program _____

Episode Name _____

Episode # (1-4095) _____

Version _____

Version # (1-4095) _____

First Air or Street Date (e.g., 2005-01-12) _____

Program Length (time) _____

Contents Info
Track layout (check one):

☐	1	2	3	4	5	6	7	8
☐	L	R	C	LFE	LS	RS	Lt	Rt
☐Other								

Leader contents ☐ 1 kHz sine-wave tone at −20 dBFS, 30 s (required) from heads:
     ☐ Pink noise at −20 dBFSrms, 30 s (optional)
     ☐ Silence, 30 s (required)
     ☐ 2 Pop on countdown leader (optional)
     ☐ Other: _____

Program starts at ☐ 01:00:00:00 Other _____

Program ends at _____

☐ Multiple program segments (detail):

Time code ☐ 29.97 DF   ☐ 29.97 NDF   ☐ 30.00 DF   ☐ 30.00 NDF

Sample rate ☐ 48.000 kHz   ☐ Other (why?): _____

Tape Geneology ☐ Original ☐ Clone ☐ Dub ☐ Simultaneous Protection

It is perhaps inevitable that edit room monitor systems will always be less expensive than sound control rooms, but that doesn't mean that they have to be put behind the picture monitor and facing away, bouncing off the wall behind. Most edit rooms will be restricted to two-channel monitoring, and this is usually adequate for cutting because most elements are delivered as mono or two-channel. So at least the two channels can be set up to span the left and right sides of the main picture monitor, and with centered listening, produce a phantom image on the screen for dialog.

The next most important thing is the frequency range of the monitor. An old saw in audio is that the product of the low-frequency and high-frequency limits of a sound system should equal 400,000. Thus 20 times 20k equals 400,000, and so does 100 times 4k. As the low-frequency limit goes up, which is what costs the most in size and money, the high-frequency bandwidth also should come down, but it often doesn't, leading to trebly sounding audio from many small monitor loudspeakers. Most edit room-style monitors go down to the 60 to 100 Hz range and miss one to two octaves of importance at the low end. Then if the program material edited on such a system is played on one with full range, bumps at the edits at low frequencies may be heard.

The way around this is to use a common-bass subwoofer for the two channels. This works for several reasons. It allows the smaller monitors to be placed relative to the picture and the subwoofer placed on the floor up against a wall or corner. With a low-enough crossover frequency such as 80 Hz, with the bass below that redirected to the sub, the system works because we generally don't hear the direction of bass as the frequency goes down. Sure we localize the higher harmonics of the bass drum hit, but that's not bass! This is no huge investment today and can save hours of frustration in mixing.

The way to use a common-bass subwoofer requires electronics called *bass management* (Figure 10-2). This system does the filtering and redirection necessary. It is routine in home receivers, and some professional systems have the capability, either as an outboard unit or built into the subwoofer. A bass manager that works for these purposes is the Martinsound ManagerMax.

The next problem is the frequency response of the monitor-room combination. Small rooms are awful in the midbass because of strong standing waves. Put out some program material with strong bass content in your

Figure 10-2 A bass manager. It high-pass filters five main channels sums and low-pass filters the five channels, and adds the LFE signal to the sum, directing it to one or more subwoofers.

room. Now move up against the back wall. Almost 99 percent of the time the bass goes up dramatically. Move into a corner: it goes up even more. This is no reflection on the monitor or its manufacturer; it is the interaction between the loudspeaker and the room. For most people, this problem is currently insoluble, and all you can do is buy a decent loudspeaker that will be smooth at the higher frequencies and hope that the lower ones will be all right. What I have done for many years and that got used on *Titanic* among others in the editing room is a system called MicroTheater® (Figure 10-3). This involves hand-tuning the equalization to the small room so that for the editor's listening location the sound field has flat frequency response. The system was also used to mix a documentary feature film about the history of electronic music called *modulations* on a desktop, and the mix translated to theaters without ever seeing a control room or dubbing stage, thus saving a lot of money in the process. Although this system remains high end, one of the techniques used in it is just beginning to emerge as available more widely in automated room equalization systems, so help is on the way. Entering the market in high-end home receivers, perhaps one day such techniques will be available for routine use in editing rooms.

For mixing 5.1-channel sound on the desktop, not just editing and mixing two-channel sound, a correctly spatialized monitor system is necessary. Necessities are the following:

- A minimum of two front loudspeakers (if center is to be rendered as a phantom) or three

- A minimum of two surround loudspeakers

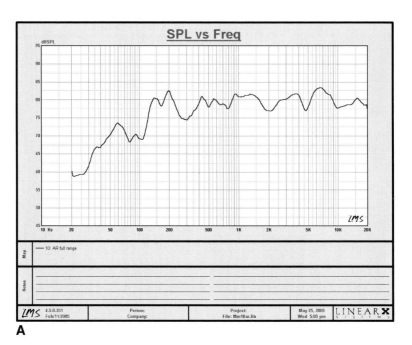

A

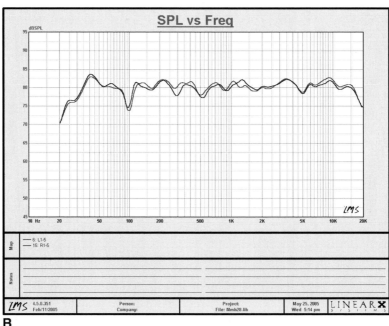

B

Figure 10-3 (a) The frequency response of a typical edit room monitor shows that it lacks bass and has uneven frequency response across the band. Measured at a typical listening location in an edit room (b) The frequency response of high-quality edit room monitor system, Microtheater. It shows a wide frequency range and smooth response over the range.

- A minimum of one subwoofer

- A bass manager circuit

- Setup such that left, center (if present), and right relate correctly to the picture so that the sound and associated picture appear in the same place. An error in placement in the horizontal plane of ±4 degrees is noticeable by professionals, and ±15 degrees is annoying. The speakers are optimally at the same height as the picture, but may be lower or higher because we hear vertical direction only about one-third as well as horizontal direction.

- Setup with left and right surround loudspeakers at ±110 degrees from front center when viewed from above. Surround speakers are usually more elevated than front speakers, mimicking theater arrangements.

- Subwoofer placed for best response. This is often the corner, which produces the most output. If two subs are available, operate them in mono from the same signal and place one in the corner and one halfway along one wall, both at the floor.

- Apply bass management

- Apply calibration as described earlier in this chapter.

Film Versus Video Mixes

The differing reference levels between cinema and home have been described, as well as the fact that a consumer 5.1 mix needs LFE redistributed to some degree from LFE only into LCR in order that the content not be lost in mixdown. There are two final points to make: (1) theatrical mixes are done to a different frequency response curve than home mixes, and (2) the sync is different for large rooms by one frame.

The different frequency response environments means theatrical mixes played at home will sound bright, whereas ones mixed on a flat desktop monitor reproduced in a cinema will sound dull. So the final mastering stage of a mix made on flat monitors for distribution into a theatrical environment is to add high-frequency shelving equalizers set to +4 dB at 10 kHz.

The consequences of film mixes sounding bright at home are overemphasis on sibilance in speech, too much apparent Foley, and sizzly sounding strings in music. These can be accommodated on receivers and controllers equipped with Home THX by switching in reequalization, which fixes this problem. But for the problem of the video mix shown theatrically, no fix is available in the cinema, so you have to build this into the master. While listening on your nice flat near-field sound system, it will sound too bright, but it will become right in the correctly tuned theater environment (SMPTE 202 and ISO 2969 standards).

Additionally, if your master is to be shown in large theaters (as opposed to small screening rooms), pull up the sound earlier relative to picture by one frame for the theatrical master, which will put it in hard sync at 47 feet from the screen.

So we've come fully to the end: you have a mix that sounds correct on your proper monitor, and now it translates into homes and cinemas. But what if you can't afford that proper monitor? The best way to proceed is to play mixes from good mixers, widely available on DVD, through your system and note what, in particular, voices sound like. The voice has the greatest recognition for most of us, and if that sounds right, a whole host of other problems can be forgiven.

Among the best times of my life are sitting in a movie theater watching the screen title crawl at the end of a wonderful film and finding a former student's name associated with a great sound track. This book attempts to bring the techniques that I teach to a wider audience and to make sound tracks accompanying moving pictures sound better. I wish that someday that sound track will be yours.

The Director's Cut

- Distinguish tapes by calling them Camera Original, Edit Master, and Delivery (or Studio) Master. Anything else is an intermediate product. The word *master* standing alone conveys almost no information because everything we use in production or postproduction except for final released materials is a master of one sort or another.
- Mono is used for cable television and low-budget video. While conventional two-channel stereo is occasionally used for legacy materials, surround sound rules today.
- LtRt matrixed surround sound delivered over two channels fits into multiple outlet chains, such as conventional broadcast, satellite and cable, VHS tape, as well as those channels that also have a 5.1 capacity: theatrical, DVD, and some HD satellite and cable services. Thus, LtRts are the most universal method of delivering surround sound.
- Audio with 5.1 channels offers greater discreteness or specificity (it can handle more signals simultaneously, presenting their direction correctly) and greater surround envelopment (two versus LtRt's single mono surround channel) for reproduction through theatrical, DVD, and some HD satellite and cable services.
- Mastering for level: Table 10-3 and the accompanying CD can be used to set the level of dialogue appropriately. The SMPTE reference level for sound accompanying pictures is −20 dBFS, and it should be used. Higher reference levels found in music recording lead to less interchangeability of product. You can test your product against others by playing good DVDs, say, and matching them for loudness.
- Only some distribution channels have 20 dB of headroom (DVD, theatrical, some HD satellite and cable services). For others, do not use all 20 dB of the headroom, because the downstream equipment and media cannot handle that much. To make a universal mix that fits all media, turn down the mix by some 5 dB and add 5 dB of peak limiting so that the maximum digital recorded level is −10 dBFS and the resulting product will fit all other media.
- Monitoring causes lots of trouble. "It sounded all right on the Avid," is frequently heard as a bromide, when what is meant is "why does it sound so bad on your professional monitoring system, Mr. Sound Mixer, when it sounded all right to me?" (under the lousy conditions of monitoring in editing room). Calibrated monitoring is a small expense compared to other things in the studio, so it should be given due consideration. It is worthwhile to listen to other products that you know well over the monitor system to see where they're at.

The Director's Cut (*Continued*)

- Bass management is necessary in virtually all monitoring systems because end users will listen to the program that way.
- There is a reason to tailor mixes specifically for the theatrical or home environments, and methods of doing so are given in the text.

Appendix: Making an Extension Microphone Cable for the Canon XL-1 Series Cameras

Purpose: To use the microphone supplied with the camera on a boom or fishpole. This makes the system much better in picking up dialog, at a minimal cost.

Parts List:

Star Quad microphone cable, such as Canare CANL-4E3-2P from Pacific Radio, www.pacrad.com, in sufficient length for your purpose. At the time of writing this, the cost was $1.55/ft.

Heat shrink and other braided tubing as necessary for a neat installation, with strain relief.

One each of the following:

3.5-mm 3-conductor male plug jack for cable, called a stereo Mini plug. Be sure the outer diameter of the shell is small enough to fit into the recess in the camera body where the microphone plugs in.

3.5-mm 3-conductor female jack socket for cable, called a stereo Mini jack.

2.5-mm 2-conductor male plug jack for cable, called a mono Micro plug. Be sure the outer diameter of the shell is small enough to fit into the recess in the camera body where the microphone power plugs in.

2.5-mm 2-conductor female jack socket for cable, called a mono Micro jack.

Directions:

    With an ohmmeter or other continuity tester, start by stripping, separately identifying, and labeling the four internal conductors at the two ends of the cable, two of which are usually white and two blue. Since we are using them for separate purposes, they must be individually identified.

    Connect one white-insulated wire to the tip of the 3-conductor male plug.

    Connect one blue-insulated wire to the ring of the 3-conductor male plug.

    Connect the other white-insulated wire at this end of the cable to the tip of the 2-conductor male plug.

    Connect the other blue-insulated wire at this end of the cable to the sleeve of the 2-conductor male plug.

    Connect the cable shield to the sleeve (the backmost conductor) of the 3-conductor shield.

    Repeat all the connections at the other end of the cable to the corresponding female sockets and pins.

    Confirm all connections with an ohmmeter for continuity and no shorts.

    Use the heat shrink and braided tubing to insulate the conductors from one another and to make a neat and strain-relieved cable assembly.

To use in practice, obtain or make a shock mount, such as the Universal Mini-Mount from Light Wave Systems (part number MM-XL1), and make a mechanical connection between it and the end of a fishpole or other boom. Make a loop of the short cable coming out of the microphone and connect it to the female end of the 3.5- and 2.5-mm cables. Strain-relieve this loop with Velcro or tape around the boom. Wrap the cable tightly around the boom, and hold it in place with one hand so that it cannot move against the boom and cause noise.

Index

CD Tracks

Track No.	Description
1	Narration: Description of this disc
2	Narration: How to calibrate the electronics of your system using the following two tracks. First is a sine-wave tone for adjustment of electronics, and second is band-limited pink noise for setting the monitor loudspeaker level.
3	1 kHz sine wave at −20 dBFS (SMPTE reference level).
4	Noise: Pink noise band limited to the range from 500 Hz to 2 kHz, at a level of −20 dBFSrms (note the peak level is higher but do not readjust for this). Use this to set the monitor level to 79 dBC slow reading on a sound level meter. This track is recorded on the left channel only. Re-route it as needed to calibrate each channel in turn.
5	Narration: Description of track 6.
6	Noise rotating among the channels left, center, right, and surround when decoded by a matrix Lt Rt decoder, such as a Dolby Pro Logic one.
7	Narration: Description of track 8.
8	30 s of 1 kHz sine-wave tone at −20 dBFS followed by a "2 pop." Use this track as a head leader, and sync the 2 pop with the correct frame of the picture countdown leader.
9	Edit Demonstration 1: A bump at an edit is solved by moving the edit point.
10	Edit Demonstration 2: A bump at an edit is solved by crossfading.
11	Edit Demonstration 3: Sometimes it is necessary to extend the background noise of a noisy shot over a quiet one to improve continuity.
12	Edit Demonstration 4: An edit that produces an incomplete sound, such as a car by, needs to have the "by" extended.
13	Microphone equalization/reverberation demonstration: Different microphone placements can be corrected with equalization and by adding reverberation where needed. In particular, lavaliere microphone sound can be equalized to sound better, and more like a boom mic.
14	Sound Process Demonstration 1: Volume graphing and hand gain riding.
15	Sound Process Demonstration 2: Compression.
16	Sound Process Demonstration 3: Limiting.
17	Sound Process Demonstration 4: Noise gating.
18	Sound Process Demonstration 5: Equalization, narration describing the following track.
19	Sound Process Demonstration 5: Equalization, pink noise is first boosted and then cut in four frequency ranges.
20	Sound Process Demonstration 6: Filters.
21	Sound Process Demonstration 7: Reverberation.
22	Sound Process Demonstration 8: Pitch shifting.
23	Sound Process Demonstration 9: Digital delay.